Streaming Media

Technologies, Standards, Applications

Tobias Künkel

WILEY

Library of Congress Cataloging-in-Publication Data

(to follow)

British Library Cataloguing in Publication Data

A catalogue record for this book is available from the British Library

ISBN 0-470-84724-7
Translated and typeset by Cybertechnics Ltd, Sheffield
Printed and bound in Great Britain by Biddles Ltd., Guildford and Kings Lynn
This book is printed on acid-free paper responsibly manufactured from sustainable forestry
for which at least two trees are planted for each one used for paper production.

Contents

Preface

The convergence of media – this is a phrase used frequently and in many situations when referring to contemporary communication strategies. With the progressive spread of ever more powerful computers and the availability of broadband Internet access, the computer has evolved from a simple worktool to the Command HQ of edutainment and communication.

The advent of graphical user interfaces, user-friendly input devices and the use of different media has created the conditions for a massive expansion both for computers and the Internet. Like computers, the Internet in its early days was only used in small doses, and you needed to be something of an expert to use it to some advantage.

The development of the World Wide Web and its hypertext documents, graphics and easy-to-use browsers was therefore decisive in gaining the consensus of the general public. Internet content became enriched with tables, graphics, images and user-friendly commands as it developed from a means of communication for specialists into a general mass medium.

Once time-discrete media of text and graphics became widely accepted, the time-based media of audio and video also became more common on the WWW. A number of different growth factors come into play here, which drive the growth of streaming media, such as:

- Increased use of Internet flat rate tariffs and broadband access, which enable more intensive use of higher quality streaming media, without the pressure of time.

- Increased user numbers and an increase in the acceptance of e-commerce on the Internet have caused greater economic attractiveness for suppliers, who now need to differentiate themselves from their competitors by resorting to innovative offers, such as using streaming media. With a general lack of Internet content, time-based media such as television, film, music and radio are seen as exceptionally profitable suppliers of content, which help create new offers and enhance existing Web sites.

The effects of these factors has become increasingly more evident, and, against this backdrop, streaming media on the Internet has developed from a technical gimmick to the innovation engine of the new Internet mass medium. Streaming technologies have not only changed the face of the Internet, but of the entire media industry. With this component, the net will finally become what recent developments have allowed it to be: an integrated media platform enabling the combination of all information represented in different forms.

The applications are various: concerts, events, fairs and congresses are broadcast live, broadcasters for different target groups are established, and the availability of motion pictures and audio for different forms of information and edutainment is commonplace nowadays.

This book aims to provide the basic technical information and practical applications that users require not only to produce and provide streaming media, but also to understand it.

Tobias Künkel
tobias@kuenkel.de

The accompanying web site

The web site accompanying this book contains many programs and tools, extensive practical examples, secondary links and additional information.
http://www.streaming-media.info

Acknowledgements

My daily work at Me, Myself & Eye Entertainment AG includes intensive analysis of current technologies and discussion in the field of streaming media. I would therefore like to thank my colleagues here who challenge me on a daily basis.

Frank Wörler has been a great help with his inexhaustible knowhow on almost everything to do with motion picture and audio.

I would especially like to thank Professor Paul Klimsa, who supported and motivated me during my studies at HTW Dresden and beyond.

And not least, this book would not have been possible without the invaluable support of my family, and especially my girlfriend, Tina Bonnekessel.

The basics of streaming technology

The victory train of streaming media as a new Internet technology has already begun its journey. During the last few years, technologies and standards have become established, and increasingly more users now recognise the benefits to be gained from film, audio and animation in the World Wide Web. It is still a young technology, which makes it essential for developers to understand the underlying concepts and ideas.

A basic understanding of streaming media requires some knowledge of network technologies and audio/video editing. Intensive development work is constantly ongoing in both fields to achieve an optimal and efficient transfer of media data, which means that application packages have a very short life cycle. Developers have to revise their work continually, which means that a sound understanding of the basics of streaming technology is the only way they can operate.

1.1 Streaming

Internet data transfer

Secure data transfer via a decentralised network is the backbone of the development of the Internet. In order to guarantee optimal fail-safe conditions and the most reliable data transfer possible, we must develop a transfer architecture capable of reacting to the failure of parts of the network in a flexible and reliable manner. This high level of failure safety was originally developed for use on the Internet for military purposes in the event of a Soviet nuclear attack on the USA. To this end, data to be sent is divided into small packets, which reach the receiver via non-predefined trunk lines over the network. The decision as to the exact transport path of the individual data packets does not rest with the sender or receiver, but with the routers stationed at network 'crossroads', based on the options available at the time.

As this architecture does not guarantee secure transport of individual packets, client and server communicate via a control connection. The client confirms the entry of each packet, or transfers the packet again if required. If data packets arrive at their target in the wrong order because of different runtimes, the receiver can sort them according to specific criteria.

This method of data transfer is perfectly suited for the download of static content such as HTML pages or graphics. As it involves time-discreet information, the mechanisms described are deployed optimally, and ensure the most reliable and rapid transfer of data.

Of course, these mechanisms can also be used for the transfer of audio- and videofiles. However, the complete download of files is a very inefficient type of transfer for time-based, resource-hungry media such as video or audio. Waiting times caused by downloads could be avoided if the client is able to begin running the file while it is being downloaded. This is where streaming technologies come in. The contents are not saved by the client and then output. Rather, a constant data stream is created by the server, which the client carries on providing in the form of audio, video or other data. So, transferred information can be output as soon as it starts reaching the player software. A certain amount of data is usually received before playback begins. This buffering ensures that playback is not compromised by short interruptions in the available bandwidth, and that there is a certain tolerance to changes in available bandwidth.

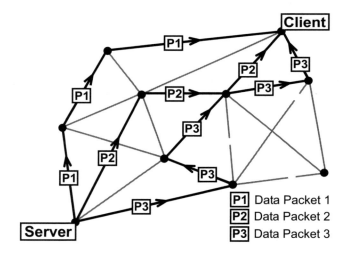

Figure 1.1 Packet-based data transfer over the Internet

The main problems of streaming media technologies are caused by the use of infrastructures, which were not actually developed for this type of data transfer. A central issue with the use of the Internet for streaming media is packet loss. If a server does not send data on schedule, or if individual packets do not reach computers because of various reasons, this does not leave much time for information to be sent again. In addition, if there is no time for information to be resent, part of the video or audio data on the client side will be missing. Streaming media technologies must therefore be able to handle the loss of small parts of information to be played back in a flexible manner.

The second main problem with data transfer, especially in streaming video, is the bandwidth restriction of Internet connections. Developers and users counter this problem with different levels of content engineering and provision (see below).

With streaming technologies, not only are otherwise unrealistically high download times of on-demand material drastically reduced, but live broadcasts also become possible. The constant data stream from the encoder via the server to the client cannot be achieved within the conventional network architecture of the Internet in this form, but requires the concepts introduced with streaming technology.

This process has many advantages from a legal point of view, as the issue of illegal reproduction of content is not raised. The client only ever receives a minimum of image or sound data, which remains cached in the intermediary memory until played back. With other downloads, reproduction of information is not without loss, or can only occur with great effort. This is currently one of the arguments in the negotiations with respective owners for illegal music and video copies via mp3, mpeg and other formats.

1.2 On-demand content and live broadcasts

There is an important distinction in the provision of streaming media content between live and on-demand content.

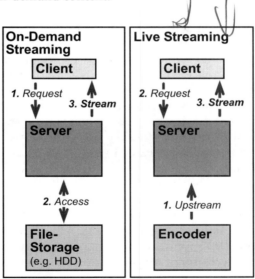

Figure 1.2 On-demand and Live streaming

Streams on demand On-demand content consists of files in the manufacturer's format, stored on the drives of Web or video servers. These are available to users at any time, and are sent on demand. The user sends a request to the server, for example by clicking on a link in a Web site to on-demand clips. The server receives this request, and begins transferring the requested file to the player. Pre-produced content is therefore made available to the user at any time.

Live Internet broadcasts
With a live broadcast, there is no file stored on the video server. Even though a file is addressed when the stream is called, this name only represents an address via which the server identifies the data stream to be delivered. This data stream is generated by an encoder, which digitalises, encodes and sends the audio or video signal to the server in real time. The server receives this data packet from the encoder, and passes it on to the client which then calls the compatible address. As opposed to on-demand streams, the same data is delivered to the user at certain intervals.

From the client's point of view, there is no difference between live and on-demand streams. In both cases, the player software receives a constant data stream at a given bandwidth, which it plays back until the server is interrupted or the user cancels the operation.

1.3 Bandwidth

Bandwidth is the technical factor which plays the largest role in the development of streaming media distribution. The user has to deal with this keyword at every level of the production and delivery process of streaming media. Bandwidth describes how much information can be transferred in a defined time over an information channel. It is measured in bits per second (e.g. Kbps or Mbps).

Server bandwidth
Internet connection bandwidth is a substantial factor in system performance as regards the provision of on-demand or live content on a streaming media server, as is the performance of hardware and software. The trend in broadband provision, in particular, places enormous demands on the network connection.

If a video clip is provided for users in modem quality (usually 34 Kbps), theoretically up to one thousand users can access the video stream simultaneously via a high-performance leased line at 34 Mbps. While dual ISDN quality (80 Kbps) cuts this capacity by almost one third, the broadband quality stream (e.g. 300 Kbps) can only be accessed by around 100 users simultaneously.

Client-side bandwidth
However, the bandwidth restrictions of Internet connections on the client side are visible to and affect all users. The types of Internet connections for private use varies from slow 28.8K modems to 2 Mbps leased lines via coaxial cable or DSL. Although the spread of broadband Internet connections is continuously increasing, a creator of streaming media content often has to consider the demands of the average modem-surfer.

When conventional content, such as text and images, is downloaded, the effect of a narrow bandwidth become evident in the slow download times, but although this constraint is annoying, the situation is still tolerable. A miscalculation in the generation of streaming media contents is a different matter. This is usually caused by distortions in the images and sound, as data is not transferred to the player quickly enough for playback. On the other hand, the main criticism of streaming media at the moment is the poor sound and image quality, which makes optimisation a necessity. Anyone wishing to provide the best quality images and sound should look carefully at the bandwidth issue.

As can be seen, transmission bandwidth is one of the most constraining factors in Internet data transfer. Especially on the 'last mile', the section of the transmission link from the end user's computer to the provider's dial-in node, the narrow-band connections of modems and ISDN cards continue to dominate. In recent years broadband Internet access over 128 Kbps has begun to gain ground amongst private users. Yet, despite all the euphoria surrounding DSL and cable modems, the fully equipped user constitutes under 5% of the Internet community in the UK. However, analysts predict a sharp increase in broadband Internet access in private households, so that in less than five years around one quarter of the UK, and almost half the United States and Scandinavia will have a high-speed Internet connection.

Table 1.1 Population percentage of Internet users and users with broadband access

	2001		2005	
	Internet users	Users with broadband access	Internet users	Users with broadband access
USA/Canada	45.0 %	14.1 %	65.0 %	53.1 %
Europe	14.3 %	3.3 %	24.5 %	24.2 %
GB	40.0 %	0.9 %	50.0 %	19.5 %

With or without broadband access, efficient use of available bandwidth will always be a requirement of data transfer in computer networks. In order to counter these problems, methods such as SureStream and compression technologies have been developed, with the aim to deliver the best possible playback quality to the end user.

1.4 SureStream/Multiple Bit Rate

These two names refer to the same technology: with SureStream or Multiple Bit Rate (MBR) technology, RealNetworks and Microsoft aim to be able to react to different Internet connection bandwidths in a more flexible manner.

The approach of these technologies is to provide several degrees of audio and video quality in one file or from one live encoder. So, if the client requests the data stream from the server, both computers first communicate over specialised protocols and negotiate how much bandwidth is available. Then the technology assesses which of the available levels of quality best corresponds to the current Internet connection bandwidth and the server starts to send the stream to the client. If the bandwidth fluctuates during transfer, the server acknowledges this, and switches up or down to the next level of quality. This guarantees that the user always gets the best quality presentation, and that playback is not interrupted, as data may have to be reloaded.

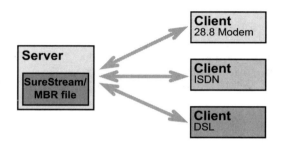

Figure 1.3   SureStream/Multibit uses several bandwidths

RealNetworks has supported SureStream since version G2 of the RealSystem. Up to eight quality levels can be defined and encoded.

Using Microsoft Windows Media the user can encode more than ten streams. Before Windows Media 9 Series, the system could not encode more than one audio quality with an MBR file. So an MBR file encoded at 20, 34, 45 and 150 Kbps and played back at 150 Kbps would have only delivered an audio stream suitable for the low bandwidth (e.g. 6 Kbps). This restriction has been removed in Windows Media 9, where a flexible combination of video- and audio streams with different bit rates is possible.

Apple QuickTime has the same type of functions as SureStream and Multibit. It calls what is known as an alternate movie, which acts as a reference to different versions of media files according to the user's Internet connection. A modem user can therefore view a video clip with a narrower bandwidth than a DSL user.

Choice of bandwidths

There are different factors which influence the available bandwidths. In each case a substantial part of the bandwidth is taken up by network overheads. As experience shows, this is somewhere between 20% and 30% of the transfer speed which is theoretically possible. It then depends on the connection made available by the provider as to whether the rest can be fully used.

SureStream/ Multibit on Web servers   Assessing the bandwidth to be used requires a special type of communication between server and player. This communication cannot take place with a normal Web server. This is also unable to select a single stream from the file and send it to the client. However, if, for example, a SureStream/MBR clip on a normal Web server were to be requested, the server would send all streams to the client simultaneously, which would of course overload any narrowband Internet connection.

Table 1.2 Typical Internet connection bandwidths

Target group	Average available bandwidth	Typical audio quota	Typical video size and image frequency
28.8K modem	20 Kbps	6 Kbps	176×132, 7 fps
56.6K modem	34 Kbps	8 Kbps	176×132, 10 fps
64K ISDN	45 Kbps	11 Kbps	176×132, 15 fps
128K Dual ISDN	80 Kbps	20 Kbps	240×180, 15 fps
DSL, cable modem	600 Kbps	64 Kbps	320×200, 25 fps

The solution to this problem is to avoid providing on-demand material in several stream qualities on Web servers, and just encode one quality. Files can then be streamed on normal Web servers via HTTP. In order to cater for different resolutions, several files will need to be placed on the server. The choice between these files can then be made manually or automatically.

In order to avoid confusion, SureStream, Multiple Bit Rate and alternate movies are all grouped together below under the term 'multistream.'

1.5   Protocols

Protocol classification   The OSI reference model (Open System Interconnection) is used for the schematic classification of network protocols. Every network protocol can be ordered and classified in this model from the network cable (physical layer) to the application (application layer). The different layers are based on each other, so a higher layer always relies on the functions of lower layers to provide functionalities, which are increasingly more oriented towards the respective application. The individual layers are also independent of each other, and can be interchanged. Interchanged overlaying layers can therefore remain unmodified, and access the functions of lower layers via standardised interfaces.

General Internet protocols

Network layer

All protocols are based on Internet protocol (IP). In the OSI reference model, IP-based transfer resides in the network layer, forming the basis for all higher protocols.

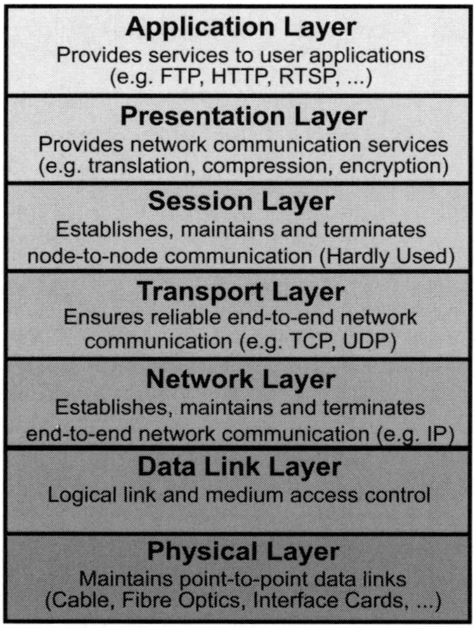

| **Application Layer** |
| Provides services to user applications |
| (e.g. FTP, HTTP, RTSP, ...) |
| **Presentation Layer** |
| Provides network communication services |
| (e.g. translation, compression, encryption) |
| **Session Layer** |
| Establishes, maintains and terminates |
| node-to-node communication (Hardly Used) |
| **Transport Layer** |
| Ensures reliable end-to-end network |
| communication (e.g. TCP, UDP) |
| **Network Layer** |
| Establishes, maintains and terminates |
| end-to-end network communication (e.g. IP) |
| **Data Link Layer** |
| Logical link and medium access control |
| **Physical Layer** |
| Maintains point-to-point data links |
| (Cable, Fibre Optics, Interface Cards, ...) |

Figure 1.4   OSI reference model

Internet Protocol (IP)   The IP-based network architecture stands out as the basis for all overlaying protocols by the following features:

• Platform independence.

• Independence from physical network types, in that IP abstracts the features of the physical network type used (Ethernet, Token Ring, etc.) for higher network layers.

• Guarantee of interoperability: independent networks can easily be connected.

This flexibility is achieved through adaptive routing and fragmentation. With adaptive routing, IP packets are not sent directly from the source host to the target host, but reach their destination via intermediate stops known as hops. Which hops are chosen for the transfer route depends on their availability, but this tends not to be strictly predefined. If a hop fails, a packet can use an alternative hop, if available.

The Internet consists of different sub-networks which communicate via Internet protocol (IP) as the lowest common denominator, and in which many different clients exist. In order to address these sub-networks and their clients, every computer has a unique address, known as the IP address. This address, 4 bytes in size, is supplied by NIC (Network Information Center – http://www.internic.net), and consists of the net segment address, and a client address within the net segment. As a byte can assume 256 conditions at 2^8, this produces an available IP address space from 0.0.0.0 to 255.255.255.255, making a maximum of almost 4.3 billion (256^4) computers on the Internet.

However, average users rarely come across IP addresses, as they usually work with easily remembered domain names. DNS are used here (Domain Name Servers), which assign the corresponding IP address to the server name requested by the user. For example, if the user enters the address http://www.internic.net in his Internet browser, a DNS is contacted, which returns the information that this server has the IP address192.0.36.35, and can be reached via http://192.0.36.35.

However, before an IP packet can be sent via a hop, the data has to be compressed as a frame. This represents an 'encapsulation' of the packet for transport through a certain sub-network. Every network has a maximum framelength, known as the Maximum Transmission Unit (MTU). If the length of a frame is larger than the MTU of the next hop, the IP packet containing the frame can be broken down into fragments. This is done using a router. These fragments become packets themselves, and are packed as frames. As their length is smaller than that of the original frame, and smaller than or equal to the MTU, they can be sent via the next hop. The target computer then will need to reassemble the individual fragments.

IP protocol is therefore a 'best effort' protocol, in that IP does not guarantee secure transmission of data packets to the target, but only guarantees the best possible effort. A data packet may get lost en route, because:

• individual bits may become damaged or lost en route

• an overloaded router may reject the packet due to lack of resources

• no path currently leads to the target address.

All functions affecting the reliability of data transfer are integrated into the following transport layer.

The primary function of IP is to accept data from TCP or UDP, pack it into datagrams, route it through the network and deliver it to the target computer. Every datagram is transported independently.

IP is therefore dependent on two concepts which aid the routing process:

• The subnet mask
  The subnet mask is a 32-bit wide mask, used to inform the local computer of other computers that are located in the local network, and of computers that can only be reached via a gateway. For example, a computer in a business network may receive information to the effect that it can only send data packets with targets from 192.149.2.0 to 192.149.2.255 locally, and all other targets can be reached via the network segment gateway.

• The IP routing table
  With the routing table, the sender recognises the IP address to which packets must be sent, intended for specific or all external network segments. In this way, one or more computers in the local network segment can communicate with the next segment, and act as a gateway.

The reason for this simple procedure is that a source host does not have to know the complete route to the target computer. It is sufficient to know where the next router is. This then directs the data packets in the same way until the data reaches its target.

On this relatively simple level, Internet protocol represents a basic functionality for the transfer of data packets via the decentralised Internet, on which protocols rely when performing further functions.

Transport layer

In the next layer up (transport layer), User Datagram Protocol (UDP) and Transmission Control Protocol (TCP) build on the functions of IPs.

TCP   TCP maintains a (virtual) connection as a connection-oriented protocol until explicitly ended. This virtual connection is known as a data stream. As a host can maintain several TCP-based connections to one or more hosts simultaneously, every connection has to be explicitly indicated. A 'sequence number' is generated from the local host and incorporated into the header of the TCP, which is then sent to the foreign host via IP. The foreign host then replies with its own sequence number, known as the 'acknowledgement number,' which in turn is made known to the local host. This then sends a reconfirmation, and begins the actual data transfer. This 'three-way handshake' ensures that both hosts know that they need to maintain the established connection.

With every datagram transferred, the sequence number increases, so the individual datagrams are numbered according to the number of bytes they contain. So, when datagrams 536 bytes in size are transferred (the standard size for TCP), where the first is marked with 0, the second with 536, the third with 1072 and so on, TCP will later be able to keep the correct sequence at the receiving end, and arrange any randomly arriving datagrams in the right order. The 'acknowledgement number' is used to confirm whether a datagram has arrived. However, datagrams are not confirmed individually, but only at regular intervals. The receipt of whole groups of datagrams is always reported by the receiver. If the first or any other from this group is confirmed as having been received, this applies to all others, as it can be seen from the sequence number whether there are any losses. If there is no confirmation following the nth plus one packet, the whole group will need to be resent.

This complicated process, which also causes fairly heavy network traffic, is used with TCP to login to remote computers or for file transfer, which requires a high reliability of transmission. Other fields in the TCP header determine the ports required and identified by the application level, and a checksum.

As regards the transfer of streaming media, the question arises as to whether these complicated confirmation mechanisms could be replaced by a more efficient use of available bandwidth.

In constrast to TCP, User Datagram Protocol (UDP) is a wireless protocol which contains no data streams. Rather, datagrams are transported independently of each other. However, this does not guarantee delivery of the individual packets. It is therefore far easier to set up than TCP. The ports required by application programs and a hash total are left in the UDP header. UDP is used for applications which do not require reliable transfer, or where a reliable transfer is given from the outset due to the network topology, which tends to be the case in local networks. Flow control and safety mechanisms to counter data loss can also be used by a protocol of the next layer.

UDP   UDP is very well suited to streaming media because of its simplicity. It allows you to react fairly flexibly to the loss of individual data packets. TCP's lack of a large 'protocol overhead' makes a large amount of bandwidth available for streaming media content.

Application layer

The next layer of the OSI reference model is Hypertext Transfer Protocol (HTTP). This was developed for the simple transfer of HTML pages, but can also be used to transport streaming media data.

HTTP is a stateless, object-oriented protocol for a distributed hypermedia information system, based on a client-server connection. It was specially designed for short response times so that the process of an HTTP operation could consciously be observed. On the Internet, HTTP uses TCP as a transport protocol. However, it is theoretically possible for HTTP to use any connection-based transport protocol.

HTTP   One feature of HTTP is the standardisation and handling of the data format of useful data. For example, it is possible to store a document at two different levels of quality. The higher quality format is sent if both client and server can handle it, otherwise the lower quality format is sent.

HTTP is based on the request/response principle, where a disctinction is made between four operations:

- Connection
  The client initiates a connection to the server, which it then confirms. On the Internet, a connection is established with TCP via port 80, but any other port could also be used.

- Request
  The client places a request with a request message.

- Response
  The server sends a response to the client (response message).

- Close
  The connection is terminated either by the server once the data has been transferred, or by the client after closing down.

HTTP can also be used for the transfer of streaming media data by configuring corresponding data types on the server, provided this supports HTTP protocol. In this way, stream data is transferred via a protocol recognised and accepted by firewalls installed on most company and academic institutions systems. Many problems which are generated from the use of a TCP- or UDP-based protocol can also be bypassed using HTTP.

1.6 Streaming media protocols

The Internet was developed for the secure transfer of data, in which reliability was clearly a priority in avoiding delays. TCP/IP based protocols were created for this type of transfer, and fulfil these requirements by reconfirmation of packet transfer. However, multimedia data has different features from conventional Internet content, and therefore requires new protocols to provide these services.

HTTP is the only application layer protocol via which streaming is possible. However, because this was developed for the transfer of static content, it does not provide any optimal conditions for streaming media transfer. As TCP is used as a basis, there are consequently larger network communication overheads used powerful enough to guarantee transfer reliability.

The implementation of new specialist streaming protocols was therefore introduced to optimise the communication processes between client and server.

Streaming media protocols can rely on both TCP and UDP in the transport layer. UDP is generally favoured because of its less complicated architecture. TCP loses valuable resources through steady communication between client and server. This is best used for transferring static content.

Streaming media protocols broaden the architecture of the Internet, and optimise the transfer of time-based media such as audio, video or multimedia conferencing.

Real Time Streaming Protocol (RTSP)

RealNetworks and Apple with open standards

Although streaming applications are easy to implement using HTTP, there are some disadvantages associated with this protocol. The central reason for modifying HTTP is the fact, that there are no mechanisms in it to control the bits tream from server to client. As you always want to get your websites as fast as possible, HTTP uses all the bandwidth it can get.

The Real Time Streaming Protocol (RTSP) is quite similar to HTTP in syntax and operation, but different to HTTP in that it provides a direct control of the bit stream. This real-time oriented protocol was developed for use in unicast and multicast networks, and is part of a family consisting of Real Time Transport Protocol (RTP), Real Time Control Protocol (RTCP), Resource Reservation Protocol (RSVP) and RTSP itself.

RTSP can be found in the application layer of the OSI reference model. It represents a robust process for streaming multimedia, and an interface for servers and players of different manufacturers, because, as an open standard, it is not subject to protection. RTSP fulfils different functions, such as multi-session control, a choice between UDP, TCP, IP multicast and RTP-based delivery mechanisms, and supervision of the set-up and authentication of sessions. Real Time Transport Protocol (RTP) forms the basis for RTSP, which reinitiates the transfer and control of real time content.

RealNetworks'
Oldie   RealNetworks and Apple use Real Time Streaming Protocol in their RealSystem and QuickTime programs. In practice, data transport, playback control, the choice between different SureStreams, and the transmission of clip information and authentications, are all achieved using RTSP. Windows Media 9 is the first version of Microsoft's product also to support RTSP.

Progressive Networks Audio (PNA)

RealNetworks' own PNA protocol was used up to version 5.0 of RealSystem until it was replaced with the RealSystem G2 based on RTSP. However, for compatibility reasons, PNA support is integrated into RealServer and RealPlayer. Both RTSP and PNA send media clips via a one-way UDP connection as standard. A parallel TCP connection is only used in the transmission of control information

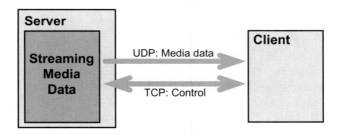

Figure 1.5 **Example of** data transport in streaming media protocols

Microsoft Media Server Protocol (MMS)

Microsoft
Streaming   Just as RTSP, Microsoft's MMS is used for the transmission of data packets and control commands from server to client. MMS is the default connection method for clients with the Windows Media Unicast Service. In this case, control commands always reach their target via TCP, while the media data is via UDP or TCP.

MMS is very similar to RTSP, which could be one of the reasons why Microsoft decided to drop this proprietary standard and use the RTSP form on Windows Media 9.

- Microsoft Media Server Protocol/UDP (MMSU)
  In this version of MMS, the server tries to send data via UDP.

- Microsoft Media Server Protocol/TCP (MMST)
  In this version of MMS, the server tries to send data by establishing a TCP connection.

- Hypertext Transfer Protocol (HTTP)
  If the first two attempts fail, the server tries to stream the data via HTTP.

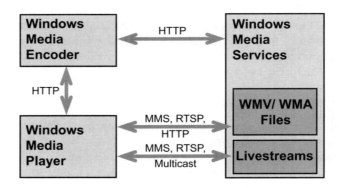

Figure 1.6 Windows media technologies protocols

Hypertext Transfer Protocol (HTTP)

As previously mentioned, HTTP is used by all major products to stream content through firewalls or across networks, which for whatever reason do not support streaming media protocols. As the majority of firewalls and all networks recognise and support HTTP, streaming content can be transferred.

The respective player receives data such as a Web site, which means that the client software also has to recognise the respective proxy settings in the business network.

The disadvantage here is the poor connection quality of HTTP streaming. As HTTP was designed for the real-time transfer of time-based media, the data stream is more prone to connection interruptions and transfer delays. This can in turn result in fluctuating or poor image quality. As with other solutions, jumping or navigating to certain points in the stream is no longer possible with HTTP transfer.

Protocol Rollover

Regardless of whether RealPlayer or Windows Media Player is being used, the user always has a choice of several protocols concerning how the Streaming Media content can be accessed. However, it is difficult for inexperienced users to know which protocol is ideal for a particular situation.

In order to relieve the user of the chore of choosing a transfer protocol, the Players of RealNetworks and Microsoft contain mechanisms that choose automatically. For this, the Player generally attempts data transmission using the following protocols, in the order presented below:

- RTSP/MMS via UDP: the ideal choice is the RTSP or MMS protocol, which uses the efficient UDP for transferring media data.

- RTSP/MMS via TCP: with this second-best option, the server attempts to send data via RTSP or MMS by establishing a TCP connection.

- HTTP: if the first two attempts fail, the server tries to stream the data via HTTP.

If the first attempt fails, the Player tries to send the data using the second or third option. The reason for it failing tends to be caused by an adjustment of the data exchange with the Internet through firewalls and proxies. These security measures mean that companies often have restricted Internet access to certain protocols and ports. As quite often specific streaming protocols are blocked, HTTP remains the only possibility left for companies, authorities and schools of accessing content with streaming media.

1.7 Splitting and Load balancing

Due to restrictions in performance and network connection a single server is not able to deliver the required bandwidth to the number of users.

A single streaming media server hits its limitations sooner or later: Its ability is always restricted by bandwidth and computer performance, and broadband streams, in particular, push connections and processors quickly to their limits.

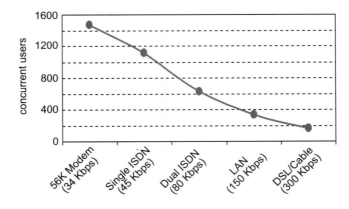

Figure 1.7 Maximum concurrent user on a streaming video server connected with 50 Mbps

Figure 1.7 shows how many clients can parallel access content with different bit rates on a server which is connected to the Net with 50 Mbps bandwidth. It becomes clear that broadband content, in particular, sets high requirements to a high-performance server infrastructure.

So, there are various factors which limit the capacity of streaming media servers:

- Connection bandwidth
- System resources (storage, memory, cpu, etc.)
- Storage capacity (for on-demand-material)

- Software limitations

- Availability

In order to counter this problem, the most obvious solution is to use several servers to deliver the same content. In this case, either the user can select the next available server, or an automatic selection process is implemented.

A simple setup is the distribution of a livestream via more than one server, where a livestream from an encoder is split up and sent to several streaming servers. A distinction in the splitting process is made between source server and splitter. The server generating the stream or receiving it from an encoder functions as a source. Other servers receive this stream from the source server, and distribute the data to clients, thus performing the function of a splitter. It follows, therefore, that a server can be both splitter and source at the same time.

Arguments in favour of splitting:

- The users will request the stream from a wide variety of locations.

- There is more than one streaming server available.

- The number of users is greater than the maximum possible number of connections of a single server.

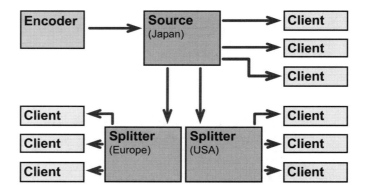

Figure 1.8 Sample splitting set-up

Push Splitting

Push Splitting involves a constant connection between source and splitter. As soon as the server receives a data stream from an encoder, it divides the stream between all splitters connected. If a client requests a live stream from a splitter, the connection to the source server is already in place, meaning that the video stream should reach the client immediately.

Pull Splitting

Pull Splitting Unsurprisingly, the alternative to Push Splitting is known as Pull Splitting, where the connection between source and splitter is only established when the first client requests the live stream from a splitter. In the event of a small number of users, this reduces bandwidth being wasted by unnecessary connections between source and splitter.

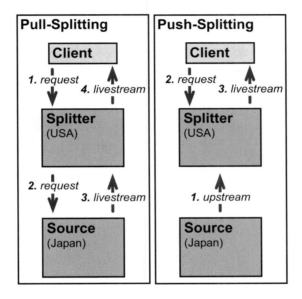

Figure 1.9 Pull- and Push-Splitting

Load balancing

Splitting functions are becoming increasingly more necessary with the growth of streaming media supply on the Internet. Single servers are very rarely able to meet the requirements of large live broadcasts. Many providers broaden the splitting capabilities of their networks with specific use of resource management, which assigns the optimal server to a client in a flexible manner according to the extent of server usage and transmission lines. These more complex setups with dozens of servers are managed by a central network operation centre, where every client request is received. A central load balancer monitors the status of every server in the network and refers every client request to the optimal server. Apart from the fact that server overloads are avoided, the load balancer can send the client to servers, to which they will have best possible connection.

Of course, not only the availability of livestreams is increased in these large scale networks. Highly frequented on demand clips can be transferred from a central file storage in the network operation centre to several servers so that users can access them under optimal conditions.

1.8 Unicasting and Multicasting

Unicasting

The total availability of information at any time is one of the main advantages of the Internet. Regardless of time and location, surfers can request text, graphics, databases and other information from servers with a minimal time delay. As opposed to something such as radio broadcasting, each client receives an individual data stream.

Multicasting is oriented to these requirements, which correspond to those of a radio broadcast rather than a connection-based data transfer in a computer network. There is no connection established here for the transfer of media data between client and server. Rather, a stream is created and directed to only those clients with certain IPs.

Unicasting corresponds to this principle with the transfer of streaming data: for every player, a new connection is opened, via which the stream and necessary control commands are transferred. This process is required when on-demand content is requested, as this makes the total availability and control of the clip possible (pause, stop, positioning). If material is available on demand, it consequently has to be delivered to each individual client via the server. The unicasting of on-demand content therefore corresponds to the conventional methods of Internet data transfer.

By contrast, with live broadcasts, all users receive identical content simultaneously. As with a radio broadcast, the data can be sent centrally and received by several clients. On the basis of what we have established so far, the main criticisms of unicasting can be highlighted:

• The server is excessively loaded, as each client receives a separate, exclusive data stream. This means high server usage, as the streams have to be generated, and network traffic is heavy due to data being sent.

• Valuable network resources are lost on the Internet, as several streams may use the same section of the transmission link to reach various clients.

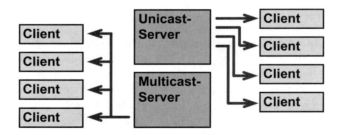

Figure 1.10 Unicasting and Multicasting

Network routers now assume a central role: they decide whether the incoming data stream should be split, as the clients addressed are located in different sub-networks. If this is the case, the stream is divided and requires further network resources. With this method, limited resources are used more efficiently than with unicasting, though certain network technologies are required to support this process. Unfortunately, this is as far as the Internet of today can take us, and multicasting is only practical for the time being in clearly identified business and academic networks. However, the use of this process is of direct interest to network administrators, and extensive efforts are currently being made in the retrofitting of infrastructures.

1.9 Embedding

Every manufacturer makes software available to users free of charge for accessing streaming media content on the Internet. This provides an optimal tool for accessing such things as RealVideo, QuickTime or Windows Media files. All software players have their own interface, designed according to manufacturer settings. If a user accesses a streaming media clip on a Web site via a link, the browser recognises this, and passes the address to the appropriate system software. From this point on, the browser has nothing more to do with the streaming media process, as the player software assumes the browser to be a separate program.

If streaming content is to be played back within HTML pages, this does not occur through the player directly, but via an appropriate browser plug-in, integrated into the browser when the player is installed. In this way, a video image can be embedded and integrated into a Web page in the same way as a static image. Embedding has the added advantage that the video and audio add to the authenticity of HTML pages. Player controls such as the play and pause buttons, time display or display panels for meta information can be configured individually.

Figure 1.11 Embedded streaming video player

Embedded players also enable discreet Web content to be synchronised with a time-based medium such as audio or video signals. Different data such as the clip title, author, running time or player status can be requested by the browser plug-in. Events can also be triggered by the plug-in, such as modifying the play status, clip title or volume. This allows video clips to be blended in, hyperlinks to appear, or browser content to be modified when the player is stopped.

The option of embedding in streaming media systems will be described in the respective chapters of this book.

1.10 SMIL

Does HTML have a sense of time? Synchronised Multimedia Integration Language (SMIL – pronouced 'smile') is a document description language written in XML. This manufacturer-independent markup language is similar in structure to HTML, but with a different purpose in mind: whereas HTML was developed for formatting text and embedding graphics, SMIL was designed for the integration of time-based media such as audio and video. Its purpose is to enable the creation of multimedia presentations on the Internet, which, similar to a television broadcast, link into one interface and synchronise time-discrete and time-based media (text, graphics, audio, video, animation).

As is the case with HTML, most media types can be embedded into Web pages using conventional means, the spatial and temporal positioning of which can cause developers major problems. Even for professional developers, overlaying images with sound, providing videos with subtitles, or even creating an entire multimedia presentation from scratch can be a major headache when one considers the countless, partly incompatible technologies on the Internet. SMIL was developed to simplify these and other Internet applications. However, as current Internet browsers do not support this standard, SMIL presentations have to be played back in specially designed browsers. RealPlayer and QuickTime Player support SMIL, with their own respective customisations.

Features of SMIL 1.0

- Layout specification and synchronisation:
  SMIL enables media objects to be positioned and determined to the last pixel. Whether it be video, audio, animation, graphics or text, SMIL enables all players to support media types which are spatially and temporally synchronised with each other.

- Links:
  SMIL can refer to all Internet documents.

- Different language versions:
  Material in different languages can be embedded in the same way as objects of different quality. The player asks which language version is being used, and different versions of media files (such as text or audio) are embedded.

- Consideration of available bandwidth:
  In SMIL, the bandwidth of the user's Internet connection can be queried, and different versions of a media file accessed accordingly. Similar to SureStream/Multibit technologies, this enables you to react flexibly to different bandwidths of Internet users.

SMIL syntax

SMIL-related links can be found on the accompanying web site.

As a derivative of XML, SMIL is a markup language, in which special tags describe when, how long, where and which media objects are represented and played back.

An SMIL file begins and ends with a `<smil>` tag, encapsulating the `<head>` and `<body>` tag. The `<switch>` tag enables the execution of statements and conditions to be combined, such as the availability of a certain transfer rate or language version of the player.

If media objects are to be represented or played back in sequence, the corresponding statements are enclosed with a `<seq>` tag. In constrast, the parallel playback of media objects is achieved by using the `<par>` and `</par>` tags. Media objects themselves are addressed and embedded using the `<video>`, `<audio>`, `<image>` and `<text>` tags. All tags can be extended using countless parameters, such as renaming, placement and other options.

Example SMIL 1.0 code

```
<smil>
 <head>
  <meta name="title" content="SMILdemo"/>
  <meta name="author" content="Tobias Kuenkel"/>
  <meta name="copyright" content="(c)2000"/>
  <root-layout width="280" height="220" background-
      color="blue"/>
  <region id="b1" left="0" top="0" width="240" height="180"/>
  <region id="b2" left="230" top="170" width="240" height="180"/>
 </head>

 <body>
  <seq>
   <switch>
     <par system-bitrate=75000>
       <audio src="audio/id75.wav"/>
       <video src="video/video75.rm" region="b1"/>
       <image src="img/logo.jpg" region="b2"/>
     </par>
     <par system-bitrate=45000>
       <audio src="audio/id45.wav"/>
       <video src="video/video45.rm" region="b1"/>
       <image src="img/logo.jpg" region="b2"/>
     </par>
     <par system-bitrate=20000>
       <audio src="audio/id20.wav"/>
       <video src="video/video20.rm" region="b1"/>
```

```
            <image src="img/logo.jpg" region="b2"/>
          </par>
        </switch>
        <audio src="audio/endsong01.mp3"/>
        <audio src="audio/endsong02.mp3"/>
      </seq>
    </body>
  </smil>
```

SMIL 2.0

After the adoption of the SMIL 1.0 standards in 1998, people in the World Wide Web Consortium (W3C) did not just sit there idly. In comparison with popular multimedia authoring solutions, the possibilities of SMIL 1.0 remain limited to the implementation of simple concepts only. Accordingly, SMIL 2.0, which was introduced in 2001, allows the construction of clearly more attractive applications. Vital new features in SMIL 2.0 are as follows:

- Animation
  Objects (videos, images, text) can be animated; they can also be moved in the presentation during playback, or have their size modified. Likewise, the volume of audio and video clips can now be modified throughout a presentation.

- Multiple windows
  A SMIL 2.0 presentation can now control several windows. In SMIL 1.0, different objects could be arranged in a single window only; using SMIL 2.0, though, these different objects can be distributed among several windows.

- Interactivity
  The behaviour of media objects can be integrated by using the mouse and keyboard. For example, a video with subtitles can only be played once you have clicked on the mouse. This clearly gives developers further possibilities with regard to designing interactive presentations.

- Transitions
  In SMIL 2.0, transitions can be defined between any objects. Whereas RealPlayer already offered this possibility for images with the proprietary RealPix-Format, now any transitions can be used, for example, between video to video, image to image or even image to video.

Since both RealNetworks and Microsoft were involved in the development of the standard, support for SMIL 2.0 was accordingly quickly implemented in RealOne Player and Internet Explorer 6.0.

Table 1.3 SMIL support

	SMIL 1.0 support	SMIL 2.0 support
Internet Explorer 5.5	●	●
Internet Explorer 6	●	●
Apple QuickTime Player 4.1	●	
Apple QuickTime Player 5	●	
Apple QuickTime Player 6	●	
RealPlayer G2	●	
RealPlayer 7	●	
RealPlayer 8	●	
RealOne Player	●	

1.11 Data compression

One of the basics of the amazing way human perception works is the deliberate loss of information. Every second, we are literally overwhelmed by visual, acoustic and tactile information. However, our nervous system is perfectly designed to filter what is required from this flood of information, so that only a small fraction of the incoming signals actually need to be interpreted in order to absorb the information they contain.

Why use compression at all?
Data compression uses this concept of human perception and the biological restrictions of our perceptive organs, in that only that information which our brain considers relevant is transferred. In the case of digital data transfer, the available bandwidth determines how much information has to be removed, and how detailed images and sound can be transmitted.

On the Internet, the problem of restricted transmission bandwidth becomes more apparent to users, and so requires particular attention. With the production of content for the public, you must adapt to transporting audio and possibly video data via a modem connection. It should be remembered that a 56.6K modem actually only delivers an average net rate of 34 Kbit/sec. Even though this value may vary from around 10 to 15 Kbit/sec, it represents an average bandwidth when we take into account protocol overheads, loss due to poor telephone connections and bottlenecks on the provider side.

When we say that not all information from the original data is transmitted, this also includes losses which occur during the compression process. We must therefore ask the question as to whether data can be compressed without any loss of data.

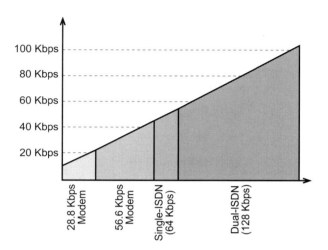

Figure 1.12 Available bandwidth with narrow-band Internet connections

Lossless compression

Run length coding The lossless compression process enables the recovery of compressed material without any loss of data whatsoever. The fundamental approach of lossy compression is the removal of redundancy, where redundancy means the duplication of information.

One example of lossless compression is run length encoding (RLE), used in fax machines, for example. In this case, a repeatedly occurring value is replaced by a code in a character string. This code describes the value and the number of repetitions. The information 'coded' in this sequence

| 61 | FFFFFF | 37BB4 | 77777 | 3 | AAAAAAAAA | 5 |

could be transmitted more efficiently by using shortcuts for strings of the same character:

| 61 | F#6 | 37BB4 | /#5 | 3 | A#9 | 5 |

As a fax often consists of large squares of plain black or white, it is better in this case not to transfer every picture element individually, but to state how often this value is repeated. Silent sequences in audio files or coloured areas in GIF images are examples where RLE is used.

Code books Compression processes are often developed for certain applications such as the optimisation of audio, video, text or program data. There are certain character strings which are repeated many times, especially in restricted application areas. All strings which occur frequently are arranged into another, similar shorter string in a code book. This code replaces the longer string in the output data.

Lossy compression

Further links on the topic of audio compression can be found on the accompanying web site. With many applications, such as those designed for text and program data compression, an exact recovery of output material is vital. However, this is not necessary in certain cases. With audio and video compression, the weaknesses of human perception described previously can be used to advantage in leaving out certain data during transfer.

If you are prepared to accept a certain degree of loss of quality, the compression factor can be increased considerably. A compromise has to be reached here between the bandwidth required and the transfer quality to be achieved.

In contrast to lossless compression, the data to be reduced is a lower priority than its characteristics in relation to human perception. Psycho-acoustic and psycho-visual models are created to decide which data can be removed on the basis of the loss tolerance determined in extensive tests.

The development of these psycho-acoustic and psycho-visual models as a mixed discipline between mathematics and human psychology is the main issue of the lossy compression process, as its quality is determined by entirely subjective factors.

Digitalisation of audio signals

Sound is carried in waves. The statement is so simple, but when these waves are saved on computer there are several points which can cause problems. The central issue is how to represent the form of these sound waves digitally, so that the analogue output signal is reconstructed to be as detailed as possible.

Figure 1.13 shows how the digitalisation process looks. The waveform audio signal is scanned with a certain frequency (scan frequency), where each instance determines the amplitude of the analogue signal. This amplitude value is assigned a numerical value, which digitally represents the amplitude value of the current point in time. How exactly this occurs depends both on how often (scan frequency) and how precisely (resolution) this amplitude value is saved.

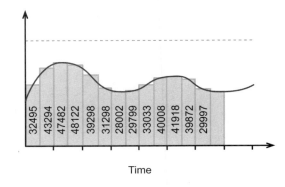

Figure 1.13 The digitalisation of an analogue video signal

As can be seen from the illustration, the output signal is represented by a wave, yet the digital values show a staircase format. This means that the status of an audio signal is always digitally saved at a certain time, but the information recorded applies to a period of time, rather than a point in time. If a signal is scanned 44,100 times per second, every digital value therefore represents the average from one 44,100th of a second. Although losses occur as the original curve is not reconstructed exactly as before, they are too small to be noticed.

This process of converting an analogue signal into digital values is known as quantisation. The losses which occur are known as quantisation noise.

There are two central factors which influence the quality of digital recording: sampling frequency and resolution. The 'wave form' of the analogue sound signal is constructed digitally, and then used to reproduce an almost identical sound on the computer or in the CD player. The number of times per second the signal is tested is very important. It is also decisive as to how precisely the determined amplitude is saved.

Resolution On a standard audio CD, the resolution at which the analogue audio signal is scanned is 16 bit. This means that 2^{16}, or over 65,000 different values can be saved. The amplitude value determined at a certain point in time is therefore digitally represented by over 65,000 values and later reconstructed.

Overmodulated audio level But what happens when the analogue audio signal level is higher than permissible? Everything probably sounds good through the speakers or on a video cassette during playback, so there appear to be no problems at analogue level. However, after digitalisation, losses can clearly be heard at overdriven points.

The reason for this dramatic consequence of overmodulation of an analogue input signal is the restricted resolution in quantisation. Analogue recording and playback devices always have a tolerance range, in which overmodulated audio signals can be processed without any dramatic loss. This may be the area marked red, which will probably be familiar from the level display of an old cassette recorder.

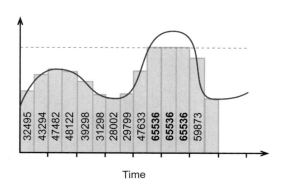

Figure 1.14 Quality loss due to overdriven audio level. The audio threshold of human hearing (simplified)

Further links on the topic of audio compression can be found on the accompanying web site.

This headroom does not exist in digital recording. If the level of the analogue input signal surpasses the permissible level, numerical values are no longer available to show this level. The highest possible value is selected, and the value is 'capped'. The losses are correspondingly high, and can clearly be heard during playback.

Human hearing can detect tones in a range from 20Hz to 22kHz, in which this highly efficient sensitivity can be strained at concerts, in the workplace or by entertainment electronics. Claude Shannon, the physicist, put forward a theory in the 1950s, stating that in order to achieve a true quality recording of audio data, the audio signal had to be scanned twice as fast in a certain frequency range. As humans can distinguish tones up to a maximum of 22kHz, the audio signal has to be scanned at around 44,000 times per second (44kHz) for us not to notice any loss in quality (quantisation noise).

Sampling frequency

Sampling frequency is usually reduced for transfer via narrowband channels such as the Internet. The frequency range for a typical audio transfer via a modem connection is usually under 44kHz. The losses incurred from a low frequency range are clearly audible from a certain point onwards, but also compromise the ability to transfer through narrowband channels at all. Transferring one audio channel alone (mono) may well spare bandwidth in narrowband connections.

Table 1.4 Frequency ranges and sampling rates

Frequency range	Sampling rate	Quality	Bandwidth required in compression
22 kHz	44 to 48 kHz	Audio CD	44,352 Kbps
15 kHz	30 to 32 kHz	Radio broadcast	2,040 Kbps
4 kHz	8 to 10 kHz	MW radio	810 Kbps
2.5 kHz	5 to 6 kHz	Telephone	58 Kbps

Uncompressed audio signals

Why not uncompressed?

In order to show the necessity of data reduction for streaming media on the Internet, the bandwidth required to transfer an uncompressed signal has been calculated below:

Sampling frequency * Resolution * Channels = Bandwith

For example, with the data on an audio CD:

44,100 (kHz) * 16 (Bit) * 2 (stereo channels) = 1411.2 Kbps

44 Modems for CD-quality sound

The uncompressed audio signal of a normal CD exceeds the typical bandwidth of a modem connection (34 Kbps) by a factor of 41. It must therefore be considered how an audio signal can be optimised and transferred in these circumstances.

Audio compression

Audio compression processes are as numerous as they are diverse. However, the traditional mp3, RealAudio format, Microsoft WMA and many others have one thing in common: they use the characteristics and weaknesses of human hearing in order to extract specific information from the data stream (irrelevance reduction). Human hearing therefore does not detect a large percentage of uncompressed data in the audio CD mentioned above. A trained ear would probably detect more information than average.

Audio threshold masking   When we analyse how sensitively the human ear reacts to certain frequencies, we can see that humans best detect sounds between 2 and 4 kHz, while a sound of 3 Hz or 16 kHz clearly has to be louder. All sounds below this threshold can therefore be removed, as they cannot possibly be detected.

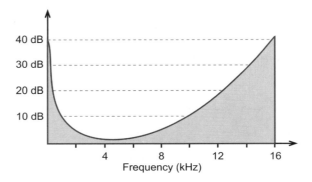

Figure 1.15 The audio threshold of human hearing (simplified)

Frequency masking   Another possibility of removing data from the audio signal comes from the audio threshold of human hearing: as we can detect a sound at, for example, 5 kHz better than at 10 kHz, this is drowned (masked) at the same time with the same volume (e.g. 20 dB). This masking effect occurs frequently in a piece of music, and therefore offers potential for data reduction.

Time masking   Human hearing is also ill adapted to abrupt changes in volume. If one sound masks another and ends abruptly, we only perceive the previously masked sound after a slight delay. This effect of 'drowning out' one sound with another continues to have an effect after the end of the masked signal, thus providing another option for removing unnoticed audio data.

Stereo redundancy   If a stereo signal is to be transferred, it would seem reasonable to examine whether the two channels must always be transferred separately, or whether certain parts of both signals are the same. For example, the melody voice in pieces of music is predominantly the same on both channels, and therefore only need transferring once.

These are only simplified possibilities of optimising a digital audio signal so that a fraction of bandwidth only is used during transfer. Exhaustive comparisons of the mp3, AAC, WMA or RealAudio compression process prove that the 1.4 Mbps rate of an uncompressed audio signal on a CD can be compressed without audible loss to a rate of 128 Kbps. When this data rate is reduced below 64 Kbps for transfer via a modem connection, losses become apparent far more quickly, yet the results are still acceptable, considering that only 2% of the original data remains.

Digitalisation of video signals

The digital recording of a video signal also runs on a simple principle, althrough much higher demands are made of the system than during audio digitalisation.

Analogue video and especially TV signals are best described by their characteristics. Since several different tv-standards exist worlwide, table 1.5 shows the size of video images and how often they are transmitted in different countries:

Table 1.5 Worldwide tv-standards

	Resolution	Frames per second	Countries (example)
NTSC	720×480	29.97	USA, Canada, Mexico, Japan
PAL	768×576	25	UK, Ireland, Germany, Spain, Italy, Australia, China, India
SECAM	768×576	25	France, Poland, Russia

For digital recording of a video signal, the colour value of each image dot in every frame has to be recorded. Ideally, 24 bit (3 bytes) per image dot is used, allowing a differentiation of about 16.8 million colour values. A video image saved in this way can be reconstructed without measurable loss.

However, as this uncompressed type of video recording makes high demands on the system, the compression process is often used to reduce these demands.

Uncompressed video signals

In comparison to audio signals, the necessity of data compression methods is more obvious with video signals, as audio has to be transmitted in addition to image data. The bandwidth required for a digital video stream is calculated as follows:

Resolution x Colour depth x Frames per second = Bandwidth

In European PAL/SECAM format, the physical resolution is 768×576 image dots at 25 frames per second. A digital representation of true colour requires a colour depth of 24 bit. The bandwidth required for an uncompressed PAL signal is calculated as follows:

768×576 (Image dots) x 24 (Bit) x 25 (fps) = 265.420.800 bps =253.1 Mbps

Corresponding to this, the necessary bandwidth for an uncompressed NTSC signal would be:

720×480 (Image dots) x 24 (Bit) x 29.97 (fps) = 248.583.168 bps = 237.1 Mbps

103 ISDN cards for moving images

To this has to be added the 1.4 Mbps of audio data. The justifiable objection now is that Internet streaming video can never be transferred at full resolution at as many frames per second. Even when the resolution is reduced to 240×180 and the image frequency to 10 fps, this still equates to a bandwidth of 9.9 Mbps, which exceeds the best performance of a dual ISDN connection (100 Kbps max) by about 100 times.

As such amounts of data could never be suitable for Internet transfer, we must ask the question as to how audio and video bandwidth requirements can be reduced, so that the average user can access such material whilst retaining the best possible signal quality. This is where we need to use data compression, comprising both lossless and lossy compression. Whereas losslessly compressed data can be reproduced in its original quality without any loss of data, this is not true with lossy compression. The data reduction achieved with lossy compression processes is high, whereby the higher the compression rate, the greater the loss of data.

Video compression

As can be seen with audio compression, a central concept of data reduction is that specific information is removed using the weaknesses and limitations of human perceptions. This occurs until the desired data rate has been reached, at which point any errors and losses are minimised as much as possible.

Data reduction in moving images uses these limitations in the same way as audio compression, on the basis that, compared to the ear, the human eye is relatively insensitive to modifications and distortions. This enables the production of a fundamentally effective process with high compression factors, which is essential given the high data rate of uncompressed video material.

In digital video data recording, it is generally assumed that the human eye has around 120 million nerve cells available for detecting brightness levels (skewers), but only about 6 million cones at the retina for registering colour information. For this reason, less memory is used in recording colour data than in recording brightness data, such as outlines and contours.

If you look at a video image, you will soon see that there are so many possibilities to remove or optimise a large part of uncompressed data in transfer without major losses.

Two-dimensional compression

In a typical moving image compression process, the individual frames are first compressed, often using Discreet Cosine Transformation (DCT). This transforms time-dependent data within the frequency domain. From a section of 8×8 pixels, the image details of the section can be described in a two-dimensional sequence in decreasing order, according to the DCT values. In the example outlined below, a block of image dots (also 8×8) is transformed. In the results, the upper left hand number represents the roughest detail, and the lower right hand number, the sharpest.

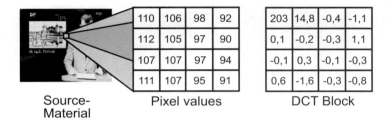

Source-Material	Pixel values			DCT Block			
	110	106	98	92	203	14,8	-0,4	-1,1
	112	105	97	90	0,1	-0,2	-0,3	1,1
	107	107	97	94	-0,1	0,3	-0,1	-0,3
	111	107	95	91	0,6	-1,6	-0,3	-0,8

Figure 1.16 Discreet Cosine Transformation

In a subsequent quantisation process, the individual values are multiplied by values in a quantisation table, and rounded. This determines which of the DCT block values can be omitted, and which image details can be permanently removed from the block. As the optimised DCT block contains countless zeros, a large amount of memory space can be saved by using a run length encoding. In contrast to DCT, this quantisation process cannot be reversed without data loss.

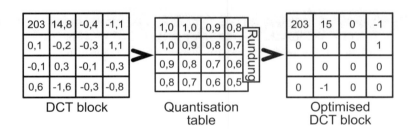

DCT block				Quantisation table				Optimised DCT block			
203	14,8	-0,4	-1,1	1,0	1,0	0,9	0,8	203	15	0	-1
0,1	-0,2	-0,3	1,1	1,0	0,9	0,8	0,7	0	0	0	1
-0,1	0,3	-0,1	-0,3	0,9	0,8	0,7	0,6	0	0	0	0
0,6	-1,6	-0,3	-0,8	0,8	0,7	0,6	0,5	0	-1	0	0

Rundung

Figure 1.17 Quantisation of the DCT block

Many of the best known video reduction processes, such as JPEG, M-JPEG or MPEG compression, are based on the quantisation of DCT blocks.

Three-dimensional compression
As well as purely two-dimensional compression of individual frames, an analysis of the three-dimensional properties of a video signal offers further possibilities in data reduction. There is an especially high redundancy potential in transferring similar image content, which should not be ignored.

In this process, a differential image, based on a keyframe, is constructed in a sequence of images, containing only the differences from the previous image. This elimination of repeatedly transferred image content provides considerable potential for reduction with appropriate video material.

A typical example for efficient use of this method is the classic 'talking heads scene,' in which one of the speakers talks in front of a static background. As there are hardly any changes occurring between individual frames, only a fraction of image data has to be transferred.

Figure 1.18 Image-sequence with high redundancy (talking head)

Figure 1.19 Keyframe with differential images

Images 1.18 and 1.19 show an image sequence of a typical 'talking head scene'. As much of the information of all five images is identical, an effective way of saving bandwidth during the transmission is to transmit only the first image and then just the information that is different to this keyframe. As you can see, the differential images contain less information than the keyframe and therefore need less bandwidth.

The movement of large objects in a video image cannot be compressed efficiently by constructing differential images. Attempts are therefore made to identify these object movements in the frame, and save only the contour of the object together with the vector of movement. The same principle is used as in camera panning shots. The existing image is moved, and only the missing part of the image supplemented.

Of course, these are only some simple examples showing how lossy video compression methods work. Those in modern standards, such as MPEG, RealVideo or Windows Media, naturally implement algorithms that have been developed over many years and that are much more complex. Nevertheless, it is becoming clear how video compression rates of 1:1000 and more can be achieved these days, and how they still provide such good results in view of the huge 'information destruction'.

Streaming video production

The technical requirements of the Internet place high demands on the components involved in the production process. Currently, relatively poor audio and video quality is accepted as normal, but we are in fact fully aware of the difference between what is good and what we have come to expect as being average quality streaming video.

The typical production process can roughly be subdivided into capture, encoding, provision and retrieval. The requirements involved in these production stages are outlined below.

2.1 Source material

A fundamental factor in the quality of the encoded stream, often underestimated by beginners, is the type and quality of the source material. The generally low quality of streaming video content often makes the user neglect this matter, which may adversely affect the end result.

Video material

Regardless of whether you are processing images or are editing existing material, it is essential that the material you end up with be of the highest possible quality. The more effort is made at this point, the better the end result will be. However, you may often have no control over the quality of the source material, so any defects will need to be corrected at later stages of production using filters.

Video noise   One of the general problems of using recording media is video noise and restricted video bandwidth, especially with consumer formats (e.g. VHS-Tapes). The problem with video noise is that the compression process used in streaming media leaves much to be desired. Granulation is not interpreted as such by the compression algorithms, and so is read as important image details. Valuable bandwidth is then wasted on transferring these interferences if no allowances are made for this process.

Figure 2.1   Video noise

Features such as sharpness, luminosity, clarity and accuracy are also indicators of an expensive format, such as Betacam SP. This tape format records in a higher resolution and higher bandwidth than consumer formats. An investment in this sense would therefore be rewarded by visibly better end results.

Table 2.1   Costs and recording quality of different recording systems

	Costs (approx.) Player/ Camera		Costs (approx.) 60 min tape	Video noise	Image Quality
Digital Betacam	£12,000	£30,000	£20	minimal	optimum
Betacam SP, Betacam SX, IMX, DVCPro	£6,000	£20,000	£12	minimal	very good
DV, DVCam	0	£1,000	£10	very little	good
DVD	n/a	£120	n/a	very little	good
SVHS, Hi-8	£170	£170	£3	visible	average
VHS	£80	£50	£1	clear	below average

However, there are, of course, further components that impact on the image and sound quality of the source material. To produce a Livecast, video cameras are required as a rule, and at the lower end of the price scale, there are considerable differences between models. An important criterion for rating the quality of cameras is – other than the format that is used (for example, MiniDV or Hi-8) – the quality of the lens system and that of the CCD. CCD (Charged Coupled Device) is the electronic component of the camera that is responsible for converting the image captured by the lens into one or more electronic signals. With basic cameras, only one CCD chip tends to be used, which possibly does not scan the complete video resolution either. CCDs in high quality cameras, on the other hand, scan the complete PAL/NTSC resolution and moreover, work in threes. Using 3 CCDs, each one of the three primary colours, red, green and blue, is scanned. Together with high quality lenses, the video signal produced from these cameras contains visibly less video noise and is significantly sharper and accurate with regard to colour.

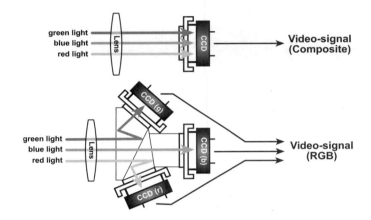

Figure 2.2 Video signal-generation in 1-CCD and 3-CCD cameras

There are different interfaces for the transmission of video signals from recorder or camera to PC. Although there are significant differences in the video quality they provide, the qualitative spectrum/spread starts at a higher level compared to camera- or recorder-equipment. So it is possible to transmit an absolutely acceptable video signal via a composite cable if the signal itself is of good quality. Nevertheless the knowledge of the different interfaces can be useful, especially when dealing with professional video equipment.

Table 2.2 Video interfaces

	Description	Remarks	Connectors
Composite	Luminance (black/white) and chrominance (colour) information is transmitted via one signal	Often found on consumer-devices and capture cards.	
		Also known as: 'FBAS'	RCA BNC
S-Video	(abbr.: Seperated Video) Luminance and chrominance information is transmited via two separate signals	Often found on better consumer-devices, cameras and capture cards. Very good interface for live-encoding.	
		Also known as: 'Y/C'	S-Video
Component	The video signal is transmitted via three separate signals: luminance and two chrominance	Professional interface, commonly used in broadcasting environments. Also known as: 'YUV'	
			BNC
SDI	(abbr.: Serial Digital Interface) The video signal is transmitted as an uncompressed digital data stream of approximately 250 Mbps.	Professional interface, commonly used in broadcasting environments.	
			BNC
Firewire	The video signal is transmitted as an compressed digital data stream of approximately 25 Mbps (DV-compression)	Very popular in semi-professional video editing. Found on every digital camcorder (DV, Digital8, etc.)	
		Also known as: IEEE1394, I-Link	Firewire

Leitmotif

If you are involved in video recording, you can considerably influence the ultimate image quality of the streaming video. The two factors that must be given priority throughout are position and motion.

Camera position

If we bear in mind the actual target audience at large, it may hardly be worth using high-detail images (totals). A user who only has a 56.6K modem connection will see an image of 176 x 132 pixels as little more than a mash of colour blocks. When recording concerts, meetings or conferences, it is essential that the camera be positioned near the speaker or artist, or that a zoom lens is available. You can then select parts of images so that the person is in focus after the encoding process. Panoramic shots of the stage, hall or audience should be used as short clips to give a sense of ambience.

Despite the poor quality of coded streams, steps can be taken at this stage of production to give the end user a positive impression by an appropriate use of camera positioning.

Camera motion

Links to major manufacturers of video editing systems and capture cards can be found on the accompanying web site. Any compression procedure worth its salt nowadays uses differential images and motion prediction to achieve the highest possible compression rate. This means that not every frame is saved in its entirety, but only the changes within a certain group of frames. If a large object, or the entire image moves (panning), this is detected and taken into account.

However, panning shots, zooms and motion in the picture require much bandwidth during recording, leaving little room for fine details. For this reason, image sequences of this kind should be kept to a minimum from a technical point of view, in order to keep as much bandwidth as possible free for detail. It goes without saying that some quick camera movements and zoom control cannot be avoided entirely. But whoever makes the decision should opt for image quality over usage, or at least minimise the speed of camera motion.

Lighting and patterns

Good lighting influences image quality considerably: even though video cameras and television can often produce reasonable images in poor light, lossy compression impacts on the way the lighting is reproduced in the final product. Sharp outlines, good contrast, bright colours and low video noise in optimum lighting conditions affect the quality of the encoded material positively, while strong contrast and shadows resulting from sunlight or spotlights have negative effects. This results in unnaturally bright surfaces and very dark shadows, with no drawing or details in them or as it is expressed in German: ', die keine Zeichnung enthalten'. As low contrast is prevalent in these overlit or underlit areas, there is a danger of loss of definition and monochrome zones after encoding.

Soft light
rec̲ᵤ̲mendation

A constant source of light is appropriate, as different lighting levels cause extensive changes in the output material. These alterations to image content must be encoded at the expense of image details, and should therefore be kept to a minimum. This problem occurs often when recording musical events, where it is usually difficult to do much about the lighting conditions. The negative effects of extreme changes in lighting can therefore be prevented by close camera positioning and by avoiding backlit shots.

Definition

When recording fine patterns such as on clothing or wallpaper, it should be remembered that this may cause shimmering in the picture, which may make these areas blurred after encoding. The rule that detailed images cause problems when enriching streaming content also applies in this context.

Direction and cutting

As mentioned previously, careful camera work is essential when creating streaming media, as every unnecessary movement wastes bandwidth. However, there are camera movements which are acceptable prior to compression. Panning shots are recognised by all compression methods. In this case, only the section of the next frame which contains new material is saved. On the other hand, zooming in and out add up to considerable increase in video material content, which will all need to be saved.

Obviously, we cannot avoid creating such dynamic elements completely. However, since the entire bandwidth is required even for a rough display in a panning shot, it would make sense to pause at the end of the pan for a few seconds, so the finer details can be broadcast.

The shot should follow these principles: every considerable change means a reduction in quality. The difference in quality between a speaker in front of a steady background and a rapidly cut music video with intermittent lighting and wild camera movements will therefore be quite substantial, even though both clips were encoded at the same bandwidth.

In practice and from a technical point of view, individual clips should be at least five to ten seconds in length.

2.2 Capturing

Capturing is the next key process in the production of streaming video. As outlined above, the source material used is the decisive factor in the ultimate quality of the video stream, and acts as a basis for further editing with capturing hardware and software.

Video and audio signals are transferred into the computer memory in different formats, resolutions and frame rates using specially installed hardware. There is a very wide range of performance, ranging from TV cards with USB connection, to professional editing facilities that cost several hundred thousand pounds. The reason for these differences was indicated in the section on video compression: editing video data with little or no compression places high demands on editing hardware and software. Affordable solutions use compression rates so high that they are unsuitable for use at professional level. Nevertheless: right now there is a technology that enables even home pcs to capture and edit video material via DV. Since every pc nowadays is equipped with a firewireport and the appropriate cameras are also affordable, video editing at a very high level is simple to do. However, the handling of a native DV-Stream with 25 Mbps also pushes a well equipped pc to its limit.

But one can take shortcuts when producing streaming video on the Internet, to avoid the requirements of traditional video editing. As well as increasing the compression rate, one can also reduce image resolution and frame rate. This means that one can use affordable computers to produce video content.

Hardware

The hardware used in streaming video production ranges from conventional editing systems to special capture cards.

The advantage with professional editing systems is that material can be processed at a higher quality, as these are designed to process full frames. Their export functions act as an interface for the production of on-demand content, making this high quality video material an ideal basis for encoding.

On the other hand, the advantage of special capture cards designed for the digitisation of Internet video data is that they usually work without time-consuming exporting operations. They can also be used for live encoding. As far as the highest possible quality recording of video signals is concerned, these solutions are less efficient than their more powerful friends, because they have less sophisticated hardware components.

Again, video capturing via firewire is a relatively young option for users which combines the good quality of professional editing systems with the cost-efficiency and easy handling of capture cards. Combined with software that supports this way of capturing video and audio firewire, it is an ideal way of generating streaming content.

Another rule which can be applied to encoding is that you get the quality you pay for. However, more economical Web solutions offer features such as live encoding, multi-card operation or hardware encoding, which has proved essential in many cases.

2.3 Encoding

Bandwidth is the key concept at this stage of production: features such as image quality, resolution, frame rate and audio quality are all connected to bandwidth. The first decision to be made, therefore, concerns the bandwidth to be encoded. In turn, this decision is linked to the target group affected.

Resolution   First, the physical resolution of the material to be encoded needs to be defined. This should be the first decision taken, as resolution is a considerable variable in the use of multistream technologies which often cannot be adapted to different bandwidths. Irrespective of whether the user has 30 or 300 Kbps of available bandwidth, the number of pixels displayed remains constant, and should therefore be adapted to suit the target group of the entire stream. It is useful to distinguish between narrowband (ISDN and less) and broadband (more than ISDN) users at this point, in order to offer both target groups an appropriate resolution. In Windows Media 9 this limitation has been removed: when encoding a multiple bit rate stream, it is now possible to define an individual resolution and frame rate for every bandwidth encoded (see below: chapter 4).

Table 2.3 Recommended resolutions of streaming video

	Ø Bandwidth	Recommended resolution	Mbps (MBytes) uncompressed
28.8K modem	20–23 Kbps	176×132	15.2 (1.9)
56.6K modem	32–35 Kbps	176×132	15.2 (1.9)
Single ISDN	45–55 Kbps	176×132	15.2 (1.9)
Dual ISDN	80–100 Kbps	240×180	25.9 (3.2)
DSL	300 Kbps	320×240	46.0 (5.8)
Cable	600 Kbps		
LAN	>1,000 Kbps	768×576 (PAL)	265.4 (33.2)

Frame rate The frame rate of the video, or the number of images displayed per second, should be somewhere between 12 and 15 frames per second (fps). Within this range, individual frames start to merge. If the frame rate falls below this level, the picture begins to get jerky. The user would be well advised to compromise between frame rate and image quality.

SureStream or Multibit encoding

Streaming without a streaming server The use of multistream techniques mainly depends on whether a normal Webserver or a streaming server is available. When using multistream concepts, client and server must be able to communicate via the available bandwidth, which is not possible using a conventional Web server. Furthermore, the server needs to be able to separate the desired audio/video stream from the file or live stream, and send only this to the client. Although transferring multistream clips via a Web server appears to work at first glance, this is not the case. This is because, when faced with a request, Web servers begin to transfer a file chronologically from beginning to end on demand. If the file contains more than one audio and video track, all versions are sent simultaneously to the client, which then plays back the best one. This is the opposite of what is required: to use bandwidth efficiently.

Links to main Internet FTP clients can be found on the accompanying web site.

Streaming with Streaming Server   If different qualities of a streaming media file are available on a Web server, several clips have to be prepared for transfer. This is when users who request streams which are available at different quality will opt for the one they want.

It is a different matter if a streaming server can communicate directly with the client. When different streaming clients such as RealPlayer, Quicktime Player or Windows Media Player are installed, users indicate which type of Internet connection they have. When a connection is made, the client sends this default setting to the streaming server. If several stream qualities are available, the server sends the data whose overall bandwidth best corresponds to the connection bandwidth.

Even though the maximum transmission bandwidth of a 56.6K modem is theoretically 56.6 Kbps, this speed is never achieved. This is partly due to connection control signals, partly due to a poor ISP connection, and, in the case of some analogue modems, partly due to the connection quality of the telephone network operator exchange. For these reasons, any estimates made regarding data rate should be lowered.

The upper limit which the various players are capable of reaching using the maximum available bandwidth of different connection types is shown in brackets in the final column of Table 2.2. In the case of each streaming client, users indicate which type of Internet connection they have (modem, ISDN, DSL, T1, etc...). For example, if it indicates ISDN, this information is sent to the streaming server. The server registers this information, then delivers the appropriate stream for the requested multistream file. If the data rate in the video file is set too high for single ISDN (e.g. 60 kbps), the server temporarily delivers the next lower quality level (e.g. 34 kbps). The user then sees a poorer image than an ISDN connection would usually allow, at least at the beginning of the transmission. However, player and server continually assess the connection quality, which, in our case, means that the server may switch to the 60 kbps stream, if the connection bandwidth allows this.

This example highlights the importance of assigning the correct bandwidth to different streams. This is what defines quality levels and therefore determines the best possible transfer between different user platforms.

In practice, it would appear that, when encoding multistreams, it makes sense to adapt to the default settings of different manufacturers' encoders. The recommendations on bandwidth and resolution outlined in Table 2.2 can be applied at this point, and enable the user to reach an optimum result quickly. Even though a multistream supply is encoded complete with its own individual settings, it is useful to follow the recommendations for different bandwidths, and also encode temporary resolutions which the client can access if the transmission bandwidth fluctuates.

Multistream and resolution   The issue of resolution in the use of multistream technologies is a delicate one. In Table 2.2 the recommended resolutions for modem and dual ISDN users are different, but both qualities cannot be produced in the one file. The provider therefore has to specify a resolution suitable for each user.

The new versions of codecs used in image compression with their improved playback quality enable a resolution of 240 x 180 for connections for modem up to DSL. Even though narrowband connections transfer fewer image details, this resolution offers DSL and modem users an acceptable compromise.

Audio

The issue of audio, a key factor in the encoding process, has not been addressed as yet. All manufacturers offer various audio codecs for different qualities and sound characteristics, which can usually be assigned to any bandwidth. However, it should always be remembered that audio signals require additional bandwidth, which should be taken into consideration along with video signal configuration.

In the case of the three software packages described here, the first decision to be made is the one regarding the codec to be used with the audio material involved. A decision usually needs to be made between speech and music, as different optimised codecs (compression/decompression processes) are offered which suit the characteristics of the respective signals. In addition, the frequency range, channel and resolution have to be specified in accordance with material, bandwidth and target group.

On-demand upload   The importance of audio data varies between negligible (e.g. for background noise only) and substantial (e.g. for music videos or speech). Bandwidth allocation therefore depends on the situation. One cannot make global recommendations; the user will need to compromise between quality and bandwidth. However, it should be remembered that because of the relatively low bandwidth required for it, audio can be transferred smoothly at good quality. So bandwidth allocation between audio and video can often give priority to audio.

2.4   Provision

Once technical specifications have been defined, the actual content production can begin. This should be made accessible to the user in the last stage of production either on a normal Web server or a streaming server.

The provision of on-demand content is usually a straightforward process: encoded clips are located on the local encoding computer and must be copied to the server. The server is often not accessible via the LAN (Local Area Network), so an FTP upload is required. This is done in a defined directory branch of the server, previously configured as the content directory. This could be either the normal HTML path of an HTTP server, or the content directory of a streaming server.

The material is available when the upload is complete, and can be requested with an appropriate player.

Live streaming   The live streaming process involves the encoder components and streaming server. A conventional Web server does not provide the functions required, and so cannot be used for broadcasting live material. In this case, a streaming server does not provide a data hosting facility, but forwards the incoming data stream from the encoder to the clients connected.

The encoder generates a data stream in the appropriate format and sends this to the server via a special Internet connection. Audio or video signals, or pre-encoded material can all be used as sources. In the latter case, a live broadcast is just simulated, as data is not encoded live; rather, it is read from an existing file and streamed to the server via a special program.

The server is configured before a 'livecast' so that it constantly plays back the data stream to a client, as long as the request is in place (e.g. the name of a certain directory or file). Following the query (and authentication, if required), the server forwards the incoming stream to the client, which then renders it and outputs it on the screen.

2.5 Requesting

After provision, the material is called from the server. The onus is now on the client to request and display the content. The player software performs this function: it contacts the server and receives the media stream. The software retrieves the address under which the material is stored either directly from the user, or from the Web browser. If the player is embedded in a Web site, the address is passed via parameters in the HTML code.

Protocol rollover   A key procedure in the streaming process is protocol rollover. This or a similar mechanism is used by the client to create a connection with the server via various network protocols. This is useful if a connection cannot be established via streaming protocols such as RTSP or MMS. Even though this guarantees optimum performance, in practice it is not often possible to use these specialist protocols. One reason for this is that security precautions in the networks of many businesses and institutions often mean that Internet access is restricted. In order to make unauthorised access to the internal network as difficult as possible, internal users can only access Internet content via HTTP protocol through firewalls.

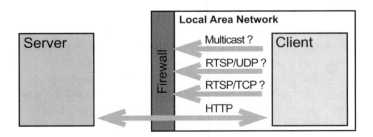

Figure 2.3 Limitation of Internet access in LANs

Firewalls   If a client attempts to access external servers from 'behind' a firewall via disabled protocols or ports, the firewall blocks this access. At this point, many programs use protocol rollover, whereby the server tries to access its target using other protocols. As RTSP and MMS use UDP in the transport layer by default and are often blocked by firewalls, a second connection set-up is usually attempted via TCP. If this also fails, HTTP is used. As the use of this protocol is essential for conventional Internet access, this is usually the best method for establishing a connection with a streaming server through firewalls. However, this is done at the expense of optimum streaming performance, as transporting data via HTTP has several disadvantages (see section 1.6 – Streaming media protocols).

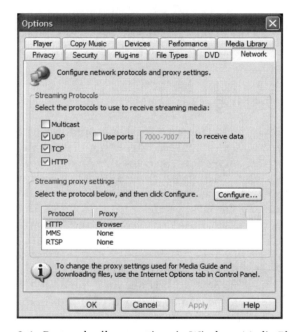

Figure 2.4   Protocol rollover settings in Windows Media Player 9

    If access to streaming media is possible in most cases, even from behind firewalls, it often fails due to incorrect player software configuration. In order to be able to communicate with the server on the Internet, the player has to be configured in the same way as the Web browser for the appropriate type of Internet connection. RealPlayer, Media Player and QuickTime Player therefore have entry fields, in which specifications such as connection type, address and firewalls ports or proxy server have to be indicated. These settings are usually displayed in most Web browsers, or the player can be instructed to use the proxy settings of the Web browser.

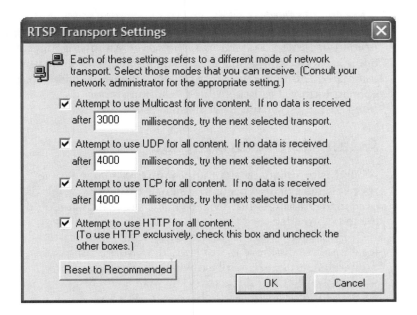

Figure 2.5 Proxy configuration in RealPOne Player

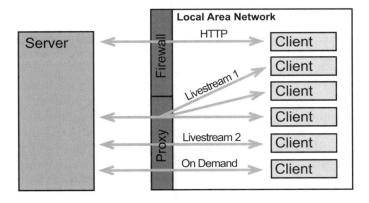

Figure 2.6 Firewall and Proxy for efficient streaming media traffic

Firewalls are necessary security facilities to protect the computers within a LAN from intruders. Nevertheless, it is possible to open them for streaming media traffic in a secure way. Instead of directing all outgoing traffic through the firewall, it is possible to setup a special gateway, which is responsible for managing all streaming data transfer between the Internet and the internal LAN. These computers are called proxies. But the main argument for using proxies is not to access streaming media through a firewall (this can be done by simply modifiing the firewall set-up), but rather to increase the efficiency of streaming media traffic. For example: when several users inside a LAN receive a livestream from the Internet, not everybody needs a dedicated connection to the server. An intelligent proxy could notice this, open just one connection to the streaming server and distribute the livestream internally. Another example are proxies which store highly frequented on-demand-content locally. The benefit for the administrator of the LAN is that the external, often cost-intensive traffic is minimised.

2.6   A sample live broadcast

A band is to broadcast their appearance at a large festival over the Internet as a special feature of a Web site. The signals from existing television cameras are to be used in the transmission. A video chat with the stars and on-demand news facilities are to be provided too.

The production of a large live event begins with planning and preparation. The legal implications have to be clarified, as does authorisation for the recording. As numerous parties are involved with the event, a written filming permit from the local authorities, producers and the management of the band is required. Third party use is also approved at this point, with a view to a future compilation of the best clips. Furthermore, light and sound engineering issues are also addressed as much as possible in relation to the best camera positions for streaming.

Discussions are to be held with technicians from the OB van (outside broadcast van) on location, and cable is laid, to which the signals from five cameras will be sent. Signals are to be transferred via an audio/video mixer, and the output signal is streamed. A video camera is also to be set up for the video chat.

Planning and preparation

Several short news reports are also to be produced. Interviews and backstage images are to be recorded using a webcam, then cut and encoded. A laptop with a firwire port is to be used as a simple editing facility. The clips are then to be forwarded as AVI videos via ethernet to the encoding PC for further editing.

A powerful computer will be required for the encoding process, as a RealVideo SureStream is encoded with five quality levels. The encoder is to be connected directly to the video server via eight bundled ISDN channels, which guarantees a bandwidth of up to 300 kbps for transferring a SureStream. A special capture card with FBAS input is to be used as an image capture device.

News on demand

On the software side, RealProducer Plus is to be used, which encodes both the on-demand clips and the live signal. The use of eight ISDN channels restricts the entire bandwidth of the live broadcast to around 400 kbps, for which reason five video streams are to be encoded at 20, 34, 45, 80 and 300 kbps.

Live encoding

In the run-up to the live event, short clips are to be produced and placed on the Real server via FTP and embedded into the Web site. During the live stream, the encoding PC will create the video stream exclusively, which first shows a compilation of clips from different cameras, followed by the video chat between the stars and the fans.

Conclusion

When used in this way, streaming offers a genuine added value compared to a standard television broadcast: spectators can see additional information before the event, view from non-broadcast camera angles, and ask the band questions after the show 'in person'. Using the most up-to-date compression technologies enables broadcasts to be of such quality that, slowly but surely, they are breaking through into the world of conventional television at a fraction of the cost.

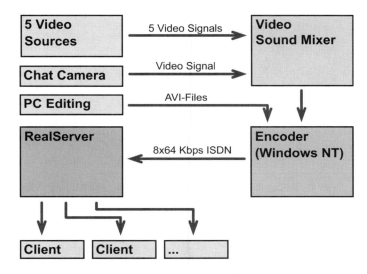

Figure 2.7 Producing a livecast (sample)

3

RealSystem

RealNetworks are pioneers in the field of streaming media. They realised the future importance of streaming media on the Internet as early as 1994. The founder of the company, Rob Glaser, was formerly Vice President of Multimedia and Consumer Systems at Microsoft, and in 1994 he launched a product named RealAudio, the true potential of which is just being realised today. RealNetworks is currently standing its ground against the strong competition from Microsoft and Apple, and is maintaining its position in broadband streaming. Nevertheless the competition is getting harder, as Microsoft in particular, seems absolutely determined to get RealNetworks' market share.

The most important and well-known product is RealPlayer, introduced in 1994 with the launch of RealAudio. Since then, the player has been installed on 80% of all Internet-capable computers. According to business reports, in the past 85% of streaming media content on the Web was distributed via RealSystem, and 350,000 hours of live material is produced weekly. The company's Web site carries part of this material, and is counted among the 25 most popular sites on the entire Web.

Pioneer work With the founding of his company (known at the time as Progressive Networks), Rob Glaser pursued his vision of Internet audio and video transfer at an early stage. The 14.4K modems available in 1994 did not allow video transfer because of their restricted efficiency, but were sufficient for transferring audio signals. At the time, this was sensational enough, as it constituted a first step in the direction of Internet multimedia. RealPlayer 1.0 was also available to download free of charge in 1994; revenue was created by customers purchasing Helix Server. Until mid-1995, RealPlayer 1.0 was downloaded over 200,000 times by business servers, and by the end of the year, one million downloads were reported.

The success of RealSystem continued, and in 1997 Progressive Networks introduced Version 4.0 of the RealPlayer, capable of supporting the transfer of video data. Around this time, Progressive Networks began to witness competition from other providers such as Xing, VDO or Vivo, who had already introduced their video solutions. Even though these companies provided increasing competition, the greatest threat to the persistent success of RealSystem came from Rob Glaser's previous employers: Microsoft.

Table 3.1 The business history of RealNetworks

April 1995	Introduction of first RealPlayer and RealAudio 1.0.
Oct 1995	Introduction of RealAudio 2.0 (15.2 kbps Voice Codec, Livecasting)
Sept 1996	Introduction of RealAudio 3.0 (Stereo, 'Near-CD quality')
Feb 1997	Introduction of RealVideo 1.0
Sept 1997	Name changed from Progressive Networks to RealNetworks
Oct 1997	Introduction of RealSystem 5.0 (Fullscreen video, streaming Flash, pay-per-view, ad insertion, increased image and sound quality of new codecs)
April 1998	Introduction of RealSystem G2 (SureStream, RealText & RealPix, RTSP and SMIL support, AVI, ASF, JPEG, MPEG, VIV und WAV support, new codecs,...) Helix Producer
Nov 1999	Introduction of RealPlayer 7 (Media Caching, Quality Optimisation)
May 2000	Introduction of RealSystem 8 (Quality optimisation, new codecs)
Sept 2001	Announcement of RealOne Platform (new versions of Player, Encoder and Server, subscription-portal with exclusive streaming content)
April 2002	Introduction of RealVideo 9 (Quality optimisation, new surround-audio-codecs)
July 2002	Announcement of Helix Community (publication of source code for 3rd party developers and open-source- community)

Due to increasing competition and innovation, especially on the part of Microsoft, development of RealSystem has been driven forward considerably during the last three years. In version 6.0, also known as G2 (Generation 2), RealNetworks introduced key features for the first time in 1998, such as SureStreaming, SMIL support and multimedia streaming, all widely acknowledged today as being powerful streaming solutions.

As for the current version of the new RealOne Player, the small tool used for audio playback has generated an SMIL-based Web browser with extensive and convenient functions for Internet access. All major media types such as video, audio, text and animation can be played back in different formats on all main computer systems with a version of RealNetworks Player software. The quality of the video and audio streams ranges from narrowband modem streams at 20 kbps to interactive video presentations in TV quality at more than 1 Mbps, in which subtitles, Internet links, picture-in-picture functions and automatic language selection are available.

Although the RealPlayer 8 is still offered for download by RealNetworks, the next level of accessing RealMedia content is now available. With RealOne Player, RealNetworks continues its strategy of evolving the RealPlayer from a simple RealMedia-access-tool to a multimedia browser integrated into the underlying operation system.

RealNetworks is currently under considerable pressure, since its main competitor, Microsoft, has proved more than once that its aggressive policy towards its fellow competitors is extremely effective. RealNetworks is standing its ground successfully, yet the limited circulation of the RealPlayer compared to the Microsoft Media Player spells dark clouds on the horizon....

3.1 Audio and video codecs

As described previously, the restricted bandwidth of the Internet requires highly efficient procedures to reduce the amount of data in image and sound transfer. As shown, the bandwidth theoretically required to transfer uncompressed material at a lower resolution exceeds a modem connection by a factor of between 300 and 750. The only method of conveying at least a rough impression of audio-visual material is to use highly efficient lossy data compression.

The procedures which enable such data reduction are written in codecs, the most important cornerstones of the streaming media system architecture (codec is an abbreviation of compression-decompression process). The entire system is measured by the quality of the data compressed using these codecs, which is why so much research is invested in this complex area.

In constrast to competitors like Apple or even Microsoft in the past, RealNetworks have always developed their own compression process, first in 1995 for the RealAudio System, and then in 1997 for RealVideo. As the core of the RealSystem, its exact technical specification is a well-kept secret, and only snippets of information ever emerge.

Video codecs

RealVideo. Very few technical details are known about the RealSystem compression procedure, so it can be assumed that video compression is based on discrete cosine transformation. This forms the basis for all moving image compression processes such as MPEG-2, Sorenson or RealVideo. It is probable that wavelet and fractal compression have also been integrated into newer versions like RealVideo 8 and 9 of the audio and video codecs, which explains the huge improvement in quality in these codec versions.

Apart from RealAudio codecs, a choice has to be made between the various RealVideo codecs due to compatibility issues. The various video codecs constitute further developments, so that ideally the most recent codec is always used. A sensible decision in favour of using an older RealVideo codec can only be made on the basis of the RealPlayer versions installed and used by the target group.

RealVideo G2

Major codec facelifting

In 1998, RealNetworks introduced RealSystem 6.0 (also known as G2 or Generation 2), a thoroughly revised product which contained not only core innovations such as SureStream, SMIL browsing or multimedia support, but also a new codec version.

A big part of RealVideo Internet content nowadays still uses this codec, and even today, some providers rely on it to encode new content. This creates compatibility issues, because using version 8 or 9 requires downloading RealPlayer 8 or the RealOne Player, which is over 4MB in size. In the past, many providers did not expect users of earlier versions of the player to download the new ones, so they relied on older codecs. In the last month, the new versions for the RealPlayer have replaced the versions G2 and 7, so that the current version of the a/v-codecs can be used without problems.

The G2 codec comes some way behind the current version of the up to date ones in terms of quality, which is understandable given the date of its introduction.

RealVideo G2 SVT

Both compression and decompression require system resources. Even though video stream playback at any bandwidth no longer pushes computers to their limits, it should be remembered that users with older computers should also be able to access streams. For this reason, SVT (Scalable Video Technology) enables the client to reduce dynamically the frame rate of the video. This means that the client itself can prevent the system from overloading.

SVT was introduced with the first update to the RealPlayer G2 (to 6.06), and is implemented in all of RealNetworks' video codec since G2. When encoding, SVT does not take into account any possible performance restrictions on the part of the client, and enables the RealPlayer to reduce the frame rate 'on the fly,' which prevents errors during playback. The material is stored in a fixed, pre-defined frame rate on the server, and the RealPlayer 'decides' whether and when to reduce the frame rate.

The RealVideo G2 SVT codec also has better loss protection mechanisms and can therefore handle the loss of individual data packets more flexibly than its predecessors.

The current versions of the Helix Producer only support G2 SVT, so the production of G2 content is only possible when using old versions of the Helix Producer.

RealVideo 8.0

The fundamental improvements in RealSystem 8.0 are in terms of quality: image quality is noticeably higher at the same bandwidth, and visibly optimised at all bandwidths. As the more complex encoding and decoding procedures of advanced codecs understandably make more demands on both encoder and client, it sometimes makes sense to use older codec versions for live encoding on slower machines.

The old RealPlayer G2 is not upwardly compatible: an automatic update for new codecs is not possible. If content in RealVideo 8 format is accessed, RealPlayer 8 is required, which may require the software to be downloaded. Normally, when accessing RealVideo 9 content via RealPlayer 8, for example, the player contacts RealNetworks and does a time-saving auto-update.

The RealVideo 8 codec brought new features to the new version of Helix Producer, which increased video quality considerably. Improved loss protection, variable bitrate encoding and two-pass encoding are innovations which can be used with more than just the current RealVideo 8 codec. They also improve video image quality in the G2 codec.

Transfer errors caused by bad connections can partly be reconstructed by coding error correction information into RealVideo streams. The majority of added information is dynamically adapted to the video data so that maximum image quality remains guaranteed. Key frames are also inserted alongside error correction information, which can increase playback quality.

Loss protection It is mostly narrowband Internet transfers which benefit from this option, as connection quality may vary in contrast to intranet transfer. If data packets go missing, this loss can be compensated for and cached using the added correction information. Using this feature does not have any negative effects on quality, so only the increased encoding time is a disadvantage in using it.

20, 45 or 300 kbps – when we mention the bandwidth of a media stream, this implies the drawback of older codecs. Transferring a constant number of bits per specified time interval is not an efficient process, as the same amount of information is transferred, regardless of current stream content.

Variable bit rate encoding (VBR) VBR encoding dynamically adapts the playback bit rate to correspond to the image content, briefly leaving more bandwidth available for important image sequences. Compatible with SureStream and live broadcasting, VBR generally improves image quality compared to CBR streams (constant bit rate), which are created by default. The best results are achieved with clips containing alternating quick and slow image sequences, as VBR enables the slower sequences to 'steal' bandwidth. This effect is far more noticeable in transfers via lower bandwidth.

Figure 3.1 shows how VBR encoding works: CBR assigns a bandwidth of 250 kbps every second, irrespective of the image content to be encoded. Using VBR, a different bandwidth can be assigned every second, with the overall bandwidth remaining at an average of 250 kbps. This type of intelligent bandwidth management is far more suitable for the transfer of time-based media via restricted bandwidths than the strict retention of default bandwidth settings.

One disadvantage of VBR is the occasional instance of increased buffer time. If the video stream begins with a scene which is difficult to encode, this is assigned substantial bandwidth, which increases buffer time as playback begins. However, a maximum buffer time can be set manually so that it remains at an acceptable level, even in extreme cases.

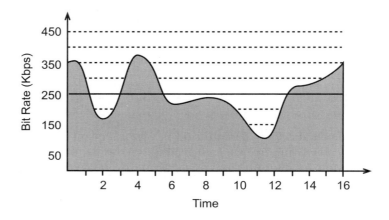

Figure 3.1   Variable bit rate encoding (VBR)

2-Pass-Encoding and VBR   In the case of two-pass encoding, an extensive analysis of the digital video clip precedes the actual encoding process. The encoder is therefore able to adapt the compression parameters perfectly to the source material, which increases the quality of the streaming video. However, encoding time can be doubled because of the analysis which is done first.

Although two-pass encoding produces better results with constant bit rates (CBR), VBR shows the best use of a preceding image analysis. The encoder knows the properties of the video clip in advance and can therefore dynamically modify the bit rate to an optimum level. Both VBR and two-pass encoding only work with video material already stored on the system hard drive.

RealVideo 9

Latest codec revisions...   With RealVideo 9, the youngest video codec of RealNetworks, the company faces competition in the sector of broadband streaming and home entertainment. The most notable new feature of RealVideo 9 is the support of higher resolutions of up to HDTV resolution (max. 2048 × 1536 pixel) and of interlaced video. According to RealNetworks, the compression rates of RealVideo 8 have been improved by 30 percent, offering VHS quality starting at 160 KBps and "Near DVD quality" starting at 500 Kbps. Furthermore, it offers the same quality at half the bit rate of MPEG-4 and at quarter the bit rate of MPEG-2 – again: according to RealNetworks.

Table 3.2 The video codec history of RealNetworks

RealVideo Codec	Player support					Notes
	One	8	G2	5	4	
RealVideo 9	•	○				Current video codec – improved quality, higher resolutions, interlaced support
RealVideo 8	•	•				Improves quality and scalability
RealVideo G2 SVR	•	•	•			Scalable Video Technology: dynamic frame rates produced on the client side
RealVideo G2	•	•	•			New video codec and introduction of SureStream
RealVideo Standard	•	•	•	•	•	Standard codec before RealSystem G2 (without SureStream)
RealVideo Fractal	•	•	•	•	•	No further support after RealSystem G2 encoder. Further support through RealPlayer

○ - available via auto-update

With this introduction, RealNetworks first of all wants to set its claim in the realm of home entertainment. Since the enormous success of DivX in past years, not only RealNetworks has realised the potential of this market segment and the new features of RealVideo demonstrate this awareness. As more and more users use their computer for transferring video and audio over the Internet, they need efficient codecs at bit rates, which are higher than in conventional streaming applications (800 to 2,000 Kbps). This was considered during the development of RealVideo 9: beneath an increased qualitative coding efficiency RealVideo now supports higher resolutions to make it ready for the demands of future HDTV applications.

Another feature is the support for interlaced video material. When RealVideo content is to be shown on conventional TV sets, the playback quality is noticeably increased when the content is stored interlaced. Above all, the movement appears to be more smooth, becauce twice as many images are displayed compared to non-interlaced video. Along with its engagement in the home entertainment sector, RealNetworks introduces RealAudio Surround, which is described below.

But, to enjoy all the new features of RealVideo 9, the client's computer has to meet high requirements. RealNetworks recommends a 750 MHz PIII for full screen, full frame rate playback of RealVideo 9 content. Of course, for smaller clips transferred via dial up connections, a lower system is adequate (200 Mhz PII). Nevertheless, these high requirements restrict the field of application for this codec: cpu power is a very limited factor, especially when used for mobile or home entertainment devices, such as DVD players. Manufacturers of such devices therefore need to wait until specialised chips for the decoding of RealVideo 9 are available, which, for example,. delays the launch of RealVideo compatible DVD-Players until mid 2003.

RealAudio codecs

RealAudio. RealNetworks released the first Internet streaming media solution in 1994 with the introduction of RealAudio. In the meantime, RealNetworks released several compression methods, used to transfer optimised audio signals of different characteristics via various bandwidths. Audio codecs can be divided into two categories, relying on the main applications of voice and music. The possible bit rates of the codec are predefined with specific values, which, of course, can be edited manually. In addition to the audience groups shown in table 3.3, there are numerous other pre-sets available, for example, for encoding surround sound or generating download-optimized clips.

Table 3.3 RealAudio standard bit rates (recommended for audio only encoding, extract)

Target audience	Voice codec	Music codec
28.8K Dial-up	16 Kbps Voice	20 Kbps Music
56.6K Dial-up	32 Kbps Voice	32 Kbps Stereo Music (High Response, RA8)
64K Single ISDN	32 Kbps Voice	44 Kbps Stereo Music (High Response, RA8)
128K Dual ISDN	64 Kbps Voice	96 Kbps Stereo Music (RA8)
150K LAN	64 Kbps Voice	132 Kbps Stereo Music (RA8)
256 Kbps DSL/cable modem	64 Kbps Voice	176 Kbps Stereo Music (RA8)
384 Kbps DSL/cable modem	96 Kbps Stereo Music (RA8)	176 Kbps Stereo Music (RA8)

RealAudio 8   At the end of the year 2000, RealNetworks significantly increased the maximum quality of its audio streams with the introduction of the new audio codec version 8. The consequential use of stereo coding constituted the most striking improvements in the narrowband area between 20 and 96 kbps. The transmission of the differences between the left and right channels has considerably improved the subjective impression of the user. The new broadband codecs in the RealAudio 8-series were the result of a venture with Sony. These codecs integrate Sony's ATRAC3 compression with bandwidths between 105 and 352 kbps, enabling audio compression in CD quality using the RealSystem. RealAudio 8 files are compatible with Sony mobile playback devices thanks to the use of Sony compression. Sony ATRAC3 compression is used in Minidisc devices and has so far taken a large share of the market.

 RealProducer distinguishes between 'voice' and 'voice with background music'. However, there are no separate audio codecs hidden behind this confusing distinction – only default settings which specify different audio codecs for certain bandwidths.

Table 3.4 RealAudio codecs

	5 Kbps	6 Kbps	6.5 Kbps	8 Kbps	8.5 Kbps	11 Kbps	12 Kbps	16 Kbps	20 Kbps	32 Kbps	44 Kbps	64 Kbps	66 Kbps	94 Kbps	96 Kbps	105 Kbps	132 Kbps	146 Kbps	176 Kbps	264 Kbps	352 Kbps
RealAudio G2 Voice	●		●	●			●	·	●		●	·		·					·		·
RealAudio G2 Music	·	●	·	●		●	●	●	●		●	·		·					·		
RealAudio G2 Music High Response	·		·				·	●	●		·			·					·		·
RealAudio G2 Stereo Music	·		·				·	●	●	●	●	●		·	●				·		
RealAudio 8 Stereo Music	·		·				●	●	●	●	●	●	●	●	●	●	●	●	●	●	●
RealAudio 8 Stereo Music High Response	·		·				·	●	●		●	●		·					·		·
RealAudio 8 Surround									●	●		·			●		●	●	●	●	●

RealAudio Surround   Along with RealVideo 9, RealNetworks presented a vital new feature for audio coding: RealAudio Surround. With regard to the growing importance of home entertainment applications, RealAudio 8 was extended to store surround audio signals. However, RealAudio Surround does not use discrete audio channels to store the surround information. Instead, it codes this information into the two Stereo signals via phase displacement, just like Dolby Pro Logic (II) and Circle Surround do it with analogue audio signals. The quality of the surround channels is not as good as with Dolby Digital/DTS, where the surround information is stored in discrete channels.

RealNetworks refers to a loss of quality when encoding non-surround signals with RealAudio surround codecs. But "field tests" have shown that RealAudio Surround sometimes produces an even better quality than its Stereo versions.

Table 3.5 RealAudio voice codec

RealAudio codec	Frequency range (kHz)	Sample rate (kHz)	Helix Producer Plus 9.0 support	RealPlayer support							
				One	8	G2	5	4	3	2	1
5 Kbps	4	8	●	●	●	●	●				
6.5 Kbps	4	8	●	●	●	●	●	●			
8 Kbps	4	8		●	●	●	●	●	●	●	●
8.5 Kbps	4	8	●	●	●	●	●	●			
15.2 Kbps	4	8		●	●	●	●	●	●	●	
16 Kbps	8	16	●	●	●	●	●				
32 Kbps	11	22.05	●	●	●	●					
64 Kbps	20	44.1	●	●	●	●					

RealAudio Surround files are fully compatible with conventional RealAudio 8 files, so no auto-update is necessary. When decoding this Matrix-Surround-Sound (4.0 or 5.1), the analogue-outputs of compatible soundcards are used.The choice of audio codec is usually left to the user's discretion in the production of RealVideo content. The user also decides which priorities are given to audio and video encoding through audio bandwidth allocation. Depending on how important the audio information is, a higher or a lower bandwidth is reserved for it. The following tables show the various RealAudio codecs, used in the encoding of both RealAudio and RealVideo streams. Codecs which are no longer used or supported by the current version of Helix Producer are not specified here.

Table 3.6 RealAudio mono music codec

RealAudio codec	Frequency range (kHz)	Sample rate (kHz)	Helix Producer Plus 9.0 support	RealPlayer support							
				One	8	G2	5	4	3	2	1
6 Kbps	3	8	●	●	●	●					
8 Kbps	4	8	●	●	●	●	●	●			
11 Kbps	5.5	11.025	●	●	●	●					
12 Kbps	4	8		●	●	●	●	●			
16 Kbps Low Response	4	8		●	●	●	●	●	●		
16 Kbps Medium Response	4.7	11.025		●	●	●	●	●	●		
16 Kbps High Response	5.5	11.025		●	●	●	●	●	●		
16 Kbps	8	22.05	●	●	●	●					
20 Kbps	10	20.05	●	●	●	●					
20 Kbps Music High Response	14.5	44.1	●	●	●	●					
32 Kbps Music	8	16		●	●	●	●	●			
32 Kbps	14,5	44.1	●	●	●	●					
32 Kbps High Response	16	44.1	●	●	●	●					
40 Kbps	11	22.05		●	●	●	●	●	●		
44 Kbps	20	44.1	●	●	●	●					
80 Kbps	20	44.1		●	●	●	●	●	●		
64 Kbps	20	44.1	●	●	●	●					

Table 3.7 RealAudio stereo music codecs

RealAudio codec	Frequency range (kHz)	Sample rate (kHz)	Helix Producer Plus 9.0 support	RealPlayer support							
				One	8	G2	5	4	3	2	1
20 Kbps Stereo	4	8		●	●	●	●	●	●		
20 Kbps Stereo	5	11.025	●	●	●	●					
32 Kbps Sereo	5.5	11.025		●	●	●	●	●	●		
32 Kbps Stereo	8	22.05	●	●	●	●					
40 Kbps Stereo	8	16		●	●	●	●	●			
44 Kbps Stereo	11	22.05	●	●	●	●					
64 Kbps Stereo	16	44.1	●	●	●	●					
80 Kbps Stereo	16	32		●	●	●	●	●	●		
96 Kbps Stereo	16	44.1	●	●	●	●					

Table 3.8 RealAudio 8 stereo music codecs

RealAudio codec	Frequency range (kHz)	Sample rate (kHz)	Helix Producer Plus 9.0 support	RealPlayer support							
				One	8	G2	5	4	3	2	1
16 Kbps Stereo	4.3	22.05	●	●	○						
20 Kbps Stereo	8.6	22.05	●	●	○						
20 Kbps Stereo High Response	9.9	22.05	●	●	○						
32 Kbps Stereo	10.3	22.05	●	●	○						
32 Kbps Stereo High Response	13.8	44.1	●	●	○						
44 Kbps Stereo	13.8	13.8	●	●	○						
44 Kbps Stereo High Response	16.0	16	●	●	○						
64 Kbps Stereo	16.0	16	●	●	○						
96 Kbps Stereo	16.0	16	●	●	○						

○: possible auto-update necessary

Table 3.9 RealAudio 8 stereo music codecs with Sony ATRAC3 technology

RealAudio codec	Frequency range (kHz)	Sample rate (kHz)	Helix Producer Plus 9.0 support	RealPlayer support							
				One	8	G2	5	4	3	2	1
105 Kbps Stereo	13.7	44.1	●	●	○						
132 Kbps Stereo	16.5	44.1	●	●	○						
146 Kbps Stereo	16.5	44.1	●	●	○						
176 Kbps Stereo	19.2	44.1	●	●	○						
264 Kbps Stereo	22.0	44.1	●	●	○						
352 Kbps Stereo	22.0	44.1	●	●	○						

○: possible auto-update necessary

Detailed information on the frequency range and sample rate of RealAudio Surround codecs is not yet available. It is fully supported by RealNetworks' Helix

Producer 9.0 and every player capable of decoding RealAudio 8 should be able to play them.

3.2 SureStreaming

RealSystem has provided a facility for encoding audio and video in a file in several qualities since version 6.0 (G2). Content can be compressed in up to ten qualities, all of which can be individually configured.

When creating SureStream content, it is important that only one video codec is used. It is therefore not possible to offer modem users a video stream in G2 codec, and a RealVideo 8 stream for dual ISDN users at the same time. However, this combination is possible by configuring the appropriate audio stream.

If only one quality of a stream is to be provided, for use by a Web server for example, it should always be encoded as a Single-Rate. Some encoding tools like the old RealProducer require some attention at this point, because if a SureStream is created in one quality, several bit rates are generated. These bit rates are used to react better to bandwidth transmission fluctuations, but they also require a streaming server. A bit rate is generated in the '28.8K modem' target group in RealProducer according to user specifications (by default 20 kbps), as well as a 17 kbps and 14 kbps version. This enables audio and video to be played back despite interruptions in transmission bandwidth (see figure 3.2). What is problematic about these additional streams in a surestream is, that the user is unable to configure them directly. One of the results of this deficit is, that when encoding a live-surestream, you cannot set the overall upstream-bandwidth precisely, since additional streams are generated automatically.

If encoded as a Single-Rate, video and audio is only compressed to the bandwidth specified by the user. In our example, this means that the Helix Producer only encodes a 20 kbps version of the stream.

Substreams   RealNetworks' latest encoding tool, Helix Producer Plus, offers a better solution for the optimal encoding of surestream content. Instead of generating the additional streams (or: 'Substreams') automatically, the user has to add them manually in Helix Producer. This gives the user full control over the different bit rates encoded in the surestream content (see below: section 3.3).

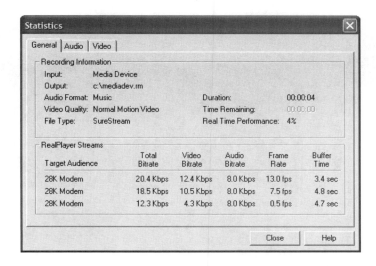

Figure 3.2 Several bit rates for one target group in the Helix Producer 8.5

3.3 Creating RealMedia content

As the central RealNetworks encoding tool, Helix Producer makes all its functions available for the production of both on-demand and live content. Audio and video data can be converted into streaming media clips, clips recorded using audio and video cards, and live broadcasts produced. The inexperienced user can rely on different samples and help functions for guidance through the production process and a simplified first configuration. Experienced users can use a wealth of integrated optimisation tools to produce the best possible results.

Central front-end elements of Helix Producer are control windows for input signal, audio level and encoded output, which enable visual control of the stream during encoding. The elements in the lower area are used to modify the encoding configuration and control the encoding process itself (see Figure 3.3).

When Helix Producer loads, a large number of options and features are visible in the main window. Despite the irritating mass of buttons and windows, the basic sequence of setting up an encoding process is easy: first of all, defining input material; secondly, setting the encoding parameters and finally, defining destinations for the material to be transferred to.

Figure 3.3 Helix Producer Plus 9.0

Encoding audio and video files

Setting Source material So, the first decision to be made entails choosing what source material should be encoded. The two main options at this point are to define a audio-/video-file or a device (sound-/video-cards) as input sources.

Existing audio and video files often have to be used to create RealMedia clips. If 'Input file' is selected in the middle left part of the main windows, the source file and target file will be queried.

Supported file formats Helix Producer Plus version 9.0 supports the following file formats for conversion into RealAudio and RealVideo format:

- Windows Video (.avi)
  - AVI 1.0 files up to 2 GB in size
  - AVI 2.0 files, including files over 2 GB in size

- Apple QuickTime (.mov, .qt, .moov)
  - DirectX 8 required

- MPEG 1 (.mpg, .mpeg, .mpa, .mp2)
  - No MPEG 2 file support
  - DirectX 8 required

- Waveform Audio (.wav)

- MPEG Layer 3 (.mp3)
  - DirectX 8 required

- Audio Interchange File Format (.aiff)

- Unix Audio (.au)

Valid sampling rates for the audio formats are 8,000, 11,025, 16,000, 22,050, 32,000, 44,100 and 48,000 Hz.

As you can see, the given compatibility list is for the Windows version of Helix Producer. Since DirectX or other software components are required for some file types and codecs, upcoming versions of Helix Producer for different operation systems may not support all of them. Platform-independent file formats, which should work with every version of RealNetworks encoding tools, are uncompressed AVI, uncompressed QuickTime (ver. 3 to 6) and WAV audio.

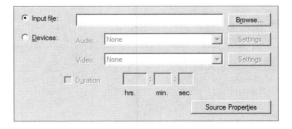

Figure 3.4 Selection of source material in Helix Producer Plus

Recording audio and video signals

In many cases, audio and video sources (video recorders, cameras, CD player, microphone etc.) are connected to the computer, and the signals encoded directly into the respective streaming media format. As shown in Figure 3.2, Helix Producer provides the source option 'Device'. When selected, the user can select the video and audio sources to be encoded from the sound, video or TV cards installed in the computer.

The installed sound card can be used in this way to record an audio signal (e.g. at a concert) directly into RealAudio format. It therefore does not need to be saved in a large WAV file and then encoded. In the case of long image and sound sequences, this can save valuable time and system resources.

Helix Producer supports all types of sound- and video-cards, which are accessible via standard windows drivers. So it is possible to capture directly from a digital video camera which is connected to the firewire port of the computer.

A new feature of the Helix Producer is the possibility to limit the duration that a live source is used for capturing. By using this, it is possible to leave long capturing jobs unattended. After the given time has expired, the capturing process is terminated automatically.

Selecting Audiences Templates

Audiences   After setting the source parameters of an encoding job, the next task is to define for what target groups the encoded material is intended and whether surestreaming is used or not. The Helix Producer presents a new interface for this, which is accessible by using the button 'Audiences' in the main program window or the menu option 'Settings' > 'Show Audiences'.

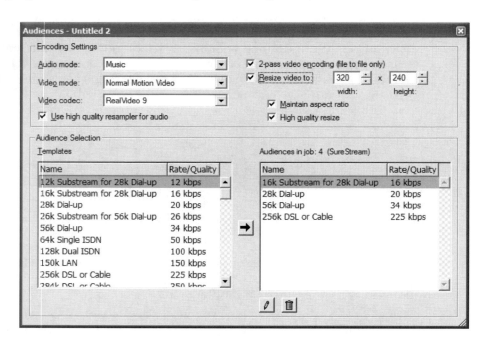

Figure 3.5 Selecting target audiences in Helix Producer Plus

Audiences templates represent different settings for audio- and videostreams encoded by the Helix Producer. The most important information an audience template contains is the overall bit rate to use for the stream, By using the lower part of the window in Figure 3.5 ('Audience Selection') the user can copy up to ten audience templates into the current job, and so define what bit rates are used to encode the streaming media.

Surestream or
Single-rate?   If there is no streaming server available to host the on-demand files, SureStreaming cannot be used and just one audience template can be selected in a

job. A normal Web server can provide RealMedia content, but is unable to extract one specific bit rate in a file from the information contained in the player and then forward it to the client. Like Livestreaming, SureStreaming requires a Helix Server for the provision of data.

Figure 3.6 Choice between narrowband SureStream and broadband Single-Rate

Another reason for using several Single-Rates instead of one SureStream is the latter's lack of flexibility. Whereas narrowband streams are often only encoded at a resolution of 176x144 pixels, this can be significantly more with broadband streams. For this reason, narrowband and broadband streams are often divided: narrowband users may receive a SureStream intended for dual ISDN users, while a Single-Rate at a higher resolution (e.g. 320x240 pixels) and higher bit rate (e.g. 300 kbps) is also offered.

The window shown in figure 3.5 not only enables the user to select the audiences templates, it also contains the settings for all audiences. These reflect how Helix Producer encodes the final streaming media.

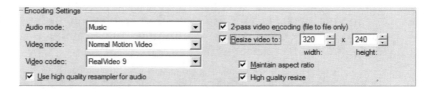

Figure 3.7   General audience settings in Helix Producer Plus

- **Audio mode**
RealNetworks offers different codecs for voice data and music data. Which of them are used with which bit rate is defined in the appropriate audience setting. Whether the voice- or music-codec of an audience-setting is used is defined by the Audio mode menu here. In case of doubt, you should always choose the Music mode, since the music codecs provide the greater range,

- **Video mode**
The Video mode settings can be used to indicate encoding preferences for the video image (normal, smooth, sharpest, slide show or no image). In this case, you indicate whether the available bandwidth will be used to represent a smooth video image, or transfer as much detail as possible. As this clearly requires more bandwidth, the SHARPEST IMAGE VIDEO option can be used to transfer fewer images per second than the SMOOTHEST IMAGE VIDEO setting. In most cases, the NORMAL MOTION VIDEO option provides a fair compromise between frame rate and image details.

- **Video codec**
As described in the section on 'Video codecs,' Helix Producer supports the 'RealVideo with SVT', 'RealVideo 8' and 'RealVideo 9' codecs. The video codec to be used for all target audiences is specified in this dialogue. It should be noted that when encoding SureStream clips, all streams use the same video codec, so a combination of codecs within one file/livestream is not possible.

- **High quality audio resampler**
Many audio codecs use a different sample rate than the one of the source material. Because of this, Helix Producer has to resample the audio. When using this filter, the encoded audio will be of a higher quality, but the encoding will take more system resources.

- **2-pass video encoding**
Helix Producer offers 2-pass-encoding for on-demand-clips. The preceding analysis doubles the encoding time, but increases the audio- and video-quality significantly.

- **Video resizing**
  As pointed out before, source material should always be of the highest quality possible, thus it is often necessary to resize the video. Activating 'High Quality Resize' slows down the encoding process, but enables the scaling of individual frames. The use of more intelligent procedures and anti-aliasing methods further optimises the end result of the encoding.

Input/Output Controls

After defining a data source for the encoding job, it is displayed in the Input window at the top left part of Helix Producer's main window (see Figure 3.3).

Audio clipping   As described in chapter 1, it is important to make sure that audio levels are set correctly. Especially when using live sources, it is important that the input signal is not over-modulated. This is signalled by the clipping indicator above the levels meter. The green part of the level monitors left of the input window indicates that the audio signal is modulated correctly. Figure 3.8 shows how a live source is encoded. The level meters show whether an audio signal is modulated correctly and the preview windows show the video image before and after encoding. As you can see, the encoded audio signal has a higher level than the input data.

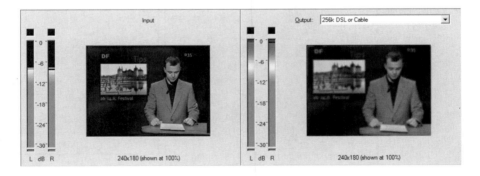

Figure 3.8 Input/Output Control in Helix Producer Plus

If there are problems with an under- or over-modulated audio source, this can be corrected by using the 'Audio Gain Control' from the 'Settings' menu (or: Ctrl-R). The audio levels of the encoded stream are also displayed left of the Output window in the main window. Another way of changing the volume of the input signals of sound cards is by using the 'Recording Mixer', which is part of every Windows installation. You can open this console by using the 'Audio Device' option in Helix Producer's 'Settings' menu or by double-clicking the speaker-icon in the Windows taskbar. In addition, many soundcards offer vendor-specific controls with some hardware-specific functions. These can also be accessed via the 'Audio Device' option.

Windows playback control can be used to mute the input signals of the sound card if necessary. Playback control is activated by double-clicking the loudspeaker icon in the Windows taskbar. The slide rule view is activated using OPTIONS/ PROPERTIES, from where features such as the microphone input level on the sound card can be specified.

Video card configuration

When using video cards for capturing video, it is often necessary to do some configuration here as well. For this, every video card driver contains control panels that can be accessed in the 'Settings' menu of Helix Producer. In most cases, these consist of two parts: the 'Video Format' and 'Video Source' dialogue, located in the 'Video Device' option of the Helix Producer 'Settings'.

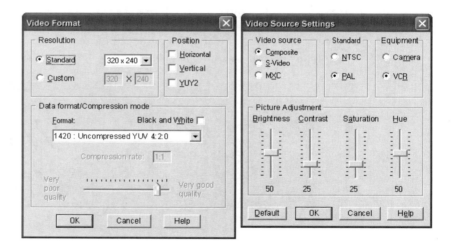

Figure 3.9 Video format and Video source panel (vendor specific)

At the 'Video Format' dialogue, a key point of the video capture settings should not be overlooked. In order to achieve optimum video quality, the largest possible video image should be captured, scaled and encoded. The size of the video image can be specified here, but it depends on the performance of the computer as to whether the image can be digitised in real time. This dialogue also contains the menu concerning what video format should be used to handle the digitised video data. It is not advisable to use a compression at this point, but to select high-quality video formats, such as YUV (component) or RGB.

At the 'Video Source' panel, the user can select the video input source, and may be able to modify brightness, saturation or contrast here. If the video card has various video inputs or supported video standards, this can be selected and configured at this point.

At the 'Output' part of Helix Producer's main window, the user can select the video stream that should be displayed. When encoding several video streams for multiple audiences, every stream encoded can be previewed this way.

Editing Audiences

Helix Producer comes with more than 20 predefined audiences templates, which represent the recommendation of RealNetworks. Nevertheless in many cases these presets have to be edited, deleted or completed with new ones.

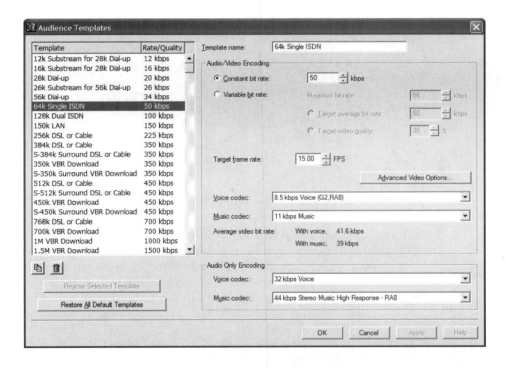

Figure 3.10   Editing Audience Templates in Helix Producer Plus

You can open the dialogue by using the 'Edit'-menu of the main program window or by double-clicking an audience template in the audience-window (shown in figure 3.5). Before editing a default audiences template, you should duplicate it by using the button under the template list. So it is possible to define your own settings according to the target group of the generated content.

It is also possible to edit audiences after copying them to an encoding job. Just double-click the audience template you want to change in the lower right part of the 'Audience' window (figure 3.5). Since the template is already copied to the current encoder job, the changes only apply for this job and will be ignored the next time used.

CBR or VBR   RealNetworks extended the support of variable bit rate encoding of Helix
Producer Plus 9.0. It can be activated here: besides setting an overall, constant bit
rate you can now activate two different types of variable bit rate coding:

- **Average bit rate**
  The first type of vbr encoding corresponds exactly to the description given in this
  chapter (see figure 3.1). It enables the encoder to use more bandwidth on
  complex parts of the video and reduce it on simple ones. The bit rate always stays
  below the maximum you define.

- **Video quality**
  The second mode of vbr coding does not use an average bit rate, but a given
  quality index. So it is not suitable for encoding streaming media, because it is
  possible that the bandwidth of a clip stays at the maximum bit rate for a longer
  time.

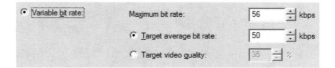

Figure 3.11   VBR encoding in Helix Producer Plus

VBR on-demand-clips are saved with the extension '.rmvb'. So it is easy to
distinguish them from cbr files (extension '.rm'), One reason why this is important
is, that you need the Helix Server 9 by RealNetwork to stream them and you cannot
stream them via the old Helix Server. VBR content has to be Single-Rate, so it is only
possible to use one vbr audience template per job.

In Europe, images are transferred at 25 fps (PAL) rather than 30 fps (NTSC).
However, RealProducer uses NTSC, so the 'Corporate LAN' settings are configured
to encode at a rate of 30 fps. This should be altered to correspond to the maximum
frame rate of the material to be encoded. For example, if an AVI file captured at 15
fps is to be converted, there is no point in encoding it at 25 fps.

Audio codecs   In the lower right part part of the Audience Templates dialogue, the selection of
audio codecs is possible. Depending on whether the sound characteristic 'Voice' or
'Music' is selected, the proper audio codec is used by Helix Producer to encode the
audio stream. Many users prefer to use the music codecs for all kinds of content,
regardless of whether it is mainly voice information. The reason for this is that
RealNetworks' voice codecs are quite out-of-date and the music ones generally
provide better quality.

Advanced video options   Furthermore, you can modify the advanced video options in the Audience Templates window (figure 3.10).

'MAXIMUM STARTUP LATENCY' specifies how much time may be taken to preload a clip before playback. This restriction may limit the user's waiting time in the case of material which is difficult to compress, as these scenes are usually taken into account in the event of variable bandwidth allocation.

The background of this option is that with variable bit rate compression, available bandwidth is dynamically adapted to the material within a certain time period. This enables scenes which are difficult to encode to be allocated more bandwidth, as there are fewer image changes to be transferred. A user may initially have to wait a long time for a stream to be buffered, as the beginning of the VBR compression may have been allocated a large amount of bandwidth. This option reduces waiting time by not allowing the buffering time at the beginning of the clip to exceed a certain amount of time.

The 'MAXIMUM TIME BETWEEN KEY FRAMES' option is fairly self-explanatory. If this period of time is set too high, image errors may occur due to the continual transfer of differential images.

As differential images only transfer image changes in the video, a complete image must occasionally be transferred. This always happens at the end of a clip, as the image content changes completely at this point. This is where the maximum time between key frames can be specified. As key frames require more bandwidth than differential images, but long differential image sequences are progressively more prone to errors with time, setting additional key frames should be carefully considered.

Audience templates   By adding extra 'LOSS PROTECTION' information to your content, it is possible to minimise the loss of data packets during the transfer from server to client.

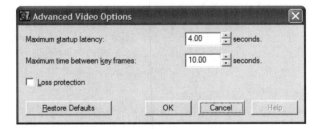

Figure 3.12 Advanced video Options of Helix Producer Plus

Audience templates are also saved as XML-files on the hard disc in the folder/ audiences/ in the program root. So it is possible to use the same setting on different encoders, make backups or send them via e-mail. It is also possible to open them with any text editor and edit their contents. Complete documentation of their syntax is part of Helix Producer's help files.

Using Video filters

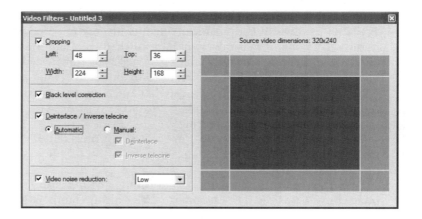

In Helix Producer, various filters can be used to optimise the input signal by using the 'Video Filters' button in the main window or by using the menu 'Settings' > 'Video Filters'.

Figure 3.13   Video filter in Helix Producer Plus

- **Cropping**
  Cropping unwanted edges is essential in the use of video cards or precaptured video files. It often happens that on TV invisible lines and colums are displayed here, but should not be encoded. You should therefore be able to crop these parts of the image.

  One of the reasons why the input image is larger than the stream becomes clear at this point. As cropping is sometimes required, the image has to be scaled up to its original size in order to obtain the required size after cropping. This is always accompanied by a loss in quality. The cropped image afterwards is scaled to the size given in the General Audience settings (see figure 3.7).

- **Black Level correction**
  Especially with simple capture cards an adjustment of image brightness can optimise the signal. In this particular case, black areas with not enough saturation are corrected,

- **De-interlace/ Inverse-Telecine Filter**
  The 25 full images of the PAL signal are transferred using twice the number of half-images. These half images consist of uneven lines, layered together by the TV device. Once the signal has been digitised, some pixels appear offset inbetween the lines of the half-images. The de-interlace filter is used to correct this effect (see figure 3.13).

The telecine filter is used to convert 24 fps film material to NTSC material at 30 fps. The task here is to create the missing frames by copying or overlapping several frames. The inverse telecine filter searches for these generated frames and removes them before the compression process in order to reduce the effects of redundant information as much as possible. When using the 25 fps European PAL standard, the telecine process does not require substantial system resources, and the results of the inverse telecine filter are therefore fairly unspectacular. In Helix Producer Plus 9.0, these two filters are combined. The software can scan for interlacing- and telecine-effects and apply the corresponding filters automatically.

• **Video noise reduction**
Using the noise filter can in many cases considerably increase compression quality. Encoding software is unable to differentiate the additional disturbances in video noise from the image details to be considered. The noise filter therefore reduces video noise as much as possible, creating an optimum basis for subsequent encoding. Helix Producer enables a distinction between high and low video noise, which the user has to specify.

Before recording: After recording: Display:
1 full frame   2 interlaced frames   interlaced

Figure 3.14   Interlacing in PAL and NTSC images

Setting Clip Information

Clip Information   Clip information presents different meta statements that are coded into the streaming media. This meta information of the clip gives the user and search engine information such as title, author, copyright, description and keywords. The contained data is displayed by the RealPlayer when called, and can act as a unique identifier of the stream. When the player is embedded into a website, it is also possible to request this information through JavaScript, etc.

Placed clearly in the foreground of the Helix Producer, the data passed to the Recording Wizard can be edited at any time, provided that the encoding process has not yet begun.

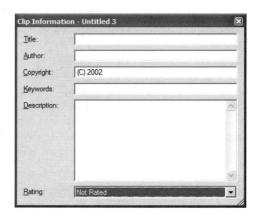

Figure 3.15   Setting Clip information in Helix Producer Plus

Setting Destinations

After defining what sources should be used for a job and setting the encoding parameters, such as audiences, filters and clip information, the Helix Producer needs to know what to do with the encoded stream. The two main options are to write it in an file (on-demand content) or to upstream it to a streaming server (livestreaming).

One of the central new features of the Helix Producer is the possibility to define more than one destination, which makes it, for example, possible to send a livestream to several streaming servers and write it to local discs at the same time.

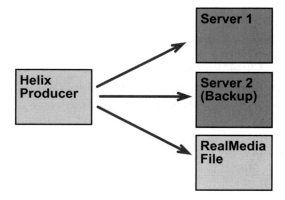

Figure 3.16   Multiple destinations in Helix Producer Plus

Setting a file destination

Setting a file destination in Helix Producer is simple. After clicking the appropriate icon in the Helix Producer main window, a folder and filename for the on-demand file can be selected. After confirming the selection, the new file destination appears in the Destinations windows in Helix Producers main window (see figure 3.15).

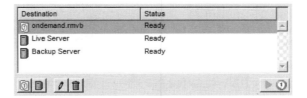

Figure 3.17   Setting destinations in Helix Producer Plus

Setting a server destination

Just like selecting a file as stream destination, one or more servers can be chosen as well. After clicking the appropriate button in the Helix Producers main window, a dialogue opens where the necessary information can be entered.

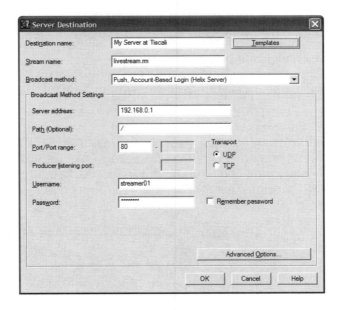

Figure 3.18   Setting a server destination in Helix Producer Plus

Standard queries regarding the Streaming Server are:

- **Destination name**
  The name which should appear in the destination window.

- **Stream name**
  This is important for subsequent addressing by the RealPlayer, which will later call the stream via this name (e.g. rtsp://Helix Server.company.uk/encoder/filename.rm).

- **Broadcast method**
  Since the new Helix Server offers different ways of sending the livestream to it, you can choose between different broadcast methods here (see below).

- **Server address**
  Either the IP address (e.g. 123.134.145.1) or server and domain name (e.g. Helix Server.company.uk).

- **Path (Optional)**
  You can enter a path, where the livestream will be accessed by the audience of the Server (e.g. rtsp://Helix Server.company.uk/encoder/MyDirectory/filename-.rm).

- **Port/Port range**
  The target port(s) on the server (for push broadcasting – see below).

- **Producer listening port**
  When using the new pull broadcast method of Helix Server, the server will request the the livestream at this port of the encoder (see below).

- **Username and password**
  Since not everybody uses a Helix Server to stream data, these are required from the login provided by the server administrator.

After entering this information and confirming, a new server destination is added to the current encoding job.

When the encoding process begins, the encoder sends data via a UDP connection, and uses a TCP connection to `communicate` with the `server`. However, as some firewalls do not support UDP transport, the Helix Producer can use a TCP connection for data transfer.

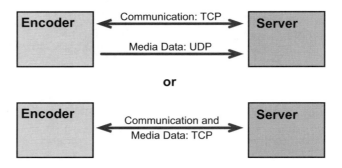

Figure 3.19 Encoder-server connection types

Furthermore, Helix Producer and Server introduced new ways to send the livestream from the Encoder up to the server.

Figure 3.20   Broadcast methods of Helix Producer Plus

With RealProducer 8 and Helix Server 8, the Encoder always first had to authenticate itself at the server (username and password) and was afterwards allowed to send the livestream to a defined port of server. The server receives the data from the encoder and forwards it to the clients connected.

Push- and   Although this 'Legacy Push' broadcasting to Helix Server G2, 7, 8 is supported
pull broadcast by Helix Producer furthermore, there are four new ways introduced, to send livestreams to a Helix Server.

1. Account-Based Push Broadcast

As the standard way of sending a livestream from the encoder to the server, the 'Accound-Based Push Broadcast' corresponds most to the old 'Legacy Push' known from Helix Server.

When using this broadcast method, the encoder first has to authenticate itself. After the server has confirmed the authentication, the encoder starts to send the livestream. When this livestream is requested by a client, the server can forward the required streaming media with no delay.

Since it offers the highest security, this broadcast method will be used when working with 3rd party ISPs or when the server administrator and the encoding staff are not in close contact.

Required information to set-up: Server address, Port at server (default: 80), Username and Password.

2. Password-Only Push Broadcast

This type of broadcast is only recommended when the encoding staff/personnel also administers the Helix Server, not only because it requires more experience to set up. Also there is no initial authentication process of the encoder, and as there are no error messages going from server to encoder, direct access to the server is needed to make sure the livestream is arriving properly.

Required information to set-up: Server address, Port Range at server (default: 30001-30020) and Password.

3. Multicast Push

In chapter 1 (see page 18) we have seen that multicasting enables several clients to receive the same data packet. With Helix Producer and Server, this method of data transfer can be used to broadcast livestream from one encoder to several Helix Servers.

This broadcast method also requires experience with administering Helix server. It is primarily designed for large isps, who need to send dozens of livestreams to several servers in their broadcast network. Another application would be the transfer of livestreams over satellites, where no return channel is available.

Required information to set-up: Server address, Port Range at server (default: 30001-30020) and Password.

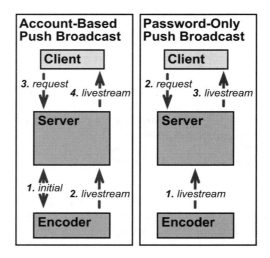

Figure 3.21 Broadcast methods in Helix Producer Plus

4. Pull Broadcast

Pull broadcasting is a completely new concept of transferring data from encoder to server at RealNetworks. Instead of sending the livestream all the time to the server, the encoder waits for the server to request it.

When starting the live-encoding, this encoder sends the information that the livestream x is now available. The server receives this information, and marks the livestream as available, although no media data is transferred yet. Only when a client requests the livestream at the server, is it again requested from the encoder and forwarded to the client.

The broadcast method should be used when doing long livecasts, which are only rarely requested by clients. The connection between server and encoder is just used 'on demand' and since this is often an multi-line dialup connection (e.g. four ISDN-lines) expenses can be lowered here.

A disadvantage is, that it takes some time to establish the connection to the encoder, and this delays the distribution of the streaming media to the clients by several seconds.

Required information to set-up: Server address, Producer listening port (default: 30031) and Password.

After defining the destinations of your broadcast, the setup of the encoding job is complete. Source material, encoding settings, filters, clip information and destinations are complete and the job can be started.

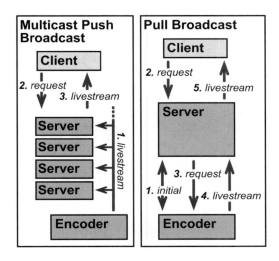

Figure 3.22 Broadcast methods in Helix Producer Plus

Working with the Job Manager

Batch encoding Before Helix Producer was introduced, one of the biggest deficits of the RealProducer versions was the lack of a batch-function in the graphical frontend. If, for example, several video files had to be encoded using RealNetworks' tools, the command line version of RealProducer had to be used (see below). This shortcoming is now corrected, as Helix Producer contains a powerful function to batch all kinds of encoding jobs.

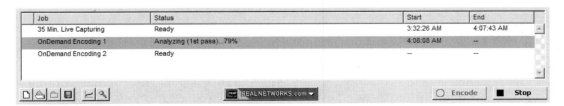

Figure 3.23 Job Manager of Helix Producer Plus

All settings of Helix Producer described previously (sources, settings, filters and destinations) are stored in a job file. When Helix producer is started and the first setting (e.g. an input source) is being made, a new encoding job is generated automatically. On the other hand, it is possible to open a new job manually by using the 'File' menu in Helix Producer.

After defining all necessary settings for the encoding job, a job can be saved. Job files have the extention .rpjf and since they are simple XML files, you can edit them with any text editor.

Organising encoding tasks in job files has various advantages:

- Batch encoding
  After selecting multiple jobs of the job manager by clicking them while Ctrl is pressed (see figure 3.21), it is possible to start the encoding of all these tasks.

- Multitasking
  While one or more jobs are already underway, it is possible to continue working with Helix Producer and define the next jobs to be rendered.

- Sharing job files
  After saving a job file, these XML files can be sent to other users or copied to any other encoder to make sure that RealMedia files are generated just the same way on different machines.

- Default jobs
  Any job in the job manager can be defined as default for every new job. So when the same settings are always needed on a certain encoder, this feature can simplify the everyday work.

The encoding process

Once you click on the ENCODE button, Helix Producer begins to render the selected jobs according to user specifications. The user can judge and influence both the end result and the runtime.

Video Preview

During encoding, one video stream of all qualities can be viewed in the preview window. Using the 'Output' menu to the right in Helix Producer's main window enables you to switch between different video versions.

Volume Control

The RECORDING MIXER command in 'Audio Device Settings' can still be used. The playback and recording control panels enable the adjustment and toggling of different input sources, even once the encoding process is underway. Live broadcasts react more flexibly to audio level adjustment.

Statistics

A detailed diagnostics window in Helix Producer allows you to monitor the encoding performance. This clearly shows that several streams are created in one

SureStream for the selected audiences, in order to be able to react more flexibly to the transmission bandwidth available.

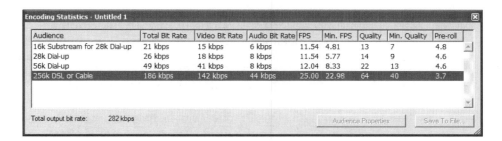

Figure 3.24 Encoding Statistics in Helix Producer Plus

The following data is displayed in the encoding statistics:

• Names of selected audiences

• Total Bit Rate of every stream in the encoding job

• The Video Bit Rate of every stream

• The Audio Bit Rate of every stream

• The current frame rate (FPS) of every video stream. After encoding, an average value is displayed

• The minimum frame rate of every video stream during an encoding process

• The quality level of every video stream. A quality index of 100% represents a video stream quality equal to the one of the source material. This helps to evaluate the loss of quality due to the applied compression method. After encoding, an average value is displayed

• The minimum quality level of every video stream during an encoding process

• The duration of the buffering necessary for accessing every video stream.

Upstream capacities   Another important item of information – especially when encoding a livestream – is the 'Total output bit rate' at the bottom of the statistics. In most cases, the upstream bandwidth available for a live broadcast is restricted. For example, if 4 ISDN lines are available, theoretically 512 Kbps upstream bandwidth could be used (4 lines x 2 channels x 64 Kbps). Due to network overhead and other factors, not more than 50–70% of this bandwidth can often be used in practice. So the 'Total output bit rate' should be higher than 250–350 Kbps. If the upstream bit rates exceeds the available bandwidth, packet loss occurs and the quality of the livestream is affected.

Additional Helix Producer tools

producer.exe

Helix Producer's command line version All Helix Producer functions can be used with the command-line program producer.exe. The program is therefore only started if prompted. All settings such as audiences, codecs or meta data are passed to the program as parameters. The advantage of using it via a prompt is that batch processes can be defined and used to convert several files into RealMedia format. Although the new job-functions in the graphical interface of Helix Producer make batch processing possible, the command line version Helix Producer can be helpful in several, special setups.

Detailed information on the producer.exe program is contained in the Helix Producer help section.

RealMedia Editor

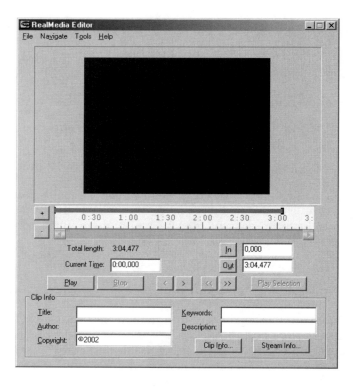

Figure 3.25 RealMedia Editor

Editing RealMeda content The RealMedia Editor is a component part of Helix Producer and the old RealProducer, enabling the additional editing of material that has already been encoded. this can be very useful when editing recorded live broadcasts, for example..

The RealMedia Editor can be launched manually from a subdirectory in the Helix Producer installation directory.

The user can navigate the RealMedia clip using a simple timeline, and set IN and OUT marks at any position. Clip information can be modified, and permission for recording– and download– can be set for a RealMedia file. Simple editing functions are also possible on the encoded video clip by using the FILE/APPEND REALMEDIA FILE function. The clips to be added have to be rendered with the exact same encoder settings, as there is no further compression at this point. The job manager of Helix Producer can be very helpful for making sure that two clips are encoded with the exact same parameters (see above).

Another feature of RealMedia Editor: 'Image maps' can be added to an on-demand file. These are text files which describe selectable fields in the RealVideo. When these fields are clicked by the user, a specific action is executed, such as displaying the company's homepage. Events are identical to image maps, except that the action is executed automatically at a certain point during playback. In order to integrate image maps and events, they have to be embedded in the RealMedia clip using RealMedia Editor. Image maps define clickable URLs at specific points in the video, and events call links automatically at certain points within the stream.

Availability

Helix Producer Plus is available from RealNetworks at around £130. The basic version can be downloaded free of charge, but contains only limited features. So only Helix Producer Plus contains important features for the encoding of RealMedia content at a professional level:

- Up to 10 audiences usable per job (just 3 in the Basic version)

- Customisable server- and audience-templates

- Job file saving

- Batch encoding

- Audio gain control

- Video cropping or scaling

- Multicast Push Broadcast

- Multiple destinations – just 1 server and 1 file destination in the Basic version

- Backwards compatibility with old RealPlayer versions (only RealVideo 9 support in the Basic version)

Helix Producer is available for a wide range of operating systems:

- Windows 98SE, ME, 2000 and XP

- Linux 2.2.x or 2.4.x on Intel platforms

There are currently no versions available for other systems, so RealNetworks additionally offers the old RealProducer Plus 8.5 for these platforms:

- MacOS 8.6 or 9.x

- Solaris 2.7 or 8 for Sparc

3.4 Delivering RealMedia content

The provision of live or on-demand content via a Helix Server is an important part of the production process. The Helix Server is scalably set out using modular technology, and grows according to user requirements. The system consists of the following components:

- Executable files
  The server 'core' called RMSERVER.EXE (Windows) or RMSERVER (Unix).

- Plugins
  Helix Server functionalities are produced and extended using various modules. These interfaces also enable other manufacturers to improve server performance and features.

- Configuration file
  The XML-based text document, RMSERVER.CFG contains all adjustable server settings.

- Licence file
  One or several files which can be used to extend the different performance features of any Helix Server installation.

- RealSystem administrator
  The administrator can configure and control all Helix Server functions using a Web interface.

- Tools
  Additional software such as Java Monitor (for monitoring server activity) or G2SLTA.

The universal streaming solution   With Helix Server, RealNetworks significantly increased the functionality of the previous/foregoing RealServer. The most important feature is the support of all important streaming media types. So not only can RealMedia content be transferred by a Helix Server, QuickTime, Windows Media, MP3 and MPEG content is also supported. This makes the Helix Server into a universal solution for media streaming.
Further functions for Helix Server are:

- Support for 'Redundant Servers', securing an optimal availability of content
- Several security features to restrict access to specific content
- 'Logging & Monitoring' modules, enabling real-time monitoring of the server and logging of all activities on the server
- Support of livecasts of RealMedia, Windows Media and QuickTime streams including live archiving of content
- 'Content Caching' providing automatic synchronisation of on-demand content on several servers
- 'Advertising' functions to deliver ads with your RealMedia streams or SMIL presentations.

A detailed server configuration is beyond the scope of this book. We have therefore assumed that an administered Helix Server is available. However, a brief summary of some central software features is outlined.

Mount points

Files and livestreams are provided by the Helix Server using what are known as mount points. These mount points appear as a subdirectory in the URL of the stream, and in the simplest case, represent a directory on the server's hard drive.

For example, the /content/ mount point could be allocated to the D:/ RealContent directory on the Helix Server using the RealSystem Administrator. A file named REALCLIP.RM at this on-demand mount point of the server 'realserver.company.co.uk' could be accessed using the URL.

```
rtsp://realserver.company.co.uk/content/realclip.rm.
```

 In practice, users often access content directories via FTP.

Not only directories are linked to mount points. Rather, these are shortcuts used by the server to decide which components should deal with the request. Before a decision is made to use a mount point in the URL, it should first be clarified which types of streaming media and data transfer are to be used.

In some cases, it makes sense to use several mount points, such as when live content is to be transferred via scalable multicast. In these cases, mount points can easily be used in sequence in the URL. The default mount point for live streams is /encoder/ for example. The /ramgen/ mount point initially returns a RAM file instead of a data stream, which activates a stream request in RealPlayer in older browsers (see below).

Table 3.10 Important mount points in Helix Server

Type of data transfer	Mount point
OnDemand	/ ('Rootdirectory') or e.g. /content/
Live streams	/encoder/
Splitting Push	/farm/
Splitting Pull	/split/
Multicasting Back-Channel	/encoder/
Multicasting Scalable	/scalable/
Authenticated	/secure/

The root directory of the server The root directory of the server is specified in the RealSystem Administrator, and is a directory on the server's hard drive in which on-demand clips will subsequently be stored. If the REALCLIP.RM file is placed in the root directory, it could be called using

rtsp://realserver.company.co.uk/realclip.rm.

If there are sub-directories with the name of a mount point in the root directory, these are not accessible, as the server always processes queries for mount points before on-demand content is accessed. These directories are therefore ignored. Live broadcasts are an interesting exception, which are only inaccessible temporarily. If a user tries to access a livestream while the server is down, this mount point is 'invalid' and the server searches in the subdirectory of the same name (e.g. /encoder/) for a file with the same name as the livestream. If found, it is streamed to the client, where failure reports are created if the live encoding fails (e.g. 'We are currently experiencing technical problems, please be patient.').

RAM files

Many (older) browsers have problems identifying RealMedia content and their association with RealPlayer. If a direct link to RealMedia clips is executed in these browsers, either an error message may appear (as RTSP protocol cannot be allocated), or, in extreme cases, you may be asked to download the entire clip.

For this reason, small meta files in text format with a .ram extension are used as a reference to RealMedia content. RAM files contain the full URL of the RealMedia content to be called (e.g. rtsp://realserver.company.co.uk/content/realclip.rm).

The Web browser can now be configured to pass files with this extension to RealPlayer to be executed. RealPlayer then uses the URLs contained in the files to access the content. This avoids error messages and enables older or incompatible browsers to access RealMedia streams.

RAM playlists

RAM files may contain one or several addresses in sequence, similar to SMIL playlists. If the user stores RAM files, they can be used as shortcuts to referenced RealMedia content at a later stage.

Player differentiation

RAM files can also be used to correct errors resulting from older RealPlayers that do not recognise RTSP protocol. As these older players ignore both rtsp addresses and the --stop-- instruction, alternative pnm addresses can be used to indicate the same content. Older versions of clips can also be passed to older players for playback, which may be helpful in finding the best compression method with different players.

Example 1 of the extended use of RAM files

```
rtsp://realserver.company.co.uk/Video01.rm
rtsp://realserver.company.co.uk/Video02.rm
rtsp://realserver.company.co.uk/Video03.rm
rtsp://realserver.company.co.uk/Advert02.rm
--stop--
pnm://realserver.company.co.uk/Video_alt01.rm
pnm://realserver.company.co.uk/Video_alt02.rm
pnm://realserver.company.co.uk/Video_alt03.rm
pnm://realserver.company.co.uk/Advert_alt02.rm
```

Passing parameters

Passing parameters to RealPlayer is another interesting option. If RealPlayer is embedded as a standalone program, and clips are not embedded in Web pages, the size of the video image or the software font could be adjusted. The following parameters are valid:

- `screensize="double"`
  The picture is scaled to double the size it was at the start.

- `screensize="full"`
  The video is played back in full screen mode.

- `screensize="original"`
  The video is played back at normal size.

- `mode="compact"`
  RealPlayer opens in compact view, in which most otherwise visible operating panels are omitted.

Example:

Example 2 of the extended use of RAM files

rtsp://realserver.company.co.uk/Video02.rm?screensize="full"

Ramgen

In order to avoid the problem of creating too many RAM files, Helix Server provides the use of a mount point called 'ramgen', which creates and returns RAM files dynamically. The ramgen mount point is therefore always used when referencing on-demand material from HTML.

This means that for our example, the file

```
rtsp://realserver.company.co.uk/content/realclip.rm
```

would be better accessed via the URL

```
http://realserver.company.uk/ramgen/content/realclip.rm
```

and embedded in our Web page. The browser retrieves the URL where the material is stored via HTTP, and passes it to RealPlayer, which then opens the address and plays back the stream.

Live streaming

In the case of live streaming, the encoding Helix Producer contacts the Helix Server and, after authentication, transmits the filename under which the livestream can be accessed on the server (e.g. 'livestream.rm'). The server then receives the stream from the encoder and waits for the /encoder/ mount point to call. If this mount point is addressed by a client, the livestream to be transmitted is identified by the filename. In our example, the livestream can be found at

```
rtsp://realserver.company.co.uk/encoder/livestream.rm
```

or

```
http://realserver.company.co.uk/ramgen/encoder/
livestream.rm
```

The option of combining different mount points becomes apparent here.

Head-end server   For live encoding, RealNetworks recommends using a head-end server on location. In this case, the encoder does not send its upstream directly to the distributing server, but to an on-site Helix Server. This is connected to the correct server (e.g. via ISDN) and functions as a source splitter. Using this head-end server guarantees that the encoder does not lose communication with the Helix Server if the connection is interrupted. When encoding resumes, the archived file of the interrupted livestream is overwritten. The head-end server responds robustly to such disturbances, and enables the Helix Producer to continue working when interrupted. Futhermore, there are several additional features of Helix Producer (see below).

Simulated livestreams

Simulated transmissions of previously encoded material are very interesting in several respects, such as in the production of Web TV stations, or the provision of standby or 'best of' programs in livecasts. For this, RealSystem uses the 'G2 Simulated Live Transfer Agent' G2SLTA.EXE at command line level.

Sample G2SLTA playlist   The G2SLTA enables the use of playlists, which refer to RealMedia files on a system hard drive in TXT format.

```
Title: MyTV
Author: Tobias Kuenkel
Copyright: ©2002 Tobias Kuenkel
D:\StreamingContent\Video01.rm
D:\StreamingContent\Video02.rm
D:\StreamingContent\Video03.rm
D:\StreamingContent\Video04.rm
D:\StreamingContent\Video05.rm
D:\StreamingContent\Advert01.rm
D:\StreamingContent\Video06.rm
D:\StreamingContent\Video07.rm
D:\StreamingContent\Video08.rm
D:\StreamingContent\Video09.rm
D:\StreamingContent\Advert02.rm
```

The example demonstrates entering meta data for the simulated livestreams. This data is then used to overwrite the title, author or copyright information of the individual clips. While RealPlayer is requesting the livestream generated by the above playlist, 'MyTV' is displayed as a title, even though the various clips probably have other titles.

The use of identical encoding settings for all RealMedia clips to be streamed is vital in simulated livecasting, as no further compression of material takes place. The STLA only accesses existing media streams and sends these to a specified server port.

A good way of testing the compatibility of RealMedia clips is the RealMedia Editor FILE/APPEND CLIP function. As this function does not transcode the material, meaning that identical streams are required in the same clip, the extent to which the two files are compatible can be tested here. If the 'Append Clip' function outputs an error, the STATISTICS function in the Editor should explain why.

G2SLTA syntax:

g2slta Host Port Username Password Livefile Playlist [-r] [-nN]

Parameter	Description
Host	Name of Helix Servers (in the domain or IP)
Port	Port number specified in server configuration (4040 by default)
Username	The name of an authorised user
Password	User password. If no password authentication is used, username and password are not required
Live file	Name of broadcast under which the livestreams can be called from the server
Playlist	Path and name of playlist to be used
-r	The SLTA streams the playlist files in random order
nN	Indicates the number of times a playlist is repeated, e.g. n3 for the playlist to be played three times. If the playlist contains four files, these are played in their entirety twice, then the first is played for a third time, so nine files are streamed in total. If -n is used, the SLTA plays the playlist infinitely

Example:

```
c:\real\realserver\bin\g2slta.exe 192.150.2.21 4040
realadmin Os45hG livefile.rm playlist.txt -n
```

The SLTA 'sends' the clips contained in PLAYLIST. TXT in the directory of the requested playlist to the Helix Server with an IP of 192.150.2.21, used by the user login 'realadmin' with 'Os45hG' as a password. This process is repeated indefinitely, and the video stream can be accessed using the RealPlayer at the following address:

```
rtsp://192.150.2.21:4040/encoder/livefile.rm
```

The virtual directory, 'encoder', is the mount point specified in the server configuration.

Embedding

RealPlayer can be integrated into a Web page using a Netscape plugin and an ActiveX control. Both technologies have the same aim: to integrate the streaming media player and its controls in an HTML page.

The following browsers are compatible with the Netscape plugin architecture, and so support the use of Netscape plugins:

- Netscape Browsers from version 3.0

- Microsoft Internet Explorer from version 3.0

- Opera from version 6.0

- Mozilla from version 1.0

The ActiveX control is a Microsoft technology, supported by the following programs:

- Microsoft Internet Explorer from version 3.0

- Any other application with ActiveX support such as Visual Basic, Visual C++, Access, Word, etc.

Both interfaces contain identical functionalities and are used in accordance with the target application.

The <EMBED> tag When embedding the RealPlayer into a website, the <EMBED> tag is used to address Netscape plugins. The compulsory parameters are SRC, WIDTH and HEIGHT, so a sample RealPlayer embedding in Netscape could look as follows:

Embedding a
RealVideo using the
<EMBED>-Tag

```
<EMBED SRC="rtsp://realserver.company.co.uk/clip.rm"
    WIDTH=240 HEIGHT=180 NAME=realPlug>
</EMBED>
```

The <OBJECT> tag Using ActiveX controls is slightly different from using Netscape plugins. Optional parameters are not written directly into the tag, but are listed as separate <PARAM> tags. In addition, an ID has to be allocated which identifies the ActiveX control in the page, similar to the NAME parameter in the Netscape plugin. Furthermore, a specific CLASSID must always be given, which identifies the control explicitly as a RealPlayer ActiveX control:

```
CLASSID="classid:CFCDAA03-8BE4-11cf-B84B-0020AFBBCCFA"
```

A simple example of a RealPlayer embedded in a Web page using an ActiveX control could also look like this:

Embedding a
RealVideo using the
<OBJECT>-Tag

```
<OBJECT ID=realPlug WIDTH=240 HEIGHT=180
    CLASSID="classid:CFCDAA03-8BE4-11cf-B84B-0020AFBBCCFA">
    <PARAM NAME="SRC" VALUE="rtsp://realserver.company.co.uk/clip.rm">
</OBJECT>
```

In practice, Netscape completely ignores the <OBJECT> tag, and Internet Explorer does not take into account an <EMBED> tag within an <OBJECT> tag. This enables both tags to be interleaved, so Internet Explorer always uses the <OBJECT> tag, and Netscape the <EMBED> tag to embed the RealPlayer.

Interleaving the
<EMBED> and
<OBJECT>-Tag

```
<OBJECT ID=realPlug CLASSID="..." WIDTH=240 HEIGHT=180>
    <PARAM NAME="SRC" VALUE="rtsp://realserver.company.co.uk/clip.rm">
        <EMBED SRC="rtsp://realserver.company.co.uk/clip.rm"
            WIDTH=240 HEIGHT=180 NAME=realPlug>
</OBJECT>
```

Embedding – a
practical example

```
<OBJECT id="realPlug1" classid="clsid:CFCDAA03-8BE4-11cf-B84B-
0020AFBBCCFA" WIDTH="240" HEIGHT="180">
    <PARAM NAME="TYPE" VALUE="audio/x-pn-realaudio-plugin">
    <PARAM NAME="CONTROLS" VALUE="ImageWindow">
    <PARAM NAME="CONSOLE" VALUE="video1">
    <PARAM NAME="SRC" VALUE="rtsp://realserver.company.co.uk/realclip.rm">
    <PARAM NAME="AUTOSTART" VALUE="TRUE">
    <embed type="audio/x-pn-realaudio-plugin"
        name="realPlug1"
        controls="ImageWindow"
        console="video1"
        src="rtsp://realserver.company.co.uk/realclip.rm"
        width="240"
        height="180"
        autostart=true>
    </embed>
</object>
```

RealPlayer Controls

As well as the RealPlayer video window, other program controls can be embedded into the Web page. This is done using the CONTROLS parameter, so embedding adjustable play buttons in Netscape browsers would look as follows:

```
<EMBED SRC="..." WIDTH=44 HEIGHT=26 CONTROLS=PlayButton>
```

And in Internet Explorer:

```
<OBJECT ID=realPlug CLASSID="..." WIDTH=44 HEIGHT=26>
    <PARAM NAME="SRC" VALUE="rtsp://realserver.company.co.uk/clip.rm">
    <PARAM NAME="CONTROLS" VALUE="PlayButton">
</OBJECT>
```

The size of the controls can be specified using the WIDTH and HEIGHT parameters. The default sizes are indicated below:

Table 3.11 Controls and slide rules in an embedded RealPlayer

Control Name	Std width	Std height	Description
ImageWindow	Depends on content		Video window, can also be controlled by right-clicking the mouse (hold mouse button in MacOS)
All	375	100	The complete RealPlayer control panel
ControlPanel	350	36	Compact version of control panel
PlayButton	44	26	Combined Play/Pause button
PlayOnlyButton	26	26	Play button
PauseButton	26	26	Pause button
StopButton	26	26	Stop button
FFCtrl	26	26	Fast forward button
RWCtrl	26	26	Rewind button
MuteCTRL	26	26	Mute button
MuteVolume	26	88	Mute button and volume control
VolumeSlider	25	65	Volume control
PositionSlider	120	26	Navigation slide rule in on-demand clip
TACCtrl	370	32	Shows information such as title, author and copyright
HomeCtrl	45	25	Real logo

Table 3.12 Information and status displays in the embedded RealPlayer

Control Name	Std. width	Std. height	Description
InfoVolumePanel	325	55	Displays clip information with volume control and mute button
InfoPanel	300	55	Displays clip information
StatusBar	300	30	Displays player status, network resources and current clip position
Statusfield	200	30	Displays player status
PositionField	90	30	Displays current position and entire length of clip

Several elements often have to be arranged in groups. Consoles are used for this purpose. These consoles each have a unique identifier, using the individual elements allocated to the different consoles. This concept is demonstrated with the introduction of the CONSOLE parameter.

Sample control grouping using a Netscape plugin

```
<EMBED SRC="rtsp://realserver.company.co.uk/clip.rm"
    WIDTH=240 HEIGHT=180 NAME=realPlug
    CONTROLS=ImageWindow CONSOLE=_master>
</EMBED>
<EMBED SRC="rtsp://realserver.company.co.uk/clip.rm"
    WIDTH=26 HEIGHT=26 NAME=realPlug
    CONTROLS=PlayButton CONSOLE=controlgroup1>
</EMBED>
<EMBED SRC="rtsp://realserver.company.co.uk/clip.rm"
    WIDTH=26 HEIGHT=26 NAME=realPlug
    CONTROLS=StopButton CONSOLE=controlgroup1>
</EMBED>
```

Sample control grouping using ActiveX control (IE)

```
<OBJECT ID=realPlug WIDTH=240 HEIGHT=180
    CLASSID="classid:CFCDAA03-8BE4-11cf-B84B-0020AFBBCCFA">
    <PARAM NAME="SRC" VALUE="rtsp://realserver.company.co.uk/clip.rm">
    <PARAM NAME="CONTROLS" VALUE="ImageWindow">
    <PARAM NAME="CONSOLE" VALUE="_master">
</OBJECT>
<OBJECT ID=realPlug WIDTH=240 HEIGHT=180
    CLASSID="classid:CFCDAA03-8BE4-11cf-B84B-0020AFBBCCFA">
    <PARAM NAME="SRC" VALUE="rtsp://realserver.company.co.uk/clip.rm">
    <PARAM NAME="CONTROLS" VALUE="PlayButton">
    <PARAM NAME="CONSOLE" VALUE="controlgroup1">
</OBJECT>
<OBJECT ID=realPlug WIDTH=240 HEIGHT=180
    CLASSID="classid:CFCDAA03-8BE4-11cf-B84B-0020AFBBCCFA">
    <PARAM NAME="SRC" VALUE="rtsp://realserver.company.co.uk/clip.rm">
    <PARAM NAME="CONTROLS" VALUE="StopButton">
    <PARAM NAME="CONSOLE" VALUE="controlgroup1">
</OBJECT>
```

The _master console The _master console sticks out like a sore thumb in the above examples. This is one of two exceptions, and indicates that the respective control is connected to all other controls on the page; it controls ImageWindow, for example. On the other hand, output can be controlled in several ImageWindows with one PLAY button. This enables several groups of buttons to be created, which correspond to various RealMedia clips. The clips assigned to a button in this way are then always output in the _master ImageWindow when the appropriate button is pressed. For example, an ImageWindow can play back different clips assigned to several play buttons on the page.

The example of embedding the RealPlayer is explained in the accompanying web site. Similar links are also listed.

The _unique console

Assigning controls to the _unique console has exactly the opposite effect. Other controls on the page do not have access to a corresponding formatted control. For example, this enables certain player windows to be controlled by buttons on the page.

Plugin control using JavaScript

As well as controlling the player using predefined controls, the embedded RealPlayer can be entirely controlled using JavaScript. This enables complete control to be embedded into the page, and many additional functionalities to be adjusted individually.

The name or individual address is an important issue in addressing RealPlayer in a page. The NAME parameter is used for this purpose with the Nestcape plugin, while ID is used with the ActiveX control.

Sample JavaScript control of the RealPlayer

```
<OBJECT ID=realPlug CLASSID="..." WIDTH=240 HEIGHT=180>
    <PARAM NAME="SRC" VALUE="rtsp://realserver.company.co.uk/clip.rm">
        <EMBED SRC="rtsp://realserver.company.co.uk/clip.rm"
            WIDTH=240 HEIGHT=180 NAME=realPlug>
</OBJECT>
<a href="javascript:document.realPlay.DoPlay()">Play</a>
<a href="javascript:document.realPlay.DoPause()">Pause</a>
<a href="javascript:alert(document.realPlay.GetTitle())">
    Clip title</a>
```

Some examples and further links can be found on the accompanying web site.

In the above example a RealPlayer is embedded, which can be started and stopped by clicking on two conventional links. In addition, the current clip title can also be displayed in a JavaScript message.

Unfortunately, Netscape, in version 6 of its Web browser, has failed to implement 'livescripting' technology. This is why, in version 6.0, RealPlayer cannot be controlled via the Netscape plugin. Since Netscape 6 does not support ActiveX, the ActiveX control does not provide a solution either, so this useful feature cannot be used for the time being.

Plugin detection

It must often be determined whether the user has installed RealPlayer before it can be embedded into the page. JavaScript and VBScript is used to verify this.

In Internet Explorer...

The RealPlayer is accessible in Internet Explorer via the installed ActiveX control. By using VBScript, an attempt is made to generate an ActiveX object. The result of this attempt allows conclusion if certain software (such as RealPlayer) is installed, and if so, which version of it.

...and in Netscape.

Netscape makes things a little easier for the developer by providing a facility to search for the plugin in JavaScript. The 'plug-in' object is used here, which contains descriptions of all plug-ins installed. In this variable, a list of all the plug-in names is available, which you can search via JavaScript to see if the name 'RealPlayer' is listed.

The accompanying web site contains a complete sample script for RealPlayer plug-in detection.

You can also check this using the ABOUT PLUG-INS command in the Netscape Help menu. A list of installed plug-ins appears, and if you look at the source code for the page, you will notice that it has been generated entirely in JavaScript. The same methods can be used to produce a plug-in detection facility in JavaScript.

Availability

The Helix Universal Server is available for different operating systems:

* Windows NT 4.0, 2000 and XP professional
* Linux 2.4.18
* gLibC 2.2.4
* FreeBSD 4.0 or 4.5
* Sun Solaris 2.7 or 2.8
* IBM AIX 4.3 or 5L
* HP UX 11.0 or 11i
* Compaq Tru64 5.1 or 5.1A

The old RealServer 8 was additionally available for the following platforms:

* Linux 2.0.x or 2.2.x
* FreeBSD 3.x
* Sun Solaris 2.6
* Irix 6.2 or 6.5

The costs for the server depend on the features included and how many concurrent streams it can manage. The Basic version can be downloaded from RealNetworks and used freely, but it only supports a maximum capacity throughput of 1 Mbps. In addition, there are Standard-, Enterprsie-, Internet- or Mobile-versions of Helix Universal Server which are optimised for different scenarios. Their pricing ranges from between £1,500 and £7,000.

3.5 Playing back RealMedia content

RealOne Player Basic and Plus

The RealOne Player is RealNetwork's solution for media playback, not only of contents in RealMedia format. This is available in two versions: RealOne Player Basic can be downloaded free of charge, while RealOne Player Plus costs around £30 to buy. Alternatively, it is included with the realONE superpass. This is a subscription service for exclusive streaming media content available for around £10 per month. RealOne Player Plus offers extended functions such as content conversion, a graphic equaliser or extended cd burning.

Version 1.0 of the RealPlayer was released in 1994, only with RealAudio support at the time. Since then the RealPlayer has undergone countless improvements and developments, and now provides all functions to access complex interactive entertainment and information content independently of a Web browser.

Figure 3.26 RealPlayer 8 Basic

With RealOne Player, RealNetworks has completely redesigned the user interface and interaction model, as well as the underlying product architecture of playback devices. The Player's new, customisable 3-pane interface allows consumers to create their own 'Play-More-Explore' media experience, by navigating between a media playback pane, a contextual information application and a fully functional embedded media browser. This model is built on standard HTML for easy authoring and was designed to support backwards compatibility with older player versions.

New features of
RealOne Player

So Player RealNetworks enhanced significantly the feature-set of its media player. Some important new features are:

- TurboPlay
  Using free additional bandwidth on broadband connections, TurboPlay minimised the time needed for buffering audio and video data.

- Support of new media types
  In RealOne Player the playback of DVD, AudioCD, Windows Media content or QuickTime MPEG-4 video is possible.

- CD burning
  It is now possible to burn audio- and video-clips directly onto cd in RealOne Player.

- Portable devices
  RealOne Player supports various portable devices to directly copy content to mp3 players etc.

- Media browser
  An integrated web browser allows a closer linking of streaming media and static web pages.

- RealAudio Surround playback

Supported formats

RealOne Player supports a wide range of media types, many of which are generally needed to design SMIL presentations.

RealMedia Data Types

Of course, the RealOne Player supports all proprietary media types of RealNetworks. In many cases this is even an exclusive feature, since RealOne Player and the old RealPlayer versions are the only applications to support RealVideo, RealPix or RealText.

RealMedia data types supported by RealOne Player:

- RealVideo (.rm)
  (see above)

- RealAudio (.rm, .ra)
  (see above)

Some examples of
RealPix and
RealText are
included on the
accompanying
web site

- RealPix (.rp)
  RealPix is not a real image format like GIF, PNG or JPEG, but can be used to enhance the presentation of these image formats in RealPlayer. RealPix enables the user to create animated slideshows containing fades, crossfades, cropping, wipes, zooming or panning, which again can be used in a SMIL presentation. RealPix files contain a simple XML code that describes the presentation of certain image files.

- RealText (.rt)
Like RealPix, RealText files contain XML code that can be edited with any text editor. With RealText, the user can create text presentations that use font formatting, timing control or animation.

3rd party file formats supported by RealOne Player

RealOne Player also supports various other open or proprietary file formats. Allthough many of them are not generally streamed, RealNetworks evolved the RealPlayer from a little streaming media player to an universal media player supporting all types of digital media types. So many supported formats, such as uncompressed WAV or AVI, are suitable for streaming use.

Third party audio formats supported by RealOne Player:

- AudioCD
- Audio Interchange File Format (.aiff)
- Liquid Audio (.lqt)
- MJuice (.mjf)
- MPEG-1 Layer 2 (.mp2)
- MPEG-1 Layer 3 (.mp3)
- MPEG-1 Layer 3 Playlists (.m3u, .pls, .xpl)
- Unix Audio (.au)
- Waveform Audio (.wav)
- Windows Media Audio (.wma)

Third party video formats supported by RealOne Player:

- Advanced Streaming Format (.asf)
- Apple QuickTime (.mov, .qt, .moov)
- Apple QuickTime MPEG-4
- Audio Video Interleave / Windows Video (.avi)
- MPEG-1 (.mpg, .mpeg, .mpa, .mp2)
- MPEG-2 on DVD
- Windows Media Video (.wmv)

Other file formats supported by RealOne Player:

- Graphics Interchange Format (.gif)
- JPEG image format (.jpg)

- Macromedia Flash (.swf)
- Portable Networks Graphics image (.png)
- Synchronised Multimedia Integration Language (.smi)

Availability

RealOne Player Basic can be downloaded free of charge from RealNetworks. It provides all functions required to access media content. RealOne Player Plus can be purchased together with RealNetworks' superPass for around £10 per month, or without superPass for around £30.

Features of RealOne Player Plus

The Plus version of RealOne Player offers extended functionalities, including:

- Advanced video controls
  to correct brightness, contrast, sharpness and hue of the video image.

- Analogue recording
  making it possible to record analogue audio signals with RealOne Player via every sound card.

- 10-band graphic equaliser
  providing much better control for the sound characteristic than the standard 3-band equaliser of the basic version.

- Crossfading
  increasing the experience of audio playlists by automatically fading from one song into another.

- Toolbar mode
  to minimize the player.

Some versions of RealOne Player Basic are included on the accompanying web site.

The portability of RealPlayer is unbeaten: no other streaming media client is available for so many platforms. Only the old RealPlayer 8 is currently available for some systems.

- Windows NT 4.0, 98, ME, 2000 or XP

- MacOS X from 10.1

- Linux 2.2x i386 based (announced)

RealPlayer 8 only:

- Linux/Alpha (Debian and Red Hat 6.2)

- Linux/Sparc (Red Hat 6.2)

- Linux PPC 2000

- Irix 6.3 and 6.5

- AIX 4.2 and 4.3

- Solaris 2.6 and 7 (Sparc)

Microsoft Windows Media

Microsoft didn't realise the importance of streaming media very early on, just as they had failed to grasp the future importance of the Internet. This has demanded not only the development of Internet Explorer, but also acknowledgement of the importance of streaming media technologies on the Internet, a phenomenon which was long underestimated. This enabled a small company, RealNetworks, not only to secure a lead in development, but also to establish itself as the unrivalled market leader in this field for some time.

However, in mid-1999, Microsoft presented a fundamental overhaul of the existing Netshow technology that already included some simple streaming functions. A software solution was launched in Windows Media Tools which provided all the necessary features for transferring streaming video and audio at high quality. The vast number of features in the current version, Windows Media 9 Series gives an initial idea of how intensive the development of Windows Media Technology has been for it to displace its two main competitors, RealNetworks and Apple, from this expanding market.

Windows Media Encoder
Particularly in the latest version, Windows Media has evolved from a bundle of streaming-related tools to an essential, integrated part of the Windows Operating System. An essential component part of Windows Media is the Windows Media Encoder, with which both livestreams and on-demand content can be created. Together with the Winows Media Player and the Windows Media Services, it forms the core of Windows Media Technology, provided by Microsoft to create and deliver any kind of streaming media content in Windows Media format. Various other tools such as the Windows Media Producer, Windows Movie Maker or Windows Media ASF Indexer provide the content developer with more options with regard to creating streaming-media-based multimedia experiences.

Windows Media Player
The Windows Media Player is distributed free of charge for accessing Windows Media content. Its widespread distribution is explained by its inclusion with Internet Explorer in Windows 98, ME, 2000 and XP —nearly all Windows platforms. According to an IDC study in 2001, Windows operation systems were used on 94% of all desktop computers. Assuming that a high percentage of them either use an up

to date Windows version (98SE, ME, 2000 or XP) or Internet Explorer, it is likely that Windows Media could theoretically be accessed by nearly every up to date Windows PC.

Yet it has to be considered that this says nothing about the percentage of installed Windows Media Player that are actually used for streaming media applications.

Windows Media Services   Microsoft Windows Media was also the first system in widespread use which provides support for using content on mobile devices. Due to early and intense cooperation with all main chip manufacturers, over 100 device manufacturers currently support Windows Media format. Thanks to these, mobile audio players, mobile phones and PDAs are all able to play back Windows Media video or audio.

Digital Rights Management   With Digital Rights Management (DRM), Microsoft provides a solution for protecting digital media from illegal use. By coding DRM information into the media stream, access to content can be restricted to certain users and certain applications. For example, usage of a DRM-secured audio file can be restricted to 3 months on a specific pc and then be transferred to two different audio devices.

Table 4.1 Windows Media technology product development

1991–1992	Windows 3.0 with Multimedia Extension 1.0 (Software-based playback of sound- and videofiles and Soundblaster device support)
1992–1996	Windows 95 and Netshow Technology (first internal tests with compression technologies and on-demand streaming)
1997–1999	Windows 98 and Windows Media Technologies 4.0 (complete revision of Netshow Technology to Windows Media Technology)
2000	Windows 2000 and ME and Windows Media Technologies 7.0 (Revision of user interface, playback quality optimisation)
2001	Windows XP and Windows Media Player 8 (CD burning, DVD playback and several small updates of Windows Media Player)
2002	Windows XP and Windows Media 9 Series (Complete update of all software components, Player, Encoder and Server

Strategy games   Microsoft decided to become involved in the streaming media market at a relatively late stage. Its very strong market position in several areas has enabled it to establish excellent sales channels for Windows Media. It can also be assumed that nearly every Windows installation includes an installation of the Windows Media Player. This makes the number of Media Players installed very high. The use of Windows and Internet Explorer has led to a rapidly increasing number of clients, to an extent where, until now, Linux- and Unix-users have been marginalised or completely ignored. However, new Media Player versions for MacOS, Pocket PCs and Palm Size PCs show that Microsoft is willing to consider non-Windows user groups in future.

Microsoft decided to focus on the development of digital media applications with the overhaul of the Netshow Technologies in the late 1990s. To catch up with the existing know-how backlog of its competitors, RealNetworks, Apple and others, Microsoft had to rely on existing, open standards , such as MPEG-4. However, in the light of the enormous performance capacity of the MPEG-4 standard, affinity for this standard was definitely a good start.

Since then, Microsoft may have distanced itself from the MPEG-4 standard for strategic reasons, and concentrated on its own Windows Media 7, 8 and 9 standards. However, this is understandable as the image quality of its own codec has increased considerably. Microsoft quickly secured a strong market position through its offensive marketing strategy, showing that its main competitor, RealNetworks, lost much of its previous market share. However, RealNetworks remains slightly in the lead in relation to the amount of content available. But this lead is decreasing, and it remains to be seen who can decide the race in the most interesting expanding market on the Internet.

4.1 Audio and video codecs

Using open standards after the revision of Microsoft Netshow Technologies was a key advantage of Windows Media Tools. Even though Microsoft imposed its own codecs, nonetheless open standards were used, and the integration of the compression technologies of other companies was supported. Using. MPEG-4 compression technology, for example, Microsoft was able to quickly catch up with its backlog in developing efficient compression technologies. As development of Windows Media continued, Microsoft continued to develop its own codecs, so that after 'Windows Media MPEG-4 Video v1, v2 and v3' the video codecs were renamed and the addendum 'MPEG-4' was omitted.

Windows Media extension confusion

Using a flexible file container like ASF enables Windows Media files similar to QuickTime to provide a platform for the integration of various compression methods. If the Windows Media Player attempts to play back files with a codec which is not installed, the player contacts Microsoft and tries to download a suitable codec. Although they all use the same format (ASF), Windows Media files can have different file extensions:

- WMA for audio files compressed with a Windows Media Audio codec

- WMV for video files compressed with a Windows Media Video codec

- ASF for an audio or video file compressed with any other codec

The reason for using various file extensions is that audio and video files should, in many cases, be played with different applications.

The introduction of versions 7, 8 and 9 of audio/video codecs has signalled a reduction in the use of the MPEG-4 standard. This is a plus point, in that the sound and image quality produced with these new codecs has been audibly and visibly improved. The downside is that Microsoft once again decided to favour the development of proprietary standards against the use of existing, open standards.

The late decision to invest massively in the streaming media market first forced Microsoft to align the development of its own video and audio codecs with other available technologies. Examples of such audio codecs are MP3 and others such as the Sipro Labs ACELP codec. In video, the MPEG-4 standard provided the basis for Microsoft's early codecs, where, for example, the ISO-compliant creation of MPEG-4 files was also supported. Today, the Windows Media Encoder 9 only supports the creation of Windows Media Video 9 streams. Whereas version 8 of Windows Media Encoder supported the encoding of standard-conform MPEG-4 video, this feature has apparently been removed in version 9.

Video codecs

As described, the early video codecs of Microsoft relied on MPEG-4 know-how to keep up with existing video compression standards, For this reason, they were named after MPEG-4, although they were not fully compliant with the official ISO MPEG-4 standard.

Today, MPEG-4 streaming solutions form their own solutions, based fully on open standards, such as RTSP, MP3, AAC and various MPEG-specifications. More on MPEG-4 is described in chapter 6.

Windows Media MPEG-4 Video v3

Microsoft presented its MPEG-4 Video even before updating the Netshow Technology to Windows Media. Microsoft MPEG-4 v1 and v2 were therefore part of the Netshow technology and one of the first MPEG-4 implementations on the market. When Windows Media Technology was introduced, Windows Media MPEG-4 Video v3 was the standard video codec of it and consequently had an enormous market presence. It generally corresponds to ISO standards, differing only in slight detail.

Microsoft has restricted itself primarily to the use of simple MPEG-4 features such as improved compression in lower bit rates, error tolerance or compression efficiency. Several extended MPEG-4 possibilities, such as the object manipulation model are not supported. Nevertheless, this codec offered a high image quality compared to its rivals at the time. Many older files available on the Internet use this Windows Media codec.

Windows Media Video V7

From version 7 upwards, Microsoft prefers its own encoder to using MPEG-4, which indicates another Microsoft aversion to ISO standards. However, the clearly optimised audio and video qualities in version 7 are a weighty argument for preferring these codecs to the older ones.

ISO MPEG-4 Video V1

In addition to its codec version 7, Microsoft offered in Media Tools 7 an option to encode streams which correspond to official ISO standards (simple profile). Microsoft was therefore still the only developer to support an open and highly developed compression method at this time. Until recently, the Microsoft ISO MPEG-4 codec has had an immense market presence, only outranged by QuickTime MPEG-4 and DivX.

As an active supporter of the MPEG-4 standard, Microsoft made more than 100 contributions to the MPEG-4 standardisation process and has patents relevant to MPEG-4 video implementations.

Windows Media Screen v7

Streaming screen content One of the most interesting improvements in Windows Media Technologies 7 was the high quality screen capture facility. This feature enables providers to use an encoder to capture screen content directly, encode it and send it to clients via Windows Media Services. This type of streaming video application, not much used up to now, has great potential for education and distance-teaching.

The Media Screen codec v7 also enables screen content to be represented more smoothly at higher resolution, and also with quick mouse movement, dialogue boxes and drop-down menus at 15 kbps. Some redundancies in screen content have been improved (colour surfaces, geometric forms, few colours), so a 70 second clip at 22 kbps only takes up just under 200 KB.

The problems involved in compression are obvious: material which is difficult to encode includes extensive image changes such as window scaling, lengthy scrolling or displaying large images with high colour density. It is also not advised to display moving image content on screen during encoding.

Windows Media Video 8

In March 2001, Microsoft announced a significant improvement in playback quality in its version 8: VHS quality at only 250 kbps and near-DVD quality at only 500 kbps were fairly weighty promises – something not uncommon in their competitors. However, the first samples on the Internet showed improved quality over Windows Media 7 at lower bit rates.

Windows Media Video 8 provided general improvement of coding efficiency and thus better playback quality at the same bit rate compared to Windows Media Video v7. The VBR encoding had been optimised and 2-pass encoding was first introduced.

The Windows Media Audio and Video 8 codecs are compatible with Microsoft Windows Media Player 7 and 6.4 by using the auto update function of the players.

Windows Media Video 9

Latest video coding   Windows Media 9 Series was introduced in September 2002 and also includes new video codecs. According to Microsoft, Windows Media Video 9 provides a quality enhancement of 15 to 50 percent compared to version 8 and needs only 50% percent bandwidth of an MPEG-4 video stream at comparable quality.

Again, in Windows Media 9 the Variable Bit Rate (VBR) encoding has been improved. It now contains a peak-constrained VBR mode, where the user specifies the maximum instantaneous bit rate allowed. This particularly optimised content played back via dial-up connections or on mobile devices.

The biggest gains compared to Windows Media Video 8 occur when encoding at high bit rates. Here, Microsoft introduced a new mode of the WMV9: Windows Media Video 9 Professional. Home entertainment use, in particular, is a central field of application for this. Windows Media Video 9 is optimised for the encoding of high definition video with resolutions that are much higher than today's tv images (1280x720 or even 1920x1080 pixels) and bit rates up to 20 Mbps. These high definition streams can be decoded by medium-range Pentium 4 PCs. Moreover, several hardware vendors such as ATI or NVIDIA have annouced hardware support to decode Windows Media 9 content, which will minimise the cpu load during playback. Home entertainment devices, such as DVD players will also support WMV9.

Windows Media Video 9 Screen

For computer-based training, Microsoft offers a new version of its Screen codec. It delivers better handling of bitmap images and screen motion with no dropped frames. A new VBR support enables delivery at very low data rates, such as from dial-up connections, with no dropped frames.

Windows Media Video 9 Image

With the new Windows Media 9 Image codec, still images can be transformed into full screen (640x480 at 20 Kbps bit rate) video using pan and zoom effects. When moving from one video sequence to another, dissolve transitions can be added, creating the effect of a fully-edited video clip. The resulting video file, compressed using either CBR or one-pass VBR encoding, can be easily shared because it is much smaller than the original image file.

Audio codecs

Sipro Labs ACELP.net

Sipro Labs ACELP.net got its name from the Algebraic Code Excited Linear Prediction (ACELP) compression procedure family, optimised for use with Internet protocol and Intel Pentium systems.

Thanks to the optimisation of package distribution at ACELP.net, the effects of transfer errors have been minimised, and error correction facilities in package loss optimised. In addition, the codec uses redundancies in frame concatenation and interlacement in order to increase transfer efficiency further. It is recommended that human voices be encoded at lower bandwidths of up to 16 kbps.

ACELP.net is outdated, but on-demand content encoded with this codec can quite often be found in combination with Windows Media MPEG-4 Video v3.

Windows Media Audio V7

The Windows Media Audio codec was developed for a wide application range from 8 kHz speech up to 48 kHz stereo music encoding. In contrast to the ACELP.net codec, the Microsoft audio codec does not use intraframe recording, a process where the codec responds robustly to errors caused by packet loss.

Microsoft advertised a clearly quicker encoding of WMA7 at qualities similar to MP3, which is confirmed when compared to the Fraunhofer encoder. However, other developers' MP3 encoders are equal in speed to the Microsoft codec, leaving only multithreading as Microsoft's advantage in speed. WMA7 much publicised claims to superiority over MP3 cannot be confirmed in this case.

Another feature of the Microsoft codec is its superior frequency range compared to all other products. Yet, despite this, its implementation does not produce the usual noise reduction of 100 dB, but only 30 dB: a clearly audible loss in quality. It could therefore be argued that Microsoft's audio compression, created under considerable pressure of time, does not compare to long-standing MP3 compression methods, even in the high end area.

Windows Media Audio 8

Version 8 of the Microsoft audio codec promised CD quality at 64 kbps. Even though experienced users would justifiably dispute this, it cannot be denied that Microsoft, just like RealNetworks with RealAudio 8, has invested much research, and actually produces an astonishingly high quality even at lower bit rates.

Windows Media Audio 9

The latest version of Microsoft's audio codecs has been significantly improved and enhanced. According to Microsoft, it can deliver 'consumer CD quality' at less than 64 Kbps, providing 20% compression improvement over Windows Media Audio 8.

One of the reasons for the better sound quality in WMA9 is the improved VBR encoding. Besides a quality-based VBR encoding, it is possible for two other VBR-modes in Windows Media Encoder. When using 'Bit Rate VBR', the stream is generated acording to an average bit rate specified. The 'Bit Rate VBR (Peak)' mode encodes a Variable Bit Rate stream that does not exceed a given bit rate. The data analysis of 2-pass encoding also optimises the quality of a VBR stream. Of course, Constant Bit Rate encoding is possible in Windows Media 9, too.

Windows Media Audio 9 Professional

The new Windows Media Audio Professional codec is aimed at the home cinema market. It can use source material with up to 24 bit resolution and 96 kHz sampling frequency (to compare: an AudioCD uses 16 bit and 44.1 kHz). Even more interesting is the option to encode multichannel digital surround sound, providing up to 8 discrete audio channels. Using this feature of Windows Media Audio the digital 5.1 surround sound of a DVD can be encoded with 128 Kbps at an acceptable quality. Doubling this bit rate to 256 Kbps enables Windows Media to encode audio streams that correspond to the sound quality of a common Dolby AC3 signal (at least 384 Kbps). Windows Media Audio Professional can currently only be played back with the Windows Media Player 9.

Windows Media Audio 9 Lossless

To store audio content at the best quality possible, Windows Media Audio 9 Lossless is introduced: different to all other codecs described in this book, WMA9 Lossless is not a lossy compression. This means that it does not alter the final decoded signal in any way, but rather compresses the audio data efficiently into a smaller data rate. So this codec is recommended for archiving audio content at an optimal quality while saving about 50–60% bandwidth. When accessing WMA9 Lossless content, the original data is rendered bit for bit identically to the original content.

Windows Media Audio 9 Lossless accomplishes this data reduction by using a method called 'Predictive Coding'. Using this, the encoder does not store every single sample like in an uncompressed wave-file, but tries to predict the correlation of subsequent samples from the previous ones. So it is possible to split a sound signal into a correlated and a noise part. Only the predicted sample and the decorrelated difference to the original data is stored. The average coding advantage amounts to an average of 50%. Other codecs using predictive coding are 'Shorten', 'Monkey Audio' or 'Sqeez'. Windows Media Audio 9 Lossless is always VBR.

Windows Media Audio 9 Voice

In addition to WMA9, WMA9 Professional and WMA9 Lossless, Microsoft introduced another audio codec. Windows Media Audio 9 Voice is different to RealNetworks voice codecs optimised for combined speech and music content. It encoded voice only and mixed content at very low bit rates at a high quality (e.g. 20 Kbps).

4.2 Multiple bit rate video

Microsoft has also supported the encoding of several stream qualities in one AV stream using the ASF (Advanced Streaming Format) since version 4.0 of Windows Media technology. In Windows Media Encoder version 7.0, the maximum possible number of bit rates has been increased from five to ten. In contrast to RealSystem, only one audio codec could be specified for all bit rates until Windows Media 9 Series.

File extensions

Microsoft recommends using the .wmv file extension for video and .wma for audio files. ASF files can be renamed accordingly, as the file format itself remains the same. For example, a distinction between Windows Media Video (.wmv) and Windows Media Audio (.wma) is required for use with mobile devices, as some devices can only output audio and video content.

Similar to RealNetworks SureStreams, several bit rates of a stream can be written into one file using multiple bit rates. The server and player then decide which of the different qualities is supplied to the user. The user-defined Internet settings configuration in the player is used for this.

Windows Media Services are required on the server side to use Multiple Bit Rate Video, as a conventional Web server does not provide these services. As with RealNetworks, a Web server would send all bit rates to the client simultaneously, which completely contradicts the purpose of multibit encoding, this being optimum use of bandwidth. When providing Windows Media content on a Web server, its operation should therefore be restricted to one target group.

Figure 4.1 shows the dialogue field specifying the computer's Internet connection. If required, this setting is sent to the streaming server, which then extracts the appropriate bitrate from a multibit stream and sends it to the client.

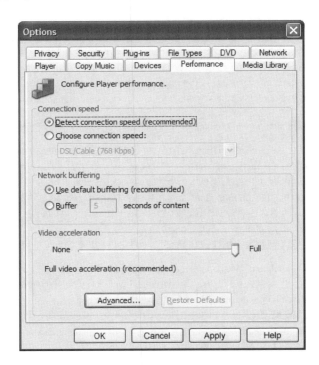

Figure 4.1   Internet connection settings in the Media Player 9

Multiple Bit Rate Audio Windows Media 9 Series includes several improvements of the Multiple Bit Rate support. So it is now possible to encode multiple audio bit rates in a Windows Media file. In previous versions, a MBR file could only contain one audio bit rate, which significantly limited the flexibility of providing multiple bit rate content. With the new Multiple Bit Rate Audio feature in Windows Media 9, a single file now can contain scalable audio content, from a 20 Kbps dial-up stream up to a 64 Kbps stream for broadband users. As with MBR video, the server and client will continually monitor connection speed and automatically scale the audio/video to match the current network speed.

Scalable Video Support
Another remarkable new feature of Windows Media 9 is the Scalable Video Support. Windows Media Encoder 9, together with Windows Media Services 9 can now create and deliver stream containing Multiple Bit Rates including multiple resolutions. A single encoding run can create one file with multiple streams optimised for each audience: e.g. 176×144 pixel video for dial-up, 240×180 for dual-ISDN and 320×240 for DSL and cable users. Windows Media 9 is the only solution to include such a feature, previous versions and RealMedia are limited to a single resolution for all their streams.

The support of Scalable Video can also simplify the capturing of several single bit rate versions of the same clip. For example, a video tape often has to be captured in various bit rates to deliver it via a web server. Using MBR with scalable video, it is possible to encode a correlative MBR file with all necessary streams in one pass. Once this is done, it is possible to extract every stream into a single bit rate file using the program 'wmstrmedt.exe' that comes with the Windows Media Encoder.

Multiple Language Audio Support
Similar to the encoding Multiple Bit Rate audio streams, it also is possible to use the Windows Media Encoder 9 to create a single file with multiple language tracks. When a Windows Media Player decodes the file, users get the sound track in their preferred language that is initially based on the Windows language setting, but which can be overridden by the user in the player software.

4.3 Creating Windows Media content

Windows Media Encoder
The Windows Media Encoder was developed as a component part of Windows Media Technology for capturing and encoding media data. Central functions include livestream encoding and the creation of on-demand clips using both existing audio and video files, and available system sound and video cards.

Capturing and encoding screen content in real time is another central feature of Windows Media Encoder, and enables new applications in distance learning, training and presentation.

Improvements
Microsoft completely revised the Media Encoder in version 9 and added many features which were previously lacking. Encoding Multiple Audio Bit Rates, support for frame accurate time codes data even via firewire, scalable video or securing live stream by using digital rights management are just some new features that will be described here.

The first striking feature on the interface is the video output in the upper area. The input and output data can be displayed in this area during runtime, scaled between 25 and 300%. This is particularly effective when both windows are displayed simultaneously, either next to each other or in splitscreen mode, as this is where compression-dependent loss comes into its own. The option to view different streams when using multibit encoding, conveniently enables the results to be assessed.

Figure 4.2 Windows Media Encoder 9 Series

The full version of Windows Media Encoder 9 Series is contained on the accompanying web site

The display of all main settings, progress and resources in the lower area of the interface has been revised in version 9 of the encoder. Data on input and output files, encoding configuration, compression progress and system resources is usually displayed here. A new feature of Windows Media Encoder 9 is the server monitoring here, which enables the user to monitor server-side statistics while broadcasting a live event. This means there is no longer a need to guess how large an audience is, or whether another server is needed to accommodate scale since there is constant feedback during the broadcast.

Program start – the New Session Wizard

Every encoding job in Windows Media Encoder is defined in a session that contains all information about sources, targets and encoding settings. When starting the program for the first time, a new session has to be defined. Session files can be saved later for future use.

When starting a new session, Windows Media Encoder launches the 'New Session' Wizard, which asks for all information required to encode live and on-demand material when the encoder is launched. Besides four New Session Wizards, the new 'Quick Start' Presets make it possible to set up sessions quickly for very common tasks with just one or two mouse clicks. Standard 'Quick Starts' are:

• Capture live content for local playback

• Capture live content for streaming (MBR)

• Convert film content to video

• Broadcast company meeting

In addition to the Quick Start presets, Windows Media Encoder 9 also contains New Session Wizards that take the user through the process of selecting sources, encoding settings, and output options so that both beginners and professionals can start working quickly. Besides defining a custom session, the user can choose between four important actions:

• broadcasting a live event from attached devices, or audio/video files

• capturing and encoding audio or video from attached devices and recording in Windows Media format

• converting an existing audio or video file into Windows Media format

• capturing screen content

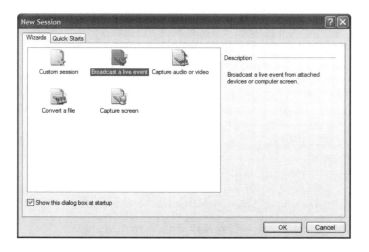

Figure 4.3 The Windows Media Encoder 9 New Session Wizards

Encoding audio and video files

Convert a file

Converting existing audio and video files into Windows Media format is one of the easiest ways of creating streaming media content. When users opt for this type of content production, they must specify the source and target files.

Input material   The following source file formats are supported by the Microsoft Windows Media Encoder:

- Advanced Streaming Format (.asf, .wmv, .wma)

- Video for Windows (.avi)

- MPEG-1 (.mpg, .mpeg)

- DVD MPEG-2 (.vob)
  – sourcing only from unencrypted .vob files
  – an approved MPEG-2 decoder has to be installed (e.g. Intervideo WinDVD, Cyberlink PowerDVD, Ravisent CinePlayer DVD)

- Waveform Audio (.wav)

- MPEG-1 Layer 3 (.mp3)

- Images (.bmp, .jpg)

Distribution methods   After selecting source and target files, the wizard asks for the distribution method that determines the encoding settings available in this session. Depending on the way the content should be distributed, the wizard preselects encoding settings that are most suitable in the next dialogue (see Figure 4.4).

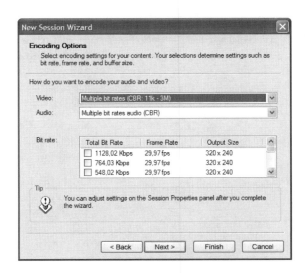

Figure 4.4   Selecting encoding settings in the New Session Wizards

Table 4.2 shows how the selection of a distribution method influences the encoding settings available in the following dialogue of the New Session Wizard.

Table 4.2 Distribution methods in New Session Wizard

	MBR	CBR	VBR	Video encoding settings selectable	Audio encoding settings selectable
File download	○	●	●	VHS to HDTV, 250–3000 Kbps	Voice-, CD- and HDCD, 6–384 Kbps, Surround
Peak constrained media	○	○	●	VHS to HDTV, 250–4000 Kbps, all with peak-constrained VBR	48–192 Kbps, Surround, all with peak-constrained VBR
Windows Media server	●	●	○	Various settings predefined for different scenarios, 10–1000 Kbps	Voice-, FM- or CD-quality, MBR audio, Surround audio, various bit rates
Web server	○	●	○	VHS, DVD, HDTV, screen capture, fullscreen, film content, highspeed content, 10–3000 Kbps	Voice-, FM- or CD-quality, Surround, 16–384 Kbps
Hardware devices	○	●	○	Predefined settings for hardware devices: Main- and Simple-Video-Profile, 160–10,000 Kbps	Audio profiles L1, L2, L3, L4 and S1, <20–384 Kbps
Pocket PC	○	●	○	Standard- or widescreen-resolution, 200 Kbps	16 or 64 Kbps
File archive	○	○	●	Quality-based-VBR encoding with index 100, 97, 95 or 75	Quality-based-VBR encoding with index 100, 90, 75 or 50, CBR with 16 or 64 Kbps

Meta Data Once the source, target and encoding settings have been selected, details such as title, author, copyright, evaluation and description are entered. As RealMedia's metadata in the RealPlayer, this information can be displayed in the Windows Media Player. Once the settings have been reviewed and the wizard closed down, the encoder is ready to begin the encoding process.

Capturing audio and video signals

Capture audio or video

Another New Session Wizard of Windows Media Encoder enables the user to record audio and video signals from connected devices in the Windows Media Format.

After selecting this option in the 'New Session Wizard', the available sources from which the user can record are displayed.

Video sources All available video devices are listed under video sources. These can be both selected and configured. For example, if a TV card is available, you can select which input source to use (e.g. tuner, FBAS, SVideo), which format corresponds to the signal (PAL, NTSC, SECAM), and whether brightness and colour values should be adjusted. The output format (resolution and colour scheme) can also be specified here.

Audio sources If several sound cards are installed on the computer, the device to be used can be selected at this stage of the wizard. Audio signal levels can also be adjusted in volume, treble and bass.

As with the RealProducer, different inputs of the chosen sound card can be selected and adjusted using the Windows record mixer (see Figure 4.5). This can be accessed by double-clicking on the speaker icon in the system tray.

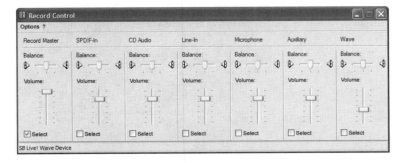

Figure 4.5 Windows XP Record Control

Once the output file has been specified, the distribution method is queried. According to the method chosen, the available encoding settings in the next dialogue are again preselected (Figure 4.4). After defining the stream's meta data, the wizard can be finished.

Live broadcasts

Although there are several similarities between RealProducer and Windows Media Encoder, the two competitors differ in a technical sense in live broadcast production. Windows Media Encoder functions as a type of mini server, and enables Windows Media Servers and clients to request the encoded live stream.

Small servers   In accordance with the principle of pull broadcasting, the wizard does not ask for the address of the distributing server, and just displays the address from which servers and clients can request the stream from the encoder. This enables Windows Media Encoder to serve up to 5 clients simultaneously. This means that a Windows Media Server does not necessarily have to be set up to provide live broadcasts to a particular, small target group.

This concept of connection between encoder and server has the decisive advantage that the encoding process becomes more robust in view of connection disturbances. For example, the Encoder carries on functioning if an ISDN connection fails.

What about Windows Media services?   However, if the target group is larger than 50, a server has to be used in order to provide for all clients simultaneously. In this case the Windows Media Services administrator needs to know the encoder address, in order to request the livestream from the encoder for further distribution.

In addition to the support of pull broadcasting, Windows Media Encoder 9 also supports push distribution of its live streams. When push broadcasting is selected in the New Session Wizard, the encoder initialises the connection to the Windows Media Services 9. When this option is selected in the wizard, the user has to specify the server name and the publishing point, from which the livestream can be requested from the server.

Figure 4.6 Specifying a streaming server for push distribution

Archiving In addition, the wizard enables the generated livestream to be archived in a local file.

Screen capturing

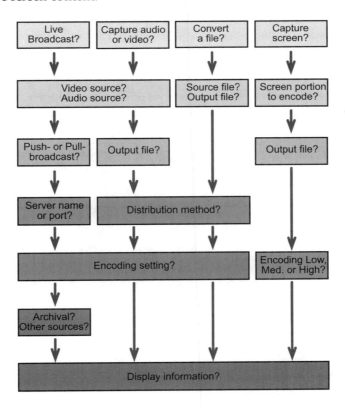
Capture screen

As well as available video sources, screen capture can also be used as an image source. In this case certain actions are recorded in definable areas of the screen surface using the improved Windows Media Video 9 Screen codec. What should be saved in the file can also be specified in more detail in the screen capture configuration:

- A specific window
  This option should be used if actions are recorded in a certain window or dialogue.
- A specific region of the screen
  In this case a section of the screen is either selected or numerically specified. This option is useful in systems with several monitors when the action is only saved on one monitor.
- The entire screen content.

Figure 4.7 Procedure for New Session Wizard in Windows Media Encoder

After selecting an output file, the wizard asks for the encoding setting to be used, giving the following three options: 'Low' (31 Kbps), 'Medium' (107 Kbps) and 'High' (259 Kbps).

After finishing the encoder configuration with a New Session Wizard, the encoding process can be started. Since the wizards only represent shortcuts to setting up the encoder for the most typical tasks, some fine tuning is often necessary.

Advanced configuration – front-end elements

The New Session Wizard provides an uncomplicated introduction to the software. In addition, the front-end of the encoder provides extra configuration facilities and different outputs for controlling the encoding process. The individual elements of the Windows Media Encoder interface are easily displayed and hidden.

The main window of Windows Media Encoder is organised in several panels. Depending on the requirements of the encoding session, the necessary panels are active or not.

Video and audio panel

Video preview   Displays for video source and encoded result are located in the upper half of the encoder interface. Several interesting features are available to the user here. The encoded video material can not only be displayed in its different bit rates, but can also be scaled between 25% and 300%. In addition, the input and output displays can be arranged at will (single, both, next to each other, splitscreen). These display options enable optimum supervision while the video data is being encoded.

Figure 4.8   Video Panel in Windows Media Encoder

The video panel is visible whenever video is encoded. On the other hand, the Audio Panel is often deactivated by default. It can be activated using the 'VIEW' menu in the main window and it contains controls for monitoring and adjusting the volume of the audio stream currently rendered. The main control is a level meter that displays the audio level. If this is overmodulated, the Windows Recording Mixer can be opened directly to adjust the volume for various inputs of the selected audio device.

Monitor panel

Detailed infomation about encoding sessions...

The monitor area of the encoder interface gives detailed information on stream configuration and the encoding process.

- Information on data input and output, encodng settings, encoding status and system status is displayed under GENERAL.
- The STATISTICS tab displays information about both the input and output audio and video, including the number of channels and sampling rate, fps, frames dropped, average bit rate, and so on.
- When a livestream is pushed to a Windows Media server, the SERVER tab displays status information on this server. It also informs the user of the number of players currently connected to the Windows Media server.
- When using pull broadcasting, the CONNECTIONS tab indicates which players and servers are currently requesting the stream during a live broadcast. The URL of the encoder can also be copied for playback.
- The EVENT LOG tab lists all the events that have occurred during the current session.
- The EDL tab displays the mark-in and mark-out times for all the clips in your EDL. The percent complete statistic for each clip in the list is also displayed.

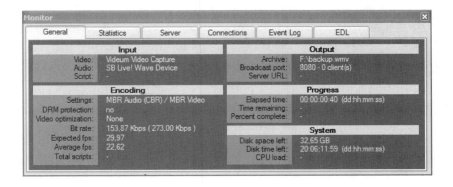

Figure 4.9 Monitor panel in Windows Media Player

Source panel

Source switching

An easily overlooked but highly innovative feature of the Windows Media Encoder is the toggling facility for switching between different audio and video sources during live encoding. Any source can be specified here, such as audio or video cards, captured clips or screen capture, and then selected in the source section during the encoding process. Sources can also be added once the live broadcast has begun.

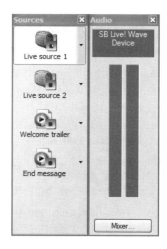

Figure 4.10   Source and Audio panel in Windows Media Encoder

This unique feature of Windows Media Encoder has many opportunities in application:

- Audio and video mixer
  The need for expensive audio and video mixers can be countered by installing more than one video card in the system, and selecting these as sources. The Media Encoder can switch between the various video signals, provided no cross-fading is required.

- Welcome trailers, error messages and farewells stills
  If existing clips are defined as a source, these can be used at the beginning, during and at the end of the live broadcast to fade messages into the livestream. The New Session Wizard supports this option.

- Online Teaching
  The toggling facility can be used to switch between video sources, clips and screen captures to broadcast live presentations over the Internet.

Script panel

If script commands are inserted into a Windows Media Stream, the player executes a specific action at a certain point during playback. Scripts are saved in a separate track, representing a separate stream just like the ones for audio or video. Script commands always consist of two sections: script type and script data. The Media Encoder has two script types by default:

- Caption script command: A free-form text is displayed.

- URL script command: An Internet address is opened in the default browser at a certain point during playback.

The third type of script commands can be defined freely and enable the user to define custom script types and execute almost any action during playback. The script type is queried by JavaScript or VBScript, and, depending on the type of command, any commands can then be executed. An example of using a custom script command is the use of a script command called 'changeImage'. The URL of an image file could be sent as script data along with audio and video. In the browser, the script event is captured by JavaScript and the information contained in the script data is then used to perform a certain JavaScript action. This will be explained in more detail later in the book (see page 143: Embedding).

Figure 4.11   Script panel of the Windows Media Encoder

Examples of using script commands in ASF files can be found on the accompanying web site

Captions can be displayed both in Windows Media Player, and the embedded player. The 'CAPTIONS AND SUBTITLES' field in the Media Player can output both text and HTML code. Any elements which can be displayed in a Web browser can also be requested and displayed here (hyperlinks, graphics, tables, etc).

The URL script command enables the default browser to open the URL sent in the script data. Not only can the requested Internet page be opened in the browser, but frames can also be addressed for output. For example, the URL

```
http://www.company.co.uk/media.htm??main
```

would open the file 'media.htm' in the frame called 'main' of the current browser.

DEVICE panel

Another new, unique feature of the Windows Media Encoder is the possibility to directly control an input device.

Direct device control

When a camera is connected to a firewire port of the computer, not only audio, video and timecode can be transferred through this connection. In this way, a camera or recorder can be controlled by Windows Media Encoder. Professional devices, such as DVCpro-, IMX-, BetaSP-, DAT- or Betacam-Players also can be connected to the serial port of the computer, if this supports the RS422 protocol (in most cases a special adapter is needed).

EDLs

Device control is especially useful, together with the new EDL (edit decision list) feature of Windows Media Encoder. When a controllable device is connected to the encoder, several clips can be specified within audio or video tapes by marking the appropriate In- and Out-timecodes in an EDL. An unlimited number of clips can be marked on one or more tapes and if more than one tape is used, the user is prompted to change it when needed. The clips do not necessarily have to be in the order in which they occur on the tape, because the software will look for the EDL point during the encoding.

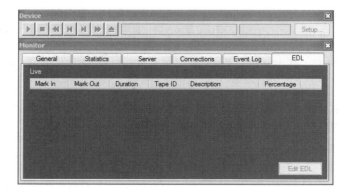

Figure 4.12 The DEVICE panel and the EDL tab of Monitor panel

Advanced configuration – Session Properties

The SESSION PROPERTIES panel contains all settings and options needed for configurating an encoding session. If a New Session Wizard was used, the settings of it can be controlled and changed here. If a Custom Session was selected in the New Session Wizard, any required detail can be entered in the SESSION PROPERTIES panel.

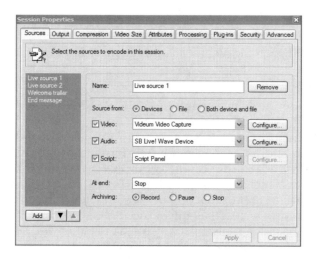

Figure 4.13 SOURCES tab of the SESSION PROPERTIES panel

The SOURCES tab

Sources can be created, edited and deleted in the SOURCES tab. Any video sources (video devices, video files or screen captures) can be combined with audio sources (sound cards, files). As well as configuring different sources, options regarding what should happen when a source ends (Stop, Loop or Roll over to another source) can be selected. If the stream is written into a local file, it also can be defined if a certain source should be recorded or if it should pause or stop the archiving.

The OUTPUT tab

Windows Media Encoder supports three different types of outputs: push- and pull-broadcasting of livestreams to Windows Media Servers and, of course, the archival into an ASF file. The OUTPUT tab enables the user to choose one or more of these output options. So a stream can be sent to a server using push distribution, be archived to a file and be requested by clients via pull-broadcasting at the same time.

The COMPRESSION tab

Customising settings   Windows Media Encoder comes with about 100 default profiles to encode audio and video content. To make the selection of proper settings easier, version 9 of Windows Media Encoder offers a menu of different distributions methods, depending on whether a file should be downloaded, streamed or distributed on CD/DVD proper audio and video profiles (see Table 4.2).

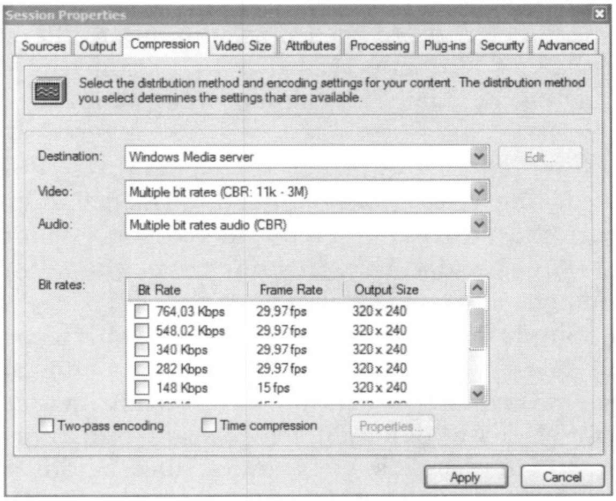

Figure 4.14 COMPRESSION tab of the SESSION PROPERTIES panel

The default settings in Windows Media Encoder are stored in the subdirectory /SETTINGS/ of the program root, defining audio and video settings separately. An XML file describes which profiles to use with which distribution methods.

Although the default profiles are a good choice in many cases, they can, of course, be freely customised by using the 'EDIT' button (see Figure 4.14). When using this function, a new window is opened where the general settings and all previously selected bit rates can be customised.

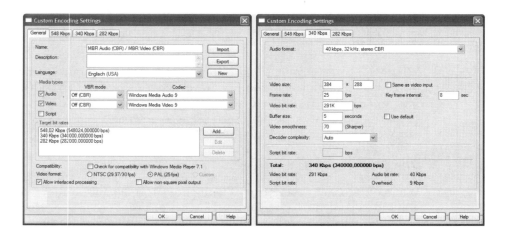

Figure 4.15   The GENERAL and a BIT RATE tab of the CUSTOM ENCODING SETTINGS

The GENERAL tab in the Custom Encoding Settings contains controls that apply to all bit rates or that are needed to administer different profiles. If another profile than the one currently loaded is to be edited, every profile file (.prx) can be imported. Accordingly, a custom profile can be exported to a local .prx file for later use.

Selecting codecs   In the Media types box of the General tab, VBR modes and codecs can be selected. Only version 9 of the Windows Media Audio codec is supported while the user can choose between several video codecs (Windows Media Video 7.1, 8, 9 and ISO MPEG-4 Video V1). In some cases, the Media Encoder is used to create uncompressed content. Although there is no danger of the quality impairments of lossy compression, the use of this option is only recommended for recording audio signals due to the high system requirements of uncompressed video processing. As shown in Chapter 1, processing long moving image content makes extremely high demands in terms of hard drive space and processor usage.

 Script commands have been described before, and just like video and audio tracks, the script command track has to be activated when this type of data is to be used.

Multiple bit rates contain more than one target bit rate. Every bit rate of the profile has it own tab in the CUSTOM ENCODING SETTINGS window. New bit rates can be added or existing ones can be deleted by using the buttons located at the middle right of the GENERAL tab.

Refining settings As some new features of the Windows Media Encoder 9 require the Windows Media Player 9 to decode the stream, it is important in many cases to make sure that the encoded content is compatible with older player versions. If the COMPATIBILITY button is checked, the user is prompted when he adjusts a setting that makes the content no longer compatible with Windows Media Player 7.1.

Every bit rate of a profile can be adjusted at its own bit rate tab of the CUSTOM ENCODING SETTINGS. Every bit rate tab contains ceveral controls:

- Audio format
  This setting determines the target audio bit rate, sampling rate, and a choice between mono and stereo. If peak bit rate based VBR encoding is used, a maximum bit rate has to be entered that will not be exceeded during encoding.

- Video size
  The image size of the encoded content can range from 16 to 2,000 pixels. When this value exceeds the image size of the source material, quality is significantly reduced. The same recommendations apply here as to the RealSystem outlined in Chapter 1.

- Frame rate
  The frame rate determines the number of frames per second (fps) in the video stream. Adjustment depends on available processor resources and the amount of moving content contained in the video. The more movement there is, the higher the frame rate has to be in order to ensure a smooth output. The hitch in using a high frame rate is its effect on the available bandwidth: the more images are encoded, the less bandwidth is available for transferring image detail. In addition, a higher frame rate makes higher demands of the encoder. The setting entered represents the maximum number of frames per second. Depending on factors such as video quality and available bandwidth, the actual frame rate achieved may be lower.

- Key frame interval
  The 'Key frame interval' setting specifies the maximum time which may elapse between the transfer of key frames. As described in Chapter 1, only differential images are usually transferred in video compression in order to save bandwidth. However, only transferring image changes increases the risk of output errors, for which reason complete key frames are transferred at regular intervals. The distance between key frames can be increased when transmitting video content with a static background, as the risk of output errors is fairly low due to little image change. The distance should therefore be greater when the video content has a lot of movement. The default setting is 8 seconds for lower bandwidths, and less for higher bandwidths.

- Video bit rate
  The bit rate to be used for the video data of the stream. It is measured in bits per

second, but the shortcuts 'K', 'M' and 'G' can be used to easily type/define larger bit rates.

- Buffer size
  Enter the number of seconds that content is to be stored for before encoding begins. A larger buffer results in better quality content, but requires more memory. When encoding content, the encoding process is delayed by the amount of time specified in the buffer; the content is also delayed by the same amount of time when streaming to a client.

- Video smoothness
  The compromise between frame rate and image detail is determined with the 'Image quality' slide rule. Depending on the setting, the encoder uses more bandwidth to represent smoother movement (more fps), and less for transferring fine image detail. At lower bandwidths, this means choosing between a detailed slideshow and smooth playback of a collection of coloured squares.

- Script bit rate
  The bandwidth available for the transfer of script commands should be chosen according to the number and content of commands to be transferred. Allocating a lower bit rate is often sufficient, as script commands are usually executed in a matter of seconds.

The VIDEO SIZE tab

Resizing The fourth tab of Windows Media Encoder's SESSION PROPERTIES is all about cropping and resizing.

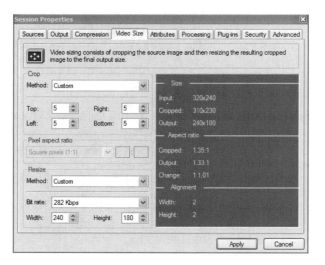

Figure 4.16 The VIDEO SIZE tab of the SESSION PROPERTIES

Cropping the source is often necessary when encoding video material that contains unwanted borders. New in Windows Media Encoder 9 are presets for cropping video to automatically meet different widescreen aspect ratios. The precropped image is displayed in the input area Video panel before encoding begins.

In the encoding profile, the image size of every video stream has already been entered. When the resize method is set to SAME AS PROFILE, the output image is stretched to meet the dimensions specified in the bit rate tab (see above). When NO RESIZE is selected, the output image is left at the dimensions of the cropped input. CUSTOM resizing makes it possible to enter custom dimensions for every bit rate encoded in the active profile.

The ATTRIBUTES tab

Optional stream meta data can be edited under ATTRIBUTES. This data on title, author, copyright, evaluation and description is displayed in Media Player, and can be queried by embedded players using JavaScript or VBScript. The Windows Media Player also displays, of course, the meta data of a stream in its status bar.

The stream details to be entered in ATTRIBUTES can be read using search programs or other applications based on the Microsoft Windows Media SDK format. In addition to display information, custom information fields, such as the date of creation, source file or editor name can also be transmitted.

The Processing tab

Video and audio filtering

Several filters are available at the Windows Media Encoder to optimise the audio and video quality before the encoding. The PROCESSING tab contains controls to activate the preprocessing video filters:

* None
  No filter is applied to the input video. This should be chosen when the input video material is already in progressive-scan display format.

* Deinterlace
  As described in Chapter 3, video is displayed in two fields, one containing all even lines and the other all odd lines. A tv set interlaces these two 'half-frames' so that a full PAL- or NTSC-video frame is displayed, Since camcorders record first the odd lines and then the even lines of a video frame, fast moving objects can already have another position when the even lines are recorded. The interference resulting from this is corrected by the Deinterlace filter.

* Inverse telecine
  Film-to-video conversion systems compensate the difference in frame rates between video (25 or 30 fps) and film (24 fps) by adding extra frames. These extra frames are redundant and can be removed by the Inverse telecine filter.

* Maintain interlacing
  One important new feature of Windows Media 9 Series is the support of interlaced video to make it ready for home entertainment applications. This video filter ensures that video interlacing is preserved in the encoded video.

Besides the video filters, the PROCESSING tab contains additional controls for audio encoding voice and surround content.

- Voice codec optimisation
  When the Windows Media Audio 9 Voice codec is used, the encoding result can be optimised by defining what type of audio is used. The codec then uses appropriate algorithms to encode plain voice data or a mix of voice and music. Alternatively, an optimisation definition file can be created that indicates the places in an input file where music starts and ends. The Windows Media Encoder help contains further information about creating optimisation definition files.

- 5.1 audio coefficients
  If multichannel audio content is encoded, all channels additionally are mixed down for output on stereo speakers. This mixdown can be customised here.

The PLUG-INS tab

Windows Media Encoder has a customisable user interface that enables developers to write transform plug-ins that customise and build upon encoding functionality.

The SECURITY tab

Using DRM Often it is important to secure digital media content to prevent uncontrolled distribution and usage. Windows Media Digital Rights Management (DRM) is an end-to-end system that offers content providers a solution for the secure distributions of digital media.

The basic principle of Windows Media DRM is that the media data is encrypted and additional information about identification, access restrictions and relevant license servers is inserted in the header of a media file.

To access a DRM secured content, a valid licence is required at the client. If this is not yet available, the client tries to connect to the licence acquisition URL stored in the header of the media content. At this URL any desired action can be defined to generate a licence for this individual client. For example, the user could be prompted to leave his e-mail address or to use various e-commerce solutions. To secure content using DRM, a licence server is required (often 3rd party).

The SECURITY tab contains controls to add new DRM profiles. These profiles contain a key, key ID, URL to the licensing server, a content ID and other information needed to encrypt the content.

Apart from restricting access rights to a content, it is possible to apply a watermark to audio or video streams. A watermark embeds a digital fingerprint into a stream. This information can be decoded to reveal information, such as copyright, terms of use and author. To work with watermarks, third party plug-ins are needed.

The ADVANCED tab

The last tab of the Session Properties contains controls for some advanced functions of Windows Media Encoder 9.

The identification name is assigned automatically and helps to identify encoders when more than one instance of Windows Media Encoder is running on the same computer.

Using DRM
The maximum PACKET SIZE of the UDP packets does by default not exceed 16,000 Bytes and is calculated during encoding. If packets are lost or fragmented during broadcast, the maximum packet size can be reduced. When broadband audio content is encoded, it sometimes can be necessary to increase the maximum packet size.

Windows Media Encoder 9 also supports timecodes that are used by professional video tapes to identify every frame recorded (e.g. on DV-, BetaSP- or Digibeta-tapes). When using a DV-tape via firewire or when controlling a BetaSP-player via RS422 as input source, the time code of the input can be stored with the encoded stream. This can be extremely useful to identify an encoded part of a video tape and find it later on the source tape. An alternative to using the time code that comes along with the input video (if any), is to create a custom time code.

The increased complexity of the Windows Media codecs requires a lot of cpu power to encode broadband streams in realtime. As a result, the encoder is often not able to handle all the captured data in realtime while encoding from devices to a file. In these cases, the captured data can be written into a temporary storage. When using the option 'Capture to hard disk first, then encode', all data is first of all written into a temporary file and is then encoded. This prevents frames from being dropped when capturing a large amount of data. Encoding stops when the minimum free disk space is reached. Storing an hour of data captured from a digital device requires approximately 15 GB of storage space.

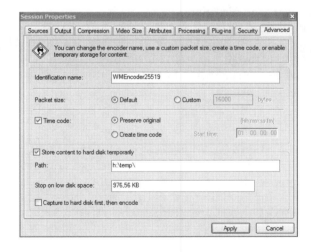

Figure 4.17 The ADVANCED tab of Windows Media Encoder SESSION PROPERTIES

The encoding process

When the START ENCODING button is clicked, Windows Media Encoder begins creating livestreams or media files. This process can be supervised and influenced by the user.

Video panel

If a video image is processed, the VIDEO panel shows either input or output, or a combination of both. The user can assess the video quality of different bit rates by toggling the output window.

Audio panel

The current audio level of the output file or sound card is displayed in the AUDIO section during encoding. Using the button below the level meter opens the Windows Record Control, where the volume of the different inputs of the sound card can be adjusted during runtime.

Monitor panel

Many display fields in the monitor panel show status information at the beginning of the encoding process. This includes the GENERAL tab, which displays information such as the total bit rate of the stream, or the intended and actual frame rate. The fields of the STATISTICS tab are also used once the start button has been pressed.

The new SERVER tab contains realtime information about the Windows Media server used to distribute a livestream.

If content is streamed live, then the CONNECTIONS tab takes on a special significance during encoding. This shows how many clients or servers are currently requesting the stream from the encoder. If there is a limited amount of bandwidth available, this may cause bottlenecks because of too many clients connecting at the same time (max. 5).

Source panel

Switching between different sources is only possible once the encoding process has begun. Sources configured in the panel can now provide real time output material for compression at the touch of a button.

Once the encoding process has begun, sources not currently being used can be modified. Other sources can also be added or removed during encoding.

Script panel

Script commands can also be added during the encoding process, provided the use of scripts in the current profile is scheduled (see figure 4.11 on page 123: Script command panel).

Ending the encoding process

If the encoding process is ended by the user, a summary of encoding results is displayed which gives a clear report of the session. This includes the bandwidths, and frame and sampling rates of the various streams created.

For example, the user can assess whether the encoder processor coped with the demands of the selected profile by comparing the expected and actual frame rates. This is reflected directly in the frame rate encoded.

In addition, the Monitor panel contains a summary of information about the encoding process after the encoding has stopped.

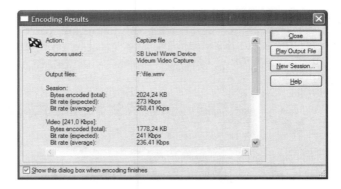

Figure 4.18 The Encoding Results display in WME 9

Further tools for content creation

Besides the Windows Media Encoder, additional tools for editing and optimising Windows Media content are located in the program directory.

Windows Media File Editor (wmeditor.exe)

Windows Media File Editor is a useful tool for editing and advancing Windows Media files. As well as trimming a file, it is possible to insert markers and script commands, edit the file's meta data and correct audio levels.

Trimming the start and the end of a media file is useful when just a part of a Windows Media file is needed, for example, when using the archival of a livecast. It is important to keep in mind that the images of a compressed video stream are organised in GOPs (groups of pictures) that start and end with a keyframe. After changing the In- and Out-points, the trimming will be done at the keyframes closest to the points. After saving the file, all data before and after the marked part is removed.

By adding markers, large files can be structured. When playing these files in the Windows Media Player, the user can select a marker and jump directly to the appropriate timecode.

Script commands have been described earlier (see Figure 4.11). If there are any script commands in the file, they are displayed and can be edited. Of course, new commands can be added, too.

The ATTRIBUTES tab contains controls to edit the meta data of a clip. If a multichannel file is used, the 5.1 audio coefficients can be edited to change the way the six audio channels are folded down for playback on stereo speakers.

When editing Windows Media Audio Professional 9 codec or the lossless format, the peak and average values of the audio signal are calculated during encoding, and those values are placed in the header of the file. During file playback, users can control the volume differences between the quietest and loudest points in the file. This is useful, for example, with content that has a wide range of volumes, and when a user does not want to have to adjust the volume manually during playback.

Meta data, markers and script commands are stored in the header of a Windows Media file. Windows Media File Editor is able to import and export this file header from/into a text file. This is an easy way to save the settings for archival or reuse purposes.

Figure 4.19 Windows Media File Editor main window

Windows Media Stream Editor (wmstreamedt.exe)

Windows Media stream editor is another tool that extends the flexibility of Windows Media. It enables the user to split or combine bit rates from existing Windows Media files into new files. For example, an encoded MBR file with various bit rates (e.g. 100, 300 and 500 Kbps) can be split up into one file containing the 100 Kbps bit rate and another containing the 300 Kbps quality. Also, only audio or video bit rates can be copied into new files. Furthermore, it is possible to combine bit rates from different files into a MBR Windows Media file.

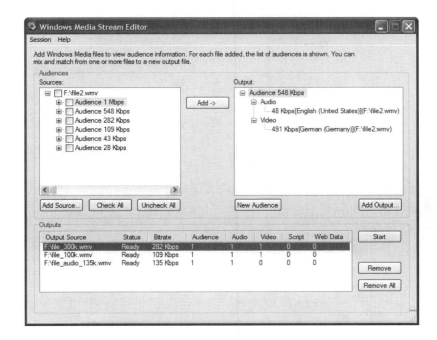

Figure 4.20 Windows Media Stream Editor

Windows Media Profile Editor (WMProEdt.exe)

The Windows Media Profile Editor contains similar controls like the COMPRESSION tab of the SESSION PROPERTIES in the Windows Media Encoder. It enables users to import any profile file (*.prx), edit it and export into another file. See above for additional information about the setup of a Windows Media Encoder profile.

Windows Media Scheduler (wmschedule.exe)

The Windows Media Scheduler helps to plan and to start Windows Media Encoder sessions at a given time. A saved session file (*.wme) can be selected and the Start (and optional Stop) Time is defined. When confirming the settings, a new task is generated in the Windows standard task scheduler.

The Windows Media Scheduler offers various applications:

- encoding tasks, which require a large amount of cpu power can be deferred to times when a workstation is not needed

- daily or weekly livecasts can be scheduled automatically

- frequent standard encoding tasks can be automated

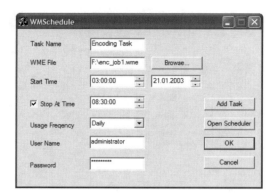

Figure 4.21   Windows Media Scheduler

Availability

Windows Media
Encoder 9 Series is
contained in the
accompanying
web site
Like all products in the Windows Media range, Microsoft provides the Windows Media Encoder free of charge.

Windows Media Encoder 9 is available for Windows 2000 and XP operating systems.

4.4   Providing Windows Media content

Windows Media Services enable administrators to set up a streaming server and to deliver all kinds of streaming media content to users over IP-based networks. Versions 4.0 and 4.1 were available for Windows NT 4.0 and 2000 and consisted of four Windows services (one for unicasting, monitoring, providing stations and providing programs). These four services are combined into one with Windows Media Services 9, which is integrated into Windows .NET Server.

As Microsoft presented with version 9, a complete revision of all components of the Windows Media Technology, as well as the Windows Media Services, have been extensively modified and improved. Many of the wishes and suggestions from the user community have been taken into consideration so that Windows Media Services 9 provide an optimal, flexible platform to deliver Windows Media content in every way possible. Central features of the server, such as Fast Streaming, Server-Side Playlists and Advertising Support or the administration interface, are described below.

Windows Media
Administrator
As with the RealServer, the Windows Media Administrator provides a set of HTML pages which enable server configuration. These pages can be used to contact and administer any Windows Media Server, provided the user has the rights to the server.

Publishing Points

Windows Media Services use publishing points to refer to directories and their media files, as well as live broadcasts. Clients request content of a server by connecting to a publishing point. There are two main types of publishing point: on demand and broadcast, which can be configured to deliver streams from different sources, such as livestreams from encoders, files or playlists.

Both of these types of publishing point can be used to deliver various content types (see below).

Table 4.3 Content types supported as sources of publishing point

Content type	Description	Example
Encoder live stream (pull)	Receives a live stream from an encoder using pull broadcasting	`http://encoder_name:port`
Encoder live stream (push)	Receives a live stream from an encoder using push broadcasting	`Push:*`
Media files	Streams single files	`c:\wmpub\WMRoot\file.wmv`
Directories	Streams files in a directory	`c:\wmpub\WMRoot\`
Publishing points	Uses publishing points on other servers as sources and forwards requested content (files or live streams) to clients	`http://server_name/pubpoint`
Playlist	Streams a playlist of several files	`c:\wmpub\WMRoot\list.wsx`
Dynamic sources	Requests playlists from dynamic sources (ASP or CGI)	`httpd://server_name/list.asp`

On-demand Publishing Points

Providing On-demand content

On-demand content is defined by the fact that each user receives their own data stream and is able to control the playback of the content. Typically, an on-demand publishing point is linked to a directory where media files are stored .

By default the server uses a default directory (SystemDrive/wmpub/WMRoot/), addressed as the default on-demand publishing point that is addressed as the server's root directory. The Home Publishing Point is not given an alias, whereby the name of the server is identical to the name of the Home Publishing Point. For example, the file TEST.ASF in this directory is requested using.

```
mms://ServerName/test.wmv
```

Subdirectories in the Home Publishing Point can also be accessed. If the TEST.ASF file is located in the SystemDrive/ASFRoot/probe/ directory, the Media Player requests

```
mms://ServerName/probe/test.wmv
```

Further on-demand publishing points can be added in order to organise Windows Media content more explicitly. These can then be used to refer to other subdirectories on the server hard drive or on network drives. For example, the file TEST.ASF could be located in the SystemDrive2/ASFDir2/probe2/ directory, where the 'extra' on-demand publishing point refers to the SystemDrive2/ASFDir2 directory. The player now requests:

```
mms://ServerName/extra/probe2/test.wmv
```

So, an on-demand publishing point provides content for clients that is used only as it is requested. If so, the server accesses the content and uses it to generate an individual data stream for the client. When a client connects to the on-demand publishing point, the content starts at the beginning and the end-user can use the playback controls on the Player to pause, fast-forward, rewind, skip between items in a playlist, or stop.

Broadcast publishing points

On the other hand, broadcast publishing points are used to organise access to live broadcasts. Publishing points are defined here which can refer to live streams from encoders, streams on another Windows Media Server, or other broadcast publishing points.

This type of publishing point is most often used when delivering live streams from encoders or broadcast publishing points on other servers. As always when receiving live streams, the clients all get the same data from the server, no matter when they connected.

In addition, it is possible to stream files and playlists (see Table 4.3) on a broadcast publishing point. In this case, the server uses one or more files to generate a live stream on the fly and send it to the clients. For example, this feature can be used to provide Internet tv stations and generate their program out of different media files. Another option is to use archive files of earlier webcasts and rebroadcast them live with little effort.

Obviously, there is no difference between on-demand and broadcast publishing points with regard to usable data sources. Rather, it is the way the media data is broadcasted by the server. Streams using sources delivered via on-demand publishing points are generated by a server just when clients request the content. Streams using sources delivered via broadcast publishing points are generated from when they are started on the encoder or server.

Server-side playlists

Content generation on demand
One of the central improvements of Windows Media Services 9 is the support of server-side playlists. Client-side playlists defined by ASX files (see below) or RAM/ SMIL files (RealMedia) are basically just lists containing information for player software of how to play several media elements. The client has to process this more or less complex playlist and initiate a connection to the streaming server for every element to be accessed. In addition, once a client-side playlist has begun, its content cannot be changed, since the player software has already downloaded it.

Windows Media Services 9 therefore introduces server-side playlists. In contrast to client-side playlists, these files (.wsx extension) are processed by the server to define several media elements in a row that should be streamed to the player. When a client accesses a publishing point that is assigned to a playlist, the server delivers one continuous stream that is generated on the fly.

Server-side playlists open a wide range of possibilities and improvements:

- Reliability and performance is increased relative to client-side playlists, because different, possibly low-performance clients don't have to process playlists instructions.

- Increased flexibility for content providers by providing the ability to change playlists dynamically during broadcasts without interruptions (change the order of clips, insert new clips, ad insertion, etc.).

- Users cannot skip clips in a playlists.

Server-side playlists can be used both with on-demand and broadcast publishing points. They can easily be edited using the build-in playlist editor of the server administration interface. Microsoft uses an SMIL 2.0 syntax at the point, so playlists can also be edited with any text editor. In addition, this XML-based format can also be generated automatically by the server, so that webcasts or server-side playlists can be dynamically created and broadcast for just one user. This provides a maximum level of personalisation, especially when inserting personal advertising.

The content of a new playlist could look as follows:

- Preproduced welcome to a product presentation (local .wmv file)

- Live broadcast from an encoder: First speaker

- Advertisements (.wmv files and images via Remote Publishing Point)

- Live broadcast from another encoder: Second speaker

- Product demonstration (local .wmv file with complemental PowerPoint slides)

- Live broadcast from first encoder: Farewell

- Still image

Although every element of the playlist may use different codecs, sizes or bit rates, the client receives one single stream with dynamically changing properties.

Client-side playlists: ASX files

References using ASX files ASF Stream Redirecting (or Windows Media Audio Redirecting) was designed to optimise playback of ASF files for the client. Similar to SMIL, playlists can be generated with these files, or advertisements displayed during playback. ASX/WAX files are text-based collections of modified XML tags which access certain functions of the Windows Media Player. These files are also known as Windows Media meta files.

ASX version 1 One possible use of the ASX format, derived from XML, is generating files which refer to ASF content. Like RealNetworks RAM files, ASX files contain the address of the content to be requested, and can be sent as e-mail attachments or saved on the hard drive. More complex functions can also be created, similar to SMIL:

- Entering alternative URLs if an address cannot be requested.

- Defining a playlist from several clips for a presentation.

- Inserting advertisements, banners or logos in a presentation.

- Playing back a short preview before the main presentation.

- Adding meta information to the content.

Microsoft insert ASX files for the same reason that RealNetworks insert RAM files: many browsers previously had problems recognising different file types and protocols. If content could not be downloaded, ASX files were used as references to content on servers. ASX version 1 provides this functionality.

ASX version 2 ASX Version 2 was extended to URL rollover functions and a direct link to an NSC file.

ASX verison 3 As part of Windows Media Technology 4.0, ASX Version 3 was extended to include the following functions:

- Playlists

Several examples for using ASX can be found on the accompanying web site
- Overwriting the meta data of a referenced ASF file:
  Details on title, author, copyright, etc. of the ASF file can be 'overwritten' by the appropriate data in the ASX file.

- Advertising
  Clickable advertising banners can be displayed at any point in the Media Player.

- Event Syntax

These are methods for toggling between a live broadcast and the media files defined in a playlist. Script commands can be received during a live broadcast, and media files can be inserted into the livestream.

Digital Rights Management

Securing content These optional Windows Media Services components enable providers to protect media content effectively. Content is encrypted, and the client requires a licence to play back or distribute the material. In addition, meta information is written into the media file which refers the user to the appropriate server for licensing, if he does not have a suitable cipher key.

A licence file is required to play back encrypted content. This specifies how often, for how long, and on which computers and mobile devices a media file may be played back.

The process for providing protected content is as follows:

- (A) Content setup
Media content is encrypted using Windows Media Rights Manager. From this point on, a key is required for playback (deciphering), which is saved in a separate file. The information specifying where the file can be licensed is added to the media file.

  The cipher key can specify how often the file can be played back, whether it can be copied to mobile devices, for how long it is valid, on which computers it may be played back, and so on.

- (B) Provision
A protected file can be provided on Web or streaming servers, distributed on CD or sent via e-mail. As the protection is implemented in the media file itself through encryption, it cannot be played back without a valid cipher key.

- (C) Installing a licence server
A database is set up to sell the cipher key. This database processes the various queries and generates the cipher key according to the licence models.

- (D) Licence sales
If users wish to play back a protected file but do not have the appropriate cipher key, they are automatically redirected to the server where they can purchase it. They would have to give a valid e-mail address, and probably pay some money.

- (E) Playing back the media file
Depending on the restrictions contained in the key, the user can play back and possibly copy the file.

Multicasting

In contrast to unicasting, data packets are sent to several receivers in the case of multicasting. As far as possible, data packets use the same transmission link, until 'duplicated' at a router and sent in different directions. This saves server and network resources, as one data packet is sent to several receivers, rather than several data packets being sent to individual clients.

The drawback in this case is the infrastructure upheaval caused in non-multicast capable networks, including the majority of the Internet. Many providers are only just beginning to convert their infrastructure, which suggests that, in future, most relevant transmission links will support multicasting. Multicasting currently attracts a lot of interest in larger corporate networks, in the production of corporate livecasts, for example. Figure 4.22 shows an application used to distribute a stream efficiently in a corporate network.

Multicasting is only supported by Windows Media Services 9 included with Windows .NET Enterprise Server or Windows .NET Datacenter Server. Here it can be activated as a property of every broadcast publishing point.

.nsc files   Multicast broadcasts are announced using a text file with a .nsc extension. A .nsc file provides clients with all necessary information, such as the server's IP address, ports, stream format or time-to-live (TTL) variable. .nsc files can be generated by the Windows Media encoder and be provided on a webserver for clients to download and execute them. Windows Media Player can receive the URL of an NSC file from an ASX file attached to an e-mail or linked on a webpage.

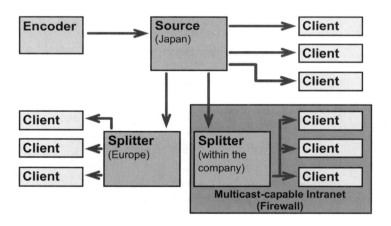

Figure 4.22   Splitting and Multicasting – sample setup

Unicast Rollover

When the Media Player opens an ASX file for a multicast station, the file instructs the player to request the appropriate NSC file, which in turn can initiate a unicast rollover.

Unicast rollover is used if a Windows Media Player does not receive the requested data packets via multicast. This may happen if a router on a transmission link does not support multicast, or if the client is located behind the multicast time-to-live (TTL) radius.

If the broadcast publishing point does not send a program, signal packets are sent instead, which the client intercepts, without passing to the unicast rollover.

The missing program from a publishing point does not necessarily force the client to establish a connection using unicast.

Once a multicast publishing point has been configured, the program has to be defined, and started.

Embedding

Like the RealPlayer, Windows Media Player uses both an ActiveX control or a Netscape plugin to embed player windows and controls into a Web page. The <OBJECT> or <EMBED> tags are used to insert different elements in the pages.

Using the Netscape plug-in   The Media Player Netscape plug-in is addressed using the <EMBED> tag. In addition to the syntax introduced with the RealPlayer, the type of embedded applications should also be passed as a parameter:

```
<EMBED SRC="mms://wmserver.company.uk/clip.asf"
        WIDTH=240 HEIGHT=180 NAME="MediaPlayer"
        TYPE="application/x-mplayer2"
        PLUGINSPAGE="http://www.microsoft.com/isapi/redir.dll?
prd=windows&sbp=mediaplayer&ar=Media&sba=plugin&">
    </EMBED>
```

The location where the browser can automatically download the plug-in is added to the TYPE parameter here, if this has not yet been installed.

Using Active X controls   Unlike the Netscape plug-in, the ActiveX control is also specified using the ClassID. For Windows Media Player this reads:

```
CLASSID="CLSID:22D6F312-B0F6-11D0-94AB-0080C74C7E95"
```

The corresponding ‹OBJECT› tag may look as follows:

```
<OBJECT ID=wmpPlug WIDTH=240 HEIGHT=180
        CLASSID="CLSID:22D6F312-B0F6-11D0-94AB-0080C74C7E95"
        CODEBASE="http://activex.microsoft.com/activex/
            controls/mplayer/en/nsmp2inf.cab#Version=6,4,5,715"
        TYPE="application/x-oleobject">
        <PARAM NAME="SRC"
            VALUE="rtsp://wmserver.company.co.uk/clip.wmv">
    </OBJECT>
```

Interleaving both tags here enables optimum content embedding without much programming required.

Due to the lack of an up to date Windows Media Player Netscape plug-in, all examples named here refer to the ActiveX control of version 7 and up and the Windows Media Player 6.4 Netscape plug-in. A Netscape plug-in will be available for the final release of Windows Media Player 9.

Windows Media Player Controls

Control bar   Unlike the RealPlayer, control elements of the Windows Media Player cannot be arranged individually and independently in a Web page. However, all controls can be displayed or removed as part of the embedded player. The following fields can be displayed using ActiveX control or Netscape plug-in parameters.

As well as playback control, the Windows Media Player control bar enables navigation through and within individual playlist chapters, and volume control.

The control bar is embedded using the parameter

```
<PARAM NAME="ShowControls" VALUE="true">
```

Different groups of elements in the bar can be displayed or removed as follows:

```
<PARAM NAME="ShowAudioControls" VALUE="true">
<PARAM NAME="ShowPositionControls" VALUE="true">
<PARAM NAME="ShowTracker" VALUE="true">
```

Figure 4.23 Windows Media Player 9 control bar

Embedding meta data The display field for outputting stream meta data can be displayed underneath video output using the following parameter:

```
<PARAM NAME="ShowDisplay" VALUE="true">
```

Figure 4.24 Windows Media Player 9 display field

Plug-in control using JavaScript

In order to embed streaming media content in Windows Media format in a Web page optimally, the Windows Media Player also enables the most important functions of the ActiveX control and Netscape plug-in to be controlled using script languages such as JavaScript, JScript or VBScript.

The instance of a Media Player in a page is addressed using its ID or its name. A simple example of an embedded Player window controlled by JavaScript would be as follows:

Sample JavaScript control of the Windows Media Player
```
<OBJECT ID="MediaPlayer" WIDTH=320 HEIGHT=240
    classid=CLSID:22d6f312-b0f6-11d0-94ab-0080c74c7e95>
    <PARAM NAME="type" VALUE="application/x-oleobject">
    <PARAM name="filename" value="clip.asf">
    <PARAM name="autostart" value="false">
```

```
<PARAM NAME="showcontrols" VALUE="false">
<PARAM NAME="showstatusbar" VALUE="false">
<EMBED TYPE="application/x-mplayer2"
    SRC="clip.asf"
    NAME="MediaPlayer"
    WIDTH=320
    HEIGHT=240
    SHOWCONTROLS=false
    SHOWSTATUSBAR=false
    AUTOSTART=false>
</EMBED>
</OBJECT>
<br>
<INPUT TYPE="BUTTON" NAME="BtnPlay" VALUE="Play" OnClick=
    "MediaPlayer.Play()">
<INPUT TYPE="BUTTON" NAME="BtnStop" VALUE="Stop" OnClick=
    "MediaPlayer.Stop()">
<INPUT TYPE="BUTTON" NAME="BtnPause" VALUE="Pause"
OnClick="MediaPlayer.Pause()">
```

As the changes between different versions of the Windows Media Player have included huge improvements and added features, the methods and properties of the Media Player 7 are incompatible with those of Version 6.4. This forces developers either to use double the amount of programming, or rely on the ActiveX control or the Media Player 6.4 Netscape plug-in.

In the above example, a Windows Media Player output window with a resolution of 320 x 240 displayed, as well as three buttons to control playback.

Plug-in detection

Several Examples for using the embedded Windows Media Player can be found on the accompanying web site
In view of the differences between Windows Media Player versions, it is important to determine whether the client has the software installed on his system, before using a Web page.

The practical use of plug-in detection can be seen on the accompanying web site. Windows Media SDK provides exclusive documentation on how to integrate the Windows Media Player into Web pages.

As in the RealPlayer, an attempt is made to initialise an appropriate control with VBScript in Internet Explorer. If this fails, then at least the Windows Media Player ActiveX control is not installed.

Netscape provides its practical 'plug-in' object here in JavaScript, enabling the search for an appropriate description.

Availability

Windows Media Service 9 Series is integrated into the Windows .NET Server series. Windows .NET Server is available in three different versions: Standard, Enterprise and Datacenter. Some features of Windows Media Services 9 are only active when it is used with Windows .NET Enterprise Server or Windows .NET Datacenter Server:

- Cache and proxy functionality
  The built-in support for 3rd party cache and proxy solutions meets the needs of companies and ISPs to manage effectively streaming content across multiple servers. Streaming economics can be optimised by conserving network bandwidth, decreasing network-imposed latency and decreasing the load on the origin servers.

- Multicast content delivery
  As described in chapter 1, multicasting can reduce the network load significantly by sending one data packet to a group of receivers. The Internet infrastructure is not fully compatible with this transfer method; it is therefore most relevant for the use in LANs and intranets.

- Fast Recovery
  The inherent high latency of wireless or satellite connections often means that content received by a client has become corrupt. To prevent inconvenient retransmissions of data packets, Forward Error Correction is used, which enables local packet correction and uninterrupted viewing of content.

- Internet authentication method (digest)
  Secure content delivery is one of the central requirements in many streaming scenarios today. The HTTP Digest authentication is an alternative to the methods supported by the Windows .NET Standard Server. A central feature of it is the possibility to flexibly limit access to streaming media content.

- Custom plug-in support
  When specific needs have to be met or Windows Media Services are to be integrated with existing applications, custom plug-ins can be created. Individual logging, custom authentication or the use of custom media sources are some examples of how the features of the server can be completely adapted to the individual's demands.

- Wireless streaming optimisations

- Event based scripting support

- Internet Group Management Protocol version 3 (IGMPv3) support

Windows Media Services 4.1 is part of Windows 2000 Server, and can be installed on Windows NT 4.0 systems, although it is questionable how long this old version will be supported by Microsoft.

4.5 Playing back Windows media content

The Windows Media Player has undergone rapid development as Microsoft's standard application for the playback of media files in different formats. From a simple media playback tool provided with all Windows installations, Windows Media Player 9 has become a comprehensive multimedia software package with extensive playback, recording and organisation functions. The new Windows Media Player 9 runs (for the time being) under Windows 98 SE, ME, 2000 and XP, and broadens the functions of an audio and video player to include a CD burner, media management and a streaming media application. For other operation systems, such as Windows 95 and NT, MacOS or PocketPCs, older versions of Windows Media Player are available.

Figure 4.25 Windows Media Player 9

The frontend of Windows Media Player 9 consists of several areas, used to control playback, display video or visualisations, search for content in the Internet, or display additional information of the loaded content.

The features bar   The features taskbar area on the right side of the main window provides quick access to the key features of the Player:

- The NOW PLAYING button is used to view video, audio visualisations and meta data of the open content. In addition, it provides a QUICK ACCESS PANEL (a right arrow) to access the player's media library and CD/DVD drives (for Audio CD, VCD and DVD playback).

- Microsoft's MEDIA GUIDE portal can be used to find featured content in the Internet.

- Audio CDs can be copied to hard disc using the COPY FROM CD button. By default, the ripped content is always encoded in Windows Media Audio format.

- The MEDIA LIBRARY of Windows Media Player 9 has been improved and offers a powerful solution to managing every kind of media content stored on the computer. Improved performance, auto updates, rating functions, and an innovative playlist management are some improvements of version 9.

- The RADIO TUNER opens a selection of featured online radios on a Microsoft website.

- Using the COPY TO CD OR DEVICE function, the user can transfer audio tracks to supported mobile devices or create an Audio CD.

- Online subscription services are listed when clicking the SERVICES button

- The SKIN CHOOSER changes the appearance of Windows Media Player by using skins.

The playback controls area at the bottom of the Windows Media Player main window contains controls for basic playback tasks, such as play and pause, fast forward and rewind functions, volume control, and a seek slider to navigate through on-demand content.

The Now Playing area in the middle of the main window contains a number of panes used to view video, visualisations, media information, audio and video controls, Internet content, or other controls. What is displayed in this part of the window depends on what function of the player is currently being used.

For more than ten years, Microsoft has been extending the complexity of its application for media content access. Starting with simple Multimedia Extensions for Windows 3.0 (1991), via the Windows Media Player 6.4 (1998), to the latest version 9: Windows Media Player today represents the core media capabilities of Windows. Some of the key features of Windows Media Player are described below.

Player skins

Design selection Windows Media Player 7 introduced a range of designs which can be created or downloaded from the Internet. A flexible interface layout allows access to all essential player functions using configurable control elements. The skins are collections of scripts, graphics, media files and texts organised as a new interface. The description and organisation of individual elements and function programming is achieved using XML. The idea of adjustable interfaces was not new when Windows Media Player 7 was introduced: this is a feature common to programs such as WinAmp, the MP3 player. However, being able to create new functions using scripts, and the total freedom in designing new skins are features unique to the Windows Media Player.

Providers can create their own skins, and download them automatically when requesting a media content. This allows a suitable player design to be offered for example with live events, attracting the user to certain brands. In addition, the user could continue to use the interface, once downloaded.

Figure 4.26 Windows Media Player 9 skins (example)

Visualisations

Media Player visualisations also were introduced with version 7 of Windows Media Player, and provided graphic audio output, in much the same way as WinAmp, the MP3 player. These visualisations consist of waveforms or frequency analyses, recycled and changed using different graphic filters (see Figure 4.25). Windows Media Player 9 came with several new visualisations and the ability to display them full-screen. Even more visualisations can be downloaded on the Windows Media website or customised by 3rd parties.

Audio CD ripping and creation

The Media Player burning function is also new, which can be used to burn CDs from various audio formats. When this feature was first presented with Windows Media Player 7, it was far from being perfected, but at this time it was a unique feature of Microsoft's media technology. In version 9, the CD burning feature has been completed with a ripping and encoding option. By default, the software encodes audio tracks directly into a Windows Media Audio 9 format that can be defined in the OPTIONS. Windows Media Player 9 also supports optional 3rd plug-ins among others for MP3-encoding. The creation of AudioCDs has been improved and now works faster and more reliably.

Media library

The Windows Media Player library browses the hard drive for media files, and lists them in a database for quick access. Here clips can be divided into various subgroups, and browsed for specific parameters using search functions.

Portable devices

From version 7.0 onwards, Media Player provides a facility to transfer content to a connected pocket PC, MP3 player, CompactFlash card, micro drive, and so on. Supported formats are ASF, WMV, WMA, WAV and MP3.

New in Windows Media Player 9

Windows Media Player 9 comes along with several new features and improvements, to meet Microsoft's design goals. Compared to Windows Media 7 and 8, the new version includes the following features and benefits.

Fast Start Streaming

No more buffering... The biggest handicap of streaming media technologies are the delays caused by buffering times. To limit buffering delays, Windows Media Player 9 uses the maximum bandwidth available of the user's connection to fill the buffer as fast as possible. For example, a user on a 1,000 Kbps DSL connection would get the 10-second buffer on a 250 Kbps stream in four seconds. Fast Start Streaming works best with broadband connections, but also with narrowband connections. Wherever there is extra bandwidth available, it is used to minimise buffering times.

Fast Cache

...or playback interruption Similar to Fast Start Streaming, the new caching feature of Windows Media Player 9 uses additional bandwidth of the user's Internet connection to buffer data ahead at a rate faster than real time on the client machine. In so doing, the likelihood of interruptions due to network issues is significantly lowered.

Scalable Video Support and Multiple Bit Rate Audio

As described above, Windows Media Format 9 supports scalable video with multiple bit rate video. Since every bit rate of multiple bit rate content can now use a separate resolution, the flexibility of the MBR feature is enhanced. In addition, multiple audio bit rates can be stored now and multiple languages can be provided in MBR content.

Mini-Player Mode

Windows Media Player 9 can be minimised and docked into the Windows taskbar. All playback controls can be used directly and video, visualisations, or media information can be displayed. To activate the Mini-Player Mode, right-click an unused part of Windows' taskbar, select TOOLBARS and then WINDOWS MEDIA PLAYER. After minimising the Windows Media Player window it will be displayed in mini-player mode.

Settings and filters

Various new filters are included with Windows Media Player 9, which can be accessed by using the SETTINGS item of the VIEW menu.

- The QUIET MODE adjusts the audio's dynamic range, so that the difference between the loudest and softest parts is reduced. The sound level is kept more uniform and can be enjoyed more at a low volume or via headphones.

- Hue, brightness, saturation and contrast of the video can be adjusted in the VIDEO SETTINGS.

- The COLOR CHOOSER allows it to freely define a colour for Windows Media Player's main window.

- CROSSFADING AND AUTO VOLUME LEVELING allows fading from one track of a playlist into the next one, and to make sure that different audio files are all played at the same volume.

- A new 10-band GRAPHIC EQUALIZER provides better control over the audio playback.

- The Play Speed Control feature allows it to change the speed content is played at rates between 1/16 and 16.

Video frame smoothing

Windows Media Player 9 can improve playback quality of low-frame-rate video by interpolating the missing frames and smoothing out the motion in the video.

Enhanced Media Library and Playlists

The Media Library of Windows Media Player 9 was improved in many respects. Performance was optimised, the frontend is better (hierarchical) organised and many features, such as track numbering, file information, or better sorting routines, were added. In addition, the software now supports ratings that can be either automatically downloaded from the Internet or modified manually.

Auto playlists are a new feature that lets users define dynamic playlists, which are updated as new music is added to the My Music folder of the computer. Auto playlists are based on descriptions of types of content, not on static lists of files (e.g. only new songs rated four stars or more and not played yet could be defined as a playlist).

Supported formats

The Windows Media Player is more developed than the RealPlayer as a universal playback software package for all time-based media types. A wide range of data formats are supported.

Streaming formats:

- Windows Media Audio (.wma)
  and Windows Media Audio meta files (.wax)

- Windows Media Video (.wmv)
  and Windows Media Video meta files (.wvx)

- Windows Media files (.asf)
  and Windows Media meta files (.asx)

- MPEG-1 and MPEG-2 (.mpg, .mpeg, .mpa, .mp2),
  including MPEG Layer-3 audio (.mp3).

All of the above formats are supported for local playback, plus the following:

- Compact Disc Audio (.cda)

- Digital Video Disc (DVD)

- Audio Video Interleaved (.avi)

- Apple QuickTime (.mov, .qt, .MooV) up to version 2

- Musical Instrument Digital Interface (.midi, .mid)

- Waveform Audio (.wav)

- Sound File (.snd)

- Unix audio (.au)

- Audio Interchange File Format (.aiff)

- Macromedia Flash (.swf)

Availability

*A version of
Windows Media
Player 9 Series can
be found on the
accompanying
web site*

All Windows Media Player versions are available for unrestricted use from the Microsoft Web site.

As you may expect, Windows Media Player 9 is available for all current Microsoft operating systems (Windows 98 SE, ME, 2000 and XP). It is recommended by Microsoft to use the XP version, as Windows Media Player 9 for Windows 98SE, ME and 2000 does not include all features of the XP version.

Windows 95 and NT users will have to play content with the older version 6.4, which does not support any of the version 9 codecs.

Windows Media Player 7.1 is available for MacOS X and MacOS 8.1 through to 9.x. No update has been announced as of yet.

QuickTime

 The Apple QuickTime architecture is a long-established open standard for the creation, integration, organisation and distribution of different types of digital media. QuickTime enables software applications to work easily and consistently with a wide range of digital media formats and codings. This integration of as many different media types as possible beyond video, audio and still images was an integral part of the development of the format from the outset.

More so than any of the other solutions described, QuickTime provides a platform for the complete integration of all digital media types. The facility for transferring streaming media is only one of many functionalities. The use of the QuickTime file format is long-established in both consumer and professional circles, as it offers an extremely flexible and convenient way of recording (not only) these types of media.

QuickTime is therefore platform-independent, extendable and designed as an open standard, which encouraged many developers to use this format in their products. For example, both Silicon Graphics and Media100 use QuickTime as the Standard Media Container of their platforms for editing professional video. On the other hand, QuickTime for many years has been used to encode video for efficient Internet downloads or cd-rom distribution.

5.1 Multitalent QuickTime

The key to the flexibility of the QuickTime format is its modular, hierarchical construction. A file always has an arbitrary number of tracks, which contain audio and video, as well as text, timecode, music/MIDI, sprite/animation, tween, MPEG, VR or 3D. All these media elements can be combined and arranged within tracks. This flexible track concept makes QuickTime a universal multimedia platform, which is a denomination that is gladly adopted by its competitors. A QuickTime file could contain anything from digital video material played in cinema quality, to a simple stream transferred via 14.4 Kbps modem connection.

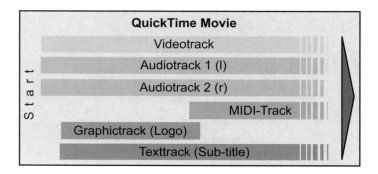

Figure 5.1 The QuickTime track concept

Media Abstraction Layer However, it is not only the flexibility of its format which guarantees QuickTime its huge fan base: its platform independence means it can be used in many different applications. The key to the flexibility and performance of QuickTime is the Media Abstraction Layer. This QuickTime basic technology is a highly developed, component-based software architecture, providing software and hardware developers with full access to QuickTime services. In addition, a plug-in interface is specified, allowing QuickTime to encompass the functions of other developers.

The QuickTime Media Abstraction Layer isolates an application (and its development) from underlying hardware concepts, and spares developers and users alike from discussing low level technologies, such as timers, storage media, video displays and frame buffers, audio mixers, synthesisers or graphics cards. The use of new hardware concepts or different hardware acceleration is massively simplified.

An application communicates via standardised methods with the QuickTime toolbox, which in turn accesses and manages the stored media data. The application receives the requested data without having to consider problems such as memory access or compression.

All services responsible for the creation, integration and playback of digital media are implemented in the Media Abstraction Layer:

- Timing and synchronisation of different tracks
- Audio, video and image compression and decompression
- Format conversion, scaling, composition and transcoding
- Audio mixing, sample rate and format conversion
- Audio and video effects, and transitions
- Capturing
- Import and export of media data
- User interface elements, e.g. for playback control, preview windows or capture dialogues

The most striking feature of the QuickTime Media Layer is the wide range of supported media types (video, audio, text, timecode, music/MIDI, sprite/animation, tween, MPEG, VR, 3D) and the provision of services for managing each media type.

Apart from the playback of each format, the support of as many file formats of other providers as possible is a central part of the QuickTime philosophy. Applications with QuickTime support enable automatic access to all supported media types, and are not restricted to the QuickTime movie format. The functionality of many video and audio formats can be extended with minimal effort. QuickTime currently supports over a dozen of the most important file formats for digital video such as AVI, OpenDML, MPEG or DV format, and can also access various formats for audio, animation or stills. The software architecture of QuickTime enables applications to access directly a large range of digital media formats.

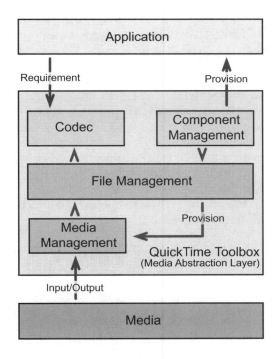

Figure 5.2 The Media Abstraction Layer in QuickTime

Streaming QuickTime

The video and audio data in a stream is arranged into separate tracks according to the QuickTime terminology. This concept is no different from the use of QuickTime as a streaming media solution. From version 3 onwards, QuickTime offers a facility for receiving multimedia streams. Its architecture enables any application with QuickTime support to play back and create streaming media clips.

Hinting   A new track type is introduced in streaming QuickTime to stream media data efficiently in ip-based networks. Additional information is saved in 'hint tracks' which enable the server to send the media data optimally.

The point of hinting is to relieve the server of computing-intensive operations. Normally, the server divides the media tracks into IP-based data packets with appropriate headings for respective bandwidths. The encoder assumes this task when generating movies, enabling the media data to be distributed more effectively.

Media is not necessarily modified in hinting. Instead, an additional hint track is added, which contains information for dispatching the corresponding media tracks on the Internet. Adding to this QuickTime concept makes QuickTime itself a fully functional streaming platform in an uncomplicated manner.

Self-contained   Hint tracks can be generated and recorded in several different ways. They are
movies   usually saved in the same file as the media tracks. An alternative method is to refer hint tracks to the media tracks of other files, and save them in separate movies ('not self-contained'). In addition, the media file and hinting information can be written together in one track. This increases the efficiency of the reading process on the server side, as a track can be read continuously, and does not have to be accessed parallel to another track.

Fast Start vs.   In QuickTime, progressive streaming is often mistaken for streaming because of
streaming   Fast Start Movies. In contrast to streaming QuickTime, Fast Start Movies are QuickTime files provided on a conventional Web server. Clients access these movies using a normal HTTP connection. Movies usually have to be downloaded in their entirety before they can be played back. However, Fast Start Movies first transfer all information required by the computer, so playback can begin before the download has finished. This enables the client to begin playback before the file has been completely received.

Figure 5.3 QuickTime Fast Start Movies

Fast Start Movies are easy to recognise, as in the control bar QuickTime displays exactly how much of the clip has been downloaded and can be played back. Anything the user has already received is saved locally, and is available at any time. In addition, the bandwidth of a Fast Start Movie is not connected to the transmission bandwidth available. If the movie bit rate exceeds the available bandwidth, playback only begins when enough of the clip has been received for the remaining download time to be less than the total length of the clip. The rest of the material can be downloaded while the movie is being played back.

Fast Start Movies guarantee 100% receipt of all image data, direct access to all material received, and a data rate independent of Internet connection bandwidth. Livecasts cannot be produced, as the user cannot access parts of a clip which have not yet been received, and the movie takes up space on the client hard drive.

Streaming QuickTime follows another approach, which corresponds to those already discussed. In true streaming, information is transferred in real time, meaning that the data required for the next output is transferred, played back and deleted. The computer receives the data to be played back from the streaming server via RTSP. This enables live broadcasts, including via multicasting, allows users to navigate material, and the clip received to be copied locally.

Alternate data rates

Using QuickTime to adapt streaming to different bandwidths is different from using RealNetworks and Microsoft SureStream/Multibit technologies. Instead of generating tracks in one movie, several movie versions are generated in QuickTime, which are logically linked with a reference movie.

The reference movie is embedded in a page (linked or embedded) and assumes the function of referring to the movie whose bit rate best corresponds to the player's default transmission bandwidth. The streamed movie uses the available bandwidth as best as possible, guaranteeing maximum playback quality.

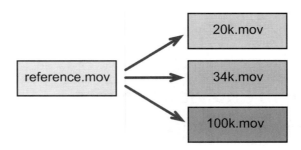

Figure 5.4 Alternate Movies in QuickTime

Upward compatibilty Furthermore, a movie or still image can be encoded in the reference movie for playback on older versions of player software, which guarantees upward compatibility for the content displayed. For example, as version 2 does not recognise the Sorenson codec, despite this being the de facto standard in QuickTime file compression, data can still be played back on the client using a 'fallback movie'. An older codec (e.g. Cinepak) has to be used when encoding a fallback movie, so it can be supported by older player versions. When using a still image, QuickTime Image Format (QTIF) should be used. This image will then be displayed instead of the video image on clients where QuickTime Player 1 or 2 is installed.

Alternate movies can also be created with the small MakeRefMovie tool, as well as professional programs such as Cleaner 5.

Product strategy

Courage to do it their way As opposed to its competitors at Microsoft, Apple has pursued a less aggressive marketing strategy, and seems keen to rely on the quality of its product. Its long-established market presence has enabled QuickTime to build up a large fan base among developers and providers. The idea of integrating streaming media services on the basis of the existing modular QuickTime concept in many ways offers a higher innovation potential than the comparatively simple solutions of its competitors.

Apple's strategic decision to go head-to-head with RealNetworks shows its courage to follow its own path in marketing its product. Using RealServer 7,8 or, of course, the Helix Server, content providers can use a server platform to sell their content and offer users two alternative streaming formats at minimal additional expense. In addition, the Apple streaming server was continued as an open source project, indicating huge further development of the product.

On the customer side, large Hollywood studios have become forerunners in the user of streaming QuickTime. However, the long wait for a live broadcast production solution has not really contributed to a huge distribution. The Sorenson Broadcaster partly reduced this deficit some years ago, and the release of the free Apple Broadcaster finally made QuickTime a rival to RealSystem and Windows Media. Increasing user numbers suggest that RealNetworks and Microsoft have to face a growing competitor in QuickTime in the realm of streaming media.

5.2 Audio and video codecs

In contrast to RealNetworks or Microsoft, Apple has not developed its own compression method. For a long time it relied instead on close partners such as Sorenson or QDesign to provide relatively highly developed codecs. However, despite considerable results in compression recently, Sorenson have lost ground to new codecs from RealNetworks and Microsoft in comparison. The latter have put great effort into optimising quality, which has proved hard to beat.

While the Sorenson Video and Qdesign Music codecs were the standard codes used in the QuickTime from version 3 to 5, Apple fortunately decided to use open standards in version 6. From there on, Quicktime supports the generation of MPEG-4 video and AAC audio content, which is completely compatible with the corresponding international standards (read more about MPEG-4 in chapter 6).

Video codecs

QuickTime uses a wide range of available codecs as a universal container for all types of media. These codecs can be used in many different applications.

Animation

The QuickTime animation codec is specially optimised for the compression of graphics containing many colour blocks. The run-length encoding process of the codec is used here, in addition to temporal encoding.

The codec uses lossless compression at the highest quality settings, while at low qualities the material is suitable for distribution on CD-ROM. However, due to its high data rates and the low data rates of the Internet, the animation codec is only suitable for transferring slideshows.

Compression and decompression do not require extensive system resources. All colour depths are supported, and an alpha channel (transparency) can also be transferred. It is recommended that one key frame per second be recorded when encoding moving images.

BMP

The BMP codec records a sequence of BMP images (Windows Bitmap) in a video track which is run-length encoded, but not temporally compressed. The data rate therefore increases in proportion to the frame rate.

This compressor is not suitable for Internet use because of its lossless compression. It is actually used to import sequences of BMP images in QuickTime. The BMP codec uses colour depths of 'millions', 256 and 16. The latter two can also be used in grayscale mode.

Cinepak

As an older QuickTime codec (developed in 1990), Cinepak is supported by all QuickTime player versions, and enables upwards compatible movies to be created, which can also be played back using Windows Media Player. On the other hand, the image qualities and compression rates do not correspond to the standards of today. Even though image quality at high data rates (higher than 1,000 Mbps, but always at least 10:1) is acceptable, images show high losses in Internet transfer.

Compressing image content requires high system resources, but images encoded by Cinepak can also be played back on older PCs.

Cinepak supports compression in 'millions of colours' and '256 colours' modes, as well as greyscale. Recording one key frame per second is recommended.

Component Video

The 3:2 compression rate of the Component Video codec is not suitable for effective content transfer over the Internet. Instead of RGB, YUV colour mode is used, where brightness values in the image are represented in 8 bit, and colour information in 16 bit. As colour information is only compressed at a factor of 2:1, the overall compression rate of 3:2 gives almost lossless compression. This is used to maximum effect, as the human eye is less sensitive to colour perception than to differences in brightness.

This codec is particularly suitable for capturing, as hardly any resources are used in compression, leaving more computing capacity for simultaneous transcoding in a livestream, for example.

Colour information is always saved at 24 bit in this codec, where every frame is a key frame (no temporal compression).

DV Stream

DV compression is used in digital video recorders and cameras which support Digital Video (DV) format. Optimal image quality is produced with a compression factor of 10:1, but the data rates linked with this are far too high to be used in Internet streaming (25 Mbps). Basically, DV codecs are based on an M-JPEG compression, which means that, depending on whether PAL or NTSC video is used, 25 or 30 JPEG images are stored in a video track.

Both compression and decompression require high system resources, which makes using this codec a convenient solution in fields where DV cassettes are used. In this case, transcoding is not required for transfer to or from the tape via firewire.

Graphics

Similar to GIF graphics, the graphics codec saves 8 bit images using temporal compression. In contrast to the animation codec, less bandwidth is required, but decompression requires higher processor power.

Unfortunately, only 256 colours are supported, which severely restricts its range of applications. On the Internet, the codec is only suitable for transferring slideshows and low-resolution content.

H.261

The H.261 codec was developed a long time ago for use in videoconferencing. Despite its relatively poor image quality, this codec works fairly reliably against package loss, and is therefore suitable for use on the Internet. Its three-dimensional compression with high compression factors makes its data rates low enough for modem transfer, even though the image quality is far below today's standards.

As it is an international standard, this compression method is available for many platforms. The YUV colour model used (see Component) compresses colour information at a 2:1 ratio.In order to achieve optimum results, a key frame should be inserted every 2–3 seconds, and a fixed data rate specified.

H.263

As a successor to the H.261 codec, H.263 compression also works very reliably in lossy environments such as the Internet. Moving image content can also be encoded in high quality and in real-time using efficient compression.

H.263 is supported by QuickTime 4 and works best at data rates under 64 kbps. Like H.261, it is an international open standard, and is available on most platforms.

The video image resolution should be set at 176×144 or 352×288 pixels; other image formats are cropped or scaled. The codec itself can specify the optimum frame rate when the user sets the value at 99.

With H.264 currently the successor to the H.263 codec about to be released, this will offer DVD-quality at bit rates of about 1 Mbps. It is developed by the Joint Video Team (JVT), and will be integrated into the MPEG-4 standard (MPEG-4 Part 10).

None

The uncompressed recording of video information contains no loss of quality whatsoever, but is wholly unsuitable for Internet streaming because of excessively high data rates.

M-JPEG

Motion-JPEG videos are essentially a sequence of JPEG images, implemented without temporal compression (key frames only). The bit rate increases in proportion to the frame rate. Either 24 bit colour or 8 bit greyscale encoding is used.

MPEG-2

Apple offers an optional MPEG-2 playback component for about £12. With this component, the QuickTime Player can open MPEG-2 content from DVDs, for example. In particular, this component is perfectly suited to users who often use MPEG-2 content as source material.

MPEG-4

As a widely accepted open standard for video compression, MPEG-4 will play an important role on the future's streaming market. Among other things the MPEG-4 specification defines a file container and of course various audio and video compression methods.

The QuickTime file format was the force behind the development.of the MPEG-4 file container. So QuickTime supports both the .mp4 file format as well as MPEG-4 compressed QuickTime movies using the .mov extension.

QuickTime 6 includes a standard implementation of the MPEG-4 video codec, featuring a versatile single-pass variable bit rate (VBR) encoder, which produces content using the MPEG-4 simple profile (see chapter 6).

Planar RGB

Videos in Planar RGB format are also not compressed, but are recorded in the RGB colour scheme. However, its bit rates are as high as the image quality produced, making it wholly unsuitable for Internet usage.

Sorenson Video

Sorenson was formerly the best QuickTime video codec for most applications. It produces high image quality at low bitrates, making this compression method ideal for use on the Internet and beyond.

Key frames should be inserted every ten seconds, and the codec automatically inserts further key frames if required (e.g. at scene changes). A fixed bit rate should be specified, but this can be 'bypassed' by using VBR encoding.

The Sorenson codec makes high demands of the processor during playback, and an up to date computer may be required for accessing broadband videos.

The 'basic edition' of the codec is distributed with QuickTime 3 to 6, and guarantees playback of all appropriately encoded streams. In addition, Sorenson-compressed clips can be created using this 'basic equipment'. However, it is seriously lacking in terms of features which are vital for producing professional level results.

Two-pass VBR encoding (Data Rate Tracking) For optimum creation of content, the more expensive 'Developer Edition' is required, available at around £300. This provides central functions such as 2-pass encoding, VBR or access protection mechanisms. All extended features of Sorenson compression are currently supported by the Discreet Cleaner application, as the developers at Discreet work closely with Sorenson in many areas. This application for professional encoding of streaming media content is described in more detail in chapter 6.

Central features of the 'Developer Edition' Sorenson video codec are Variable Bitrate Encoding (VBR), media keys for creating access restrictions, optimised key frame setting and optimised scaling in playback (temporal scalability).

Sorenson was the first provider to integrate video compression with variable bit rates into its product. Sorenson extended VBR by a variable which can be used to define by which factor the bitrate of a clip may vary. It can therefore be specified how dynamically the data rate is adapted to the image content, where on average the predefined bitrate is adhered to. If the value is set to zero, encodings with a constant bitrate can be produced. If the value is set to 100, the bitrate depends entirely on the content of the image. A high bit rate variance is permitted with

Internet applications in order to guarantee maximum quality with restricted bandwidths.

Media keys   Media keys are used to restrict access to movies. A password is assigned and written into the track while the video is being encoded. For example, media keys can be used in computer games in order to prevent the end sequence from being displayed before certain levels have been completed. Streaming videos on unsecured Web pages can also be protected from unauthorised access.

Automatic key frames   When key frames are set automatically, the differences between two frames are identified, and the encoder is forced to set a key frame when a certain limit value is exceeded. This limit, after which a key frame is inserted, is defined by the user, and should be set so that key frames are inserted at the beginning of each scene. If this value is set too low, too many key frames are generated, which wastes unnecessary bandwidth during transfer.

Another feature enables slow computers to play back Sorenson clips in higher bit rates. If a client processor becomes overloaded when decompressing a stream, QuickTime interrupts the video and only plays back audio until the next key frame. By interrupting video playback, further interference can be prevented during encoding.

Temporal scalabilty   Sorenson video enables clients to leave out frames at a 2:1 or 3:2:1 ratio, relieving the pressure on the processor. This feature is predominantly used in CD-ROM distribution, as current computers are rarely troubled by Internet streams with low data rates.

Video

General...   The video codec only achieves good image quality at high bit rates, which rules out Internet usage. The compression which occurs is both spatial and temporal. Even though the quality is slightly lower than that of Cinepak, the advantage of the video codec is that compression and decompression do not require as many system resources by comparison.

Audio codecs

AAC

AAC (Advanced Audio Coding) is an open audio compression standard, designed as a successor of MP3, and building up on the experiences with MP3. Already in 1997, AAC was integrated into the MPEG-2 standard, but was not very well received due to the high popularity of MP3 at this time. Along with MPEG-4, AAC was completed with 'MPEG-4 Tools' to maximise the coding efficiency, For example, the 'Perceptual Noise Substitution' (PNS) takes advantage of the fact that every noise signal sounds the same. Instead of coding every noise signal, the encoder just saves information about noise power and the frequency band.

AAC is structured in 'Profiles', each supporting various combinations of 'MPEG-4 Tools'. The AAC implementation of QuickTime 6 just supports 'AAC LC' (Low

Complexity). Presumably only MPEG-2 AAC is used by QuickTime 6, which can be encoded with 16 to 256 Kbps.

Generally, AAC is one of the most advanced open audio compression standards available today, even though QuickTime does not support the latest profiles of it. Implementing more advanced AAC profiles, such as 'Long Time Prediction' (LTP) or 'Spectral Band Replication' (SBR) would have maximised the effectiveness of the codec. Nevertheless, the audio quaility achieved by the AAC codec of QuickTime 6 is similar to one of its competitors from Microsoft or RealNetworks.

IMA 4:1

The IMA audio codec has been an integral part of QuickTime since version 2.1, and provides fairly good sound quality at reasonable compression rates. 16 bit audio is compressed at a ratio of 4:1, so a 22 kHz audio track requires a data rate of 80 kbps. IMA is therefore unsuitable for streaming media applications, as the sampling rate of a 44.1 kHz stereo signal would have to be reduced to an unacceptable 4 kHz for transfer via a 28.8K modem.

QualCom PureVoice

PureVoice was specifically developed for compressing speech signals. However, its optimisation for the distinct characteristics of the human voice yield unsatisfactory results from anything other than voice signals.

PureVoice compresses at a factor of 9:1 in the 'full' setting and 19:1 at 'half'. PureVoice can therefore be used for streaming media applications, even though its quality and bandwidth requirements fall considerably short of newer codecs.

QDesign Music

The QDesign music codec was the standard audio compressor for QuickTime 3, 4 and 5, and both its compression rates and quality are comparable to those produced using MP3.

QDesign Music makes comparably high demands of the decoding computer as well as the encoder.

QuickTime 3 to 5 contains the 'Basic Edition' of the QDesign Music Encoder, which is particularly impressive for its efficient compression of music signals with high frequency ranges at smaller bandwidths. Music, speech and sound effects can be reduced to a guaranteed usable quality by a factor of 100:1. Qdesign's efficient compression makes it especially suitable for use in streaming media applications. Version 2, provided with QuickTime 4, was improved further, and produces even higher qualities at lower bit rates.

As with the Sorenson video codec, a 'professional edition' would cost around £250 to be able to use all features of the codec, which among others enables encoding at higher bit rates. All audio tracks encoded with QDesign Music 1 or 2 can be played back with the standard QuickTime Player, but the Professional Edition should be used for optimal content production.

5.3 Creating QuickTime content – On Demand

QuickTime Player Pro The QuickTime Player Pro Version 6 enables files to be created and edited in streaming QuickTime format. It cannot be used for production of livestreams.

Figure 5.5 QuickTime Player 6 Pro

The QuickTime Player can be downloaded from Apple free of charge. This simple version enables access to all supported file types, but not saving and exporting functions. These are the central features of the Pro Version. You can get these by purchasing an unlock key which activates these and other functions in the QuickTime player.

The only difference from the Standard player when accessing files is that the QuickTime Player Pro Version can also access sequences of single images.

Contrary to what its simple interface suggests, the QuickTime Player Pro is not only a small tool for playing back QuickTime movies, but is a complete solution for accessing, editing and saving different content types.

As the Apple QuickTime Player Pro combines both playback functions and encoding tools, the program provides more facilities than suggested at first glance.

Opening files

As the name indicates, the QuickTime Player is a software package for playing back digital media types such as movies, audio, images or animations. The range of supported file types is therefore considerably large:

Table 5.1 Files and media types supported by QuickTime 6

Digital Video:	Animation and 3D:
QuickTime Movie	3D Meta File (3dMF)
DV Stream	Animated GIF
DVCPro Stream	FLC
MPEG-4 (MP4)	Macromedia Flash 5
OpenDML	PICS
SDP	Virtual Reality (VR)
Video for Windows (AVI)	

Still Images	Digital Audio
BMP	AIFF/AIFC
FlashPix	AU
GIF	Audio CD Data (Mac)
JFIF/JPEG (JPEG 2000 on MacOS only)	WAV
MacPaint	MPEG Layer 1 & 2
Photoshop	MPEG Layer 3
PNG	Sound Designer II
Silicon Graphics Image File	System 7 Sound
QuickDraw GX Picture	MIDI
QuickDraw Picture (PICT)	Standard MIDI
QuickTime Image File	General MIDI
Targa Image File	Karaoke
TIFF	Text

In addition to locally saved files, the QuickTime Player can access streams on the Internet (on-demand or live). The address of the desired movie can be entered using OPEN URL.

Opening image sequences

A special feature of the QuickTime Player Pro is the facility to open image sequences. Some programs allow you to export videos or animations (e.g. Adobe AfterEffects or Macromedia Flash) by exporting a sequence of still images. These image sequences can be opened and converted into any supported format.

A noteworthy feature of this option is the facility to specify the playback length of individual images (between 1/30 and 10 seconds). This also enables you to specify the playback length of individual images, which will later be inserted into another movie as captions.

Figure 5.6 The FILE menu in QuickTime Player 6 Pro

QuickTime Player Capturing

One of the differences from the RealNetworks and Microsoft encoders is that the QuickTime Player cannot digitise signals directly from sound and video devices. This has to be done by another program, which then returns completed files to the QuickTime Player Pro.

Importing files

In most cases, the FILE/OPEN MOVIE and FILE/IMPORT options perform the same function. However, PICT and text files are exceptions, as these have to be imported rather than opened.

In MacOS, the QuickTime Player can also import songs from audio CDs. Like media files, these are opened in the player via the IMPORT dialogue, and can be exported at will.

Saving files

An appropriate name

The FILE/SAVE and FILE/SAVE AS commands enable the currently opened clip to be saved in a location of the user's choice. These commands always save the file in the original format with the same configuration (compression, resolution, etc.): transcoding is not possible at this stage.

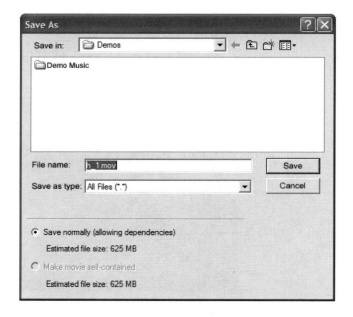

Figure 5.7 The FILE/SAVE As dialogue in QuickTime Player

QuickTime Movies always have a .MOV extension, which should always be retained when files are renamed. If this is not observed, when transferring movies on the Internet, the browser may not know which application or plug-in to assign to this file type, which may cause the file to be played back incorrectly.

Because of the wide range of different systems and browsers, there are a number of points to be noted when providing files for Internet use.

• Some systems (e.g. Unix) differ from Windows in their use of upper and lower case letters when renaming files. Caution should be exercised when renaming and embedding files in Web pages. On a Linux server, the file Clip1.mov may not be the same file as clip1.mov.

- Inserting blank spaces into filenames is a source of errors. For example, a file named 'CLIP HOLIDAY.MOV' should be renamed 'CLIP_HOLIDAY.MOV' or CLIPHOLIDAY.MOV'.

- Special characters should not be used in filenames. Ideally, only alphanumeric characters (a-z, A-Z, 0-9) and the underscore (_) should be used. A full stop may also be used, but only to separate the filename from the file extension.

Self-contained and dependent movies

External references The QuickTime architecture stands out by way of its hierarchical organisation of movie information into tracks, a unique feature which makes it highly flexible. A movie is an organisational unit which refers to tracks. In turn, the tracks refer to smaller organisational units (media data), and so on. The difference it makes to the user and relevant file information is that the media data to which it refers can also be saved in other movies.

For example, a QuickTime movie can refer to video and audio data, and play back on request, despite the data not being saved in the same file. This considerably reduces file size, as it only has to save reference information rather than actual media data.

The relative path of the target file and a hash total are saved in the reference, so the data file may no longer be edited or moved in relation to the QuickTime movie.

Recording dependent movies is interesting in different ways, especially when saving references to clips and broadcasts on the Internet.

Saving streaming clips

Internal references When a movie is accessed on the Internet, it can still be saved locally. This occurs either using the appropriate QuickTime Player command, or by holding the left mouse button down over a movie embedded in a Web site.

However, much to the disappointment of many users, the media data is not written in the local file. Instead, the URL of the clip, the current point in the timeline (except in live broadcasts) and user settings (e.g. volume) are written into the .MOV file. If this is recalled, the computer connects to the server and attempts to play back the file in the appropriate settings over the Internet.

Saving as a Fast Start Movie

QuickTime supports a special kind of HTTP 'streaming', using which QuickTime movies can also be played back via a Web server. In Fast Start Movies, all relevant information required by the client to begin the playback process is transferred at the beginning of the transmission. However, the internal organisation of the QuickTime movie has to be correct for this type of transfer to be carried out efficiently.

As well as references to external files, a QuickTime movie can also contain internal references. The QuickTime Player Pro can be used to select part of a movie and insert it at another point. However, instead of inserting the media data in the appropriate track at this stage, only an internal reference is created, which refers to the place of insertion. This saves computing time and hard drive space, but the movie can no longer be played back correctly in Fast Start mode.

Flattening

If the movie is saved using the FILE/SAVE command, these internal references are written in the file. If the 'Make movie self contained' option is chosen in the FILE/ SAVE AS dialogue box, flattening occurs. This closes all internal references, and regenerates the media data if required, so all tracks contain the media data to be played back chronologically. Movies saved using the FILE/SAVE AS option will always have the Fast Start feature.

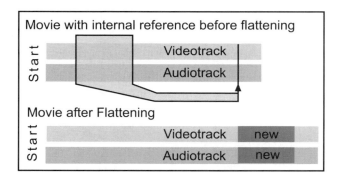

Figure 5.8   Internal references and flattening

Exporting files

Supported file formats   One of the central features of the QuickTime Player Pro Version is the facility for exporting opened files. The QuickTime movie export function supports various formats, which can in many cases be individually adjusted using predefined properties:

Digital Video:

- MPEG-4

- QuickTime Movie (.MOV, .MOOV)
  – Predefined settings for export as a streaming movie at 20, 40 or 100 Kbps; high or low motion with music or voice audio.
  – Other presets for distribution on CD-ROM in Sorenson or Cinepak codec

- Audio/Video Interleaved (.AVI)
  – Presets for CD-ROM distribution and animation coding

- DV Stream
  – Predefined settings for export as NTSC or PAL video and 32 or 44.1 kHz (12 or 16 Bit) Audio

- Hinted Movie

- FLC
  – MacOS or Windows colour palette at 12 or 30 images per second

Digital Audio:

- Audio Interchange File Format (.AIFF)
  – 11.025, 22.05 or 44.1 kHz, mono or stereo at 8 or 16 Bits

- System 7 Sound (.SND)
  – 11.025, 22.05 or 44.1 kHz, mono or stereo at 8 or 16 Bits

- Waveform Audio (.WAV)
  – 11.025, 22.05 or 44.1 kHz, mono or stereo at 8 or 16 Bits

- uLaw
  – 8.0, 11.025, 22.05 or 44.1 kHz and mono or stereo

The settings mentioned here are only suggestions, and can be modified using the OPTIONS button.

The facility for creating streaming clips using the QuickTime Player export function is particularly interesting. As mentioned previously, just as movies with the Fast Start option can be created for Fast Start streaming, genuine streaming QuickTime clips can also be created.

Creating streaming movies

The QuickTime player can receive multimedia streams from version 3 upwards, and every application which supports QuickTime can be used to receive and play back streaming QuickTime clips.

Hinting Before an existing track can be streamed, it has to be 'hinted'. In the hinting process, the data of every track is analysed and a hint track created for each one, containing information on optimum dispatch conditions for the media data via a network.

If a movie has already been correctly compressed, it can be prepared for streaming using the HINTED STREAMING setting. In this case, the movie data is analysed and hint tracks are generated, which enable the data to be streamed via a server. The media data itself remains unmodified here, and does not need to be recompressed.

Hint tracks are usually saved in the same movie as the media tracks. However, another method is to configure the hint tracks to refer to media tracks on other movies, and save them in separate movies (dependent). Alternatively, the media data could be directly implemented in the hint track, which increases the efficiency of the reading process on the server side.

The purpose of hinting is to relieve the server of computing-intensive operations. The server would usually have to divide the media tracks into IP-based data packets, with corresponding headers for respective bandwidths. Hinting removes the need for this, and takes into account both static and dynamic protocol information, such as packet size.

Media and file types in streaming

QuickTime supports the playback of many media types, but only some of these can be streamed.

Audio and Video streaming
    Audio and video can of course be streamed. The key issue here is to use the correct codec, so the little bandwidth available is used optimally during transfer to the end user. It is recommended that the Sorenson codec be used in conjunction with the QDesign Music codec.

Streaming MIDI music
    QuickTime also supports the streaming of MIDI music. As this only requires a low bandwidth, it can be used on the Internet. In order for MIDI music to be embedded correctly, it must only be inserted after audio and video compression, else it will be rendered in the normal audio tracks.

Figure 5.9 FILE/EXPORT in QuickTime Player 6 Pro

Streamed Images   Streaming still images runs the risk of irregular bit rates, as images require high bandwidth for a very short period in transfer. However, streaming still images is also supported.

Text in a QuickTime movie   Streaming text can be used for creating subtitles or displaying extra links.

Of course, QuickTime 6 supports MPEG-4 streaming, too. In this case, two options are available: the QuickTime file container using MPEG-4 and AAC coding can be used, or the MPEG-4 file container can be used for streaming not only to the QuickTime Player.

Adjusting export settings

QuickTime Player Pro provides groups of default settings which greatly simplify the compression and hinting of content for the most important target groups (20, 40 and 100 kbps), when encoding QuickTime movies. These settings therefore have to be adjusted frequently in order to produce optimal content. This is done using the OPTIONS dialogue in the export window.

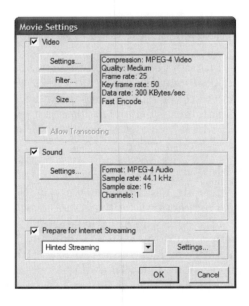

Figure 5.10   Export options in QuickTime Player Pro

The user can specify in the export options whether, and if so, how, video, audio or hint tracks are written into the movie.

Adjusting the Video settings   The most important field in video track configuration is the SETTINGS, where the codec, compression quality, number of key frames and frame rate are all selected. A choice between all available codecs can be made here, which is especially useful for Internet transfer using the Sorenson codec. The field for determing video bit rate is essential in the production of streaming QuickTime movies, as this value, along with the audio bit rate, determines the overall bandwidth of the movie.

QuickTime Player Pro also provides a number of filters, which enable the optimisation of material, and even defamiliarisation. In addition to the colour, brightness and contrast controls, relief, outline and colouring filters can be used, sharp and smooth edges defined, film damage rendered or blending effects inserted. These extensive image editing facilities are unique to QuickTime Player Pro, and confirm its claim that it is more than just a playback and conversion tool (see below for more information about QuickTime video filters).

Finally, the size of the video image can be specified. If the image is not to be exported in output size, the user can define a separate resolution to which the image will be scaled during the exporting process.

Adjusting the audio settings
In audio settings, only the codec, sampling rate, data format and channels can be adjusted. Apple recommends the QDesign Music Codec for music signals, but for optimal use you will need to buy the full version. The MPEG-4 Audio (AAC) codec is recommended for coding audio signals in QuickTime 6, since this is the most advanced audio compression available here.

The bitrate of the audio codec should also be specified, so the overall bandwidth of the movie corresponds to the intended target group (modem, ISDN, broadband, etc.).

Adjusting hint tracks
The hint track can be adjusted in the last export options field. Since the default setting produces optimal results in most cases, we only need to mention one option here. The hint track can be optimised using the 'OPTIMIZE HINTS FOR SERVER' option in SETTINGS. This means that the media and hinting information is written together in one track, which increases read access efficiency, as the server will not need to skip from one track to the next.

Alternate Movies

Until now, streaming QuickTime movies have been produced at a fixed bandwidth. However, for Internet transfer there should be a facility for providing content to different target groups with modified qualities, so the exact bitrate which uses the available transmission bandwidth optimally is available to as many users as possible. In order to relieve the end user of having to choose between several different clip versions, QuickTime offers alternate movies.

Reference Movies
A reference movie is a QuickTime movie which takes into account the settings of the QuickTime player or plug-in, and refers to alternate movies. When an alternate movie is called, depending on the Internet connection and QuickTime version installed, it can either refer to a suitable movie, or play back media data saved directly in the reference movie.

Media data can therefore be saved in a reference movie, and played back if none of the alternate movies fulfils the requirements of the QuickTime player or bandwidth. As QuickTime supports alternate movies from version 3 onwards, the standard data in the reference movie is output if an older client is installed.

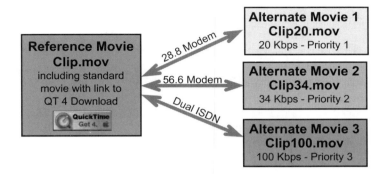

Figure 5.11 Sample alternate movies in QuickTime

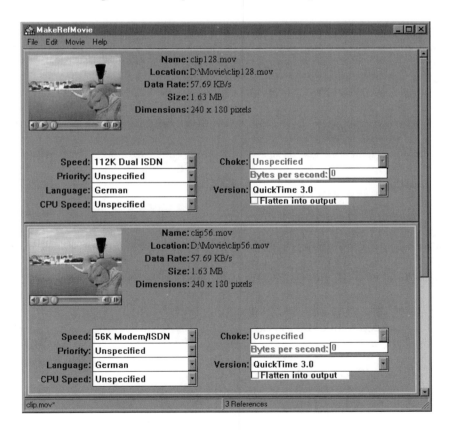

Figure 5.12 MakeRefMovie Tool

Alternatively, if alternate movies are supported, the reference movie can refer directly to those alternate movies stored in the same directory. If they refer to streaming clips on the Internet, an appropriate Fast Start movie has to be generated. This causes the appropriate movie to be called and saved in the QuickTime player. A Fast Start movie is then stored locally, which only contains a reference to the streaming clip on the Internet. The Fast Start movie is now copied and embedded into the directory for reference movies. The reference movie therefore refers to the saved Fast Start movie, which in turn refers to a streaming clip on the Internet.

For example, they may be alternate movies for bandwidths of 20, 34, 45 and 80 kbps, the URLs of which are referred to by a reference movie. A still image containing the URL for the QuickTime 4 download is also saved in the reference movie, which is output on older clients and those with 14.4K modem connections.

Other QuickTime Player Pro features

Presenting movies

This QuickTime Player Pro option enables movies to be displayed in full screen mode, and allows the user to specify a scaling at which the movie is displayed, while the rest of the screen remains black.

Figure 5.13   Presenting movies in QuickTime Player Pro

Playback options

The Movie command in the QuickTime player menu bar activates several playback options. The endless loop function begins playback again once the movie has ended, while the Movie/Loop Back and Forth option plays the movie backwards once it has ended, and then normally again when it has reached the beginning.

Playing back clips   QuickTime Player Pro enables the user to specify a clip in the timeline, and save or edit it, or insert it into another movie. The MOVIE/PLAY SELECTION ONLY option allows the user to select and play back a clip.

Playing back all frames   The MOVIE/PLAY ALL FRAMES option is fairly self-explanatory. It allows the user to specify that all frames in a movie be played back, even though it may overload the processor. This enables an uncompressed video track to be played back and checked, even though the computer does not have the system resources to play back the image in real time.

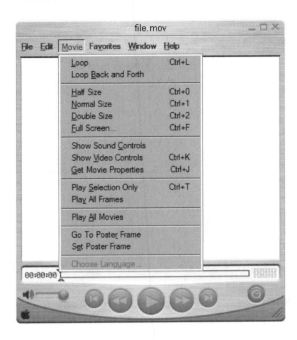

Figure 5.14 The MOVIE menu in QuickTime Player 6 Pro

Playing all movies If several movies are open, they can be played back simultaneously using the MOVIE/PLAY ALL MOVIES command. This naturally requires a sufficiently powerful computer.

Scaling The playback window of a movie can be enlarged or reduced from the bottom right hand corner. In addition, the QuickTime player has a toggling facility to switch between half, normal, double and full size display.

Title images The poster image of a movie is an abitrary frame used to introduce the movie. The MOVIE/GO TO POSTER FRAME and MOVIE/SET POSTER FRAME options respectively display and specify this image.

Language versions If several language versions are saved in a QuickTime movie, these can be selected using the MOVIE/CHOOSE LANGUAGE dialogue.

Movie properties

The MOVIE/GET MOVIE PROPERTIES menu item in the QuickTime player enables all information relevant to the movie and all tracks to be displayed, and partially edited. General information on the movie, video and audio tracks is particularly relevant in the production of streaming media.

Figure 5.15   Movie information in QuickTime Player

General movie   The general movie information contains the following fields:
information
- General
  This field displays size, bit rate and track number (standard).

- Annotations
  What is known as meta data in RealProducer or Windows Media Encoder is known as annotations in QuickTime. A number of parameters can be entered here, including information on artist, album, author, copyright, product, data source and so on. Thus fields can be added, edited and deleted by the user.

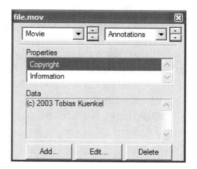

Figure 5.16   The ANNOTATION field in Movie Information

- Auto Play
  (De)activate this feature for the movie.

- Files
  All files to which there are external references in the movie are displayed here. If the movie itself contains the media data, there are no external references, so only the filename of the movie is displayed.

- Colors
  If an image or video is saved in 256 colours (8 bit), a colour table may have to be allocated to guarantee true colour representation. This can be done using the 'Colors' field.

- Size
  Displays the size (resolution) of the entire movie.

- Controllers
  The QuickTime Player has different interfaces, each with different facilities. The player usually works with the movie controller, which contains the Play and Stop buttons, volume control and other controls (see Figure 5.5). However, QuickTime VR Panoramas, for example, require another interface due to different requirements. If the movie control panel is not activated, the player opens the movie in a standard window.

Figure 5.17 The CONTROLLER panel in Movie Information

- Preview
  The QuickTime player File/Open dialogue displays a preview of the selected file. It has to be specified which part of the movie is previewed. This could even be an appropriate section of a different movie, pulled into this window using drag&drop.
  By default, the preview is the poster frame in MacOS, and the first ten seconds of the movie in Windows.

- Time
  Displays the current position in the movie, total length and selections.

Information about video tracks In addition to the standard fields displayed by default, the following fields are particularly relevant to the properties of a video track:

- Alternate
  Alternate tracks can be specified, similar to alternate movies. A language can be specified for a video track, and subtitles inserted. If the QuickTime player is installed in a different language, an alternative video track can be specified which does not contain subtitles.

- Frame rate
  Playback not only indicates how many frames per second are saved in movies, but also how many frames per second are displayed during playback. The extent to which the computer manages playback in real time can also be seen.

- Layers
  If a movie contains several video tracks, it is important to specify which movie is played at back on which layer. For example, if a graphic is placed over the video image, a graphic with an alpha channel (transparency) is created and inserted into the movie as a new video track. Which of the two video tracks is visible in the movie is determined by the layer on which it is located.

- Format
  The resolution of the video or still image is output in the 'format' field. If the image in the QuickTime player has already been scaled, the actual resolution is displayed without scaling. The colour depth and codec used are also displayed.

- Graphics mode
  The QuickTime player enables the graphics mode to be specified, including transparency and masking settings. The 'transparency' graphic mode enables a colour to be selected and displayed transparently: a function useful in titles and logos.

- Size
  In contrast to the 'format' field, the 'size' field enables the scaling, orientation, position and distortion to be modified. These modifications do not affect the image material itself, but its representation in QuickTime. If an image is downscaled, image information is lost. The image or video can then be rescaled to its original output size without any loss in quality.

- Mask
  Another facility for specifying image transparency is the definition of a static mask. A mask is a black and white image whose white areas define which part of the video track will be transparent. This information can also be saved directly in the alpha channel of an image.

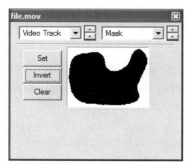

Figure 5.18 The 'Mask' field in Movie Information

Information on audio tracks In addition to standard fields such as 'GENERAL', 'ANNOTATIONS', 'FILES' and 'FORMAT', one field is particularly interesting in audio tracks:

- Volume
  As well as the volume of an audio track, balance, treble and bass can also be controlled. When a track is played back, an equaliser can be controlled in addition to the audio level.

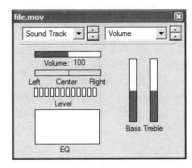

Figure 5.19 The 'Volume' field in Movie Information

Inserting tracks

If part of a movie is moved or inserted into another movie, it is usually inserted as a new track, but not without affecting the existing content. For example, a video may be interrupted for an inserted frame to be played back. However, this is not preferable if the frame contains a logo to be displayed in the video.

The command which performs this insertion is 'ADD SCALED', and is selected from the EDIT menu, or by using the keyboard shortcut Ctrl+Alt+⇧ (Ctrl+apple in MacOS). This allows the content of the clipboard (e.g. a still frame from another movie) to be inserted into the selected area of a movie, without affecting playback. The layers, masks or graphics mode functions can be used to specify which part of a video track is visible, and the volume control in Movie Information enables several video tracks to be mixed.

Availability

Costs The basic version of the QuickTime Player can be obtained from Apple free of charge. The user downloads an installer, which receives the required data from the Internet and installs the software. A version which can be installed without an Internet connection is also available.

The QuickTime Player Pro contains all the functions described here for creating and editing content, and can be purchased for around £20.

Availability QuickTime has always been available as an integral part of the Apple Macintosh operating system, and was made available for Windows in 1990. Other versions are not reported.

5.4 Creating QuickTime content – Livestreams

The QuickTime Player Pro cannot be used to produce livestreams; this requires the applications of other manufacturers. In addition to a streaming server and computer with video hardware, a 'broadcaster' is also a technical necessity in the production of livestreams.

Similar to the RealProducer or Windows Media Encoder, a broadcaster digitises and encodes the input signals from audio or video hardware and sends the generated A/V stream to a video server for transmission. As the real time encoding of Sorenson or MPEG-4 compressed streams is very computing-intensive, this process makes high demands of the system.

The choice of broadcaster is currently very clear: until QuickTime 6 was released, only Sorenson provided an appropriate tool, which also runs under MacOS and Windows. Since Apple now offers a separate free tool for live encoding, Sorenson Broadcaster has not been developed further. Apple's QuickTime Broadcaster is available only for MacOS X and supports all QuickTime codecs including MPEG-4 and ACC.

Using Sorenson Broadcaster

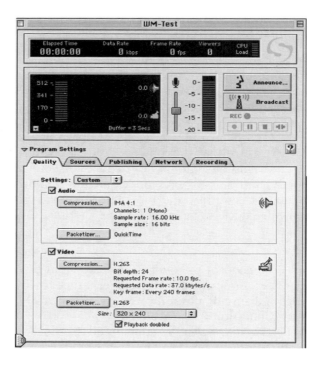

Figure 5.20 Sorenson Broadcaster 1.1

*The Link to the
Sorenson download
page is contained on
the accompanying
web site*

Just like the QuickTime Broadcaster, the Sorenson Broadcaster offers an easy-to-use interface. Users can set up a livecast with just a few mouse clicks, and help inexperienced users to handle the most common situations.

Preparing a live broadcast with the Sorenson broadcaster is quite straight forward, in comparison to the competitors from RealNetworks and Microsoft:

(a) Choice of audio and video sources.
USB cameras and video cards can be used as a video source. The latest Macs also have a DV or Firewire interface, which can also be used as video sources in new versions of QuickTime.
The standard Mac hardware can normally be used as an audio source, but a Firewire interface can also be used. Sending audio directly is also supported by an audio CD.

(b) Choice of compression and data rate.

(c) Choice of multicast or several unicast addresses for transfer (e.g. the IP address of the streaming server).

(d) Start of stream.

Announcement files

In contrast to the RealServer or Windows Media Services, the user cannot call the QuickTime livestream directly from the server. Small files are used here which contain a description of the session and client instructions for requesting the stream. These announcement files are provided directly on the streaming server and embedded into the referenced Web pages. If a client calls a file, this query is received by the server, and the livestream sent to the client.

Announcement files are automatically generated by the broadcaster and have an .SDP extension. After being placed in the content directory on the server they can be published, at which point the .sdp extension is dropped. The LIVESTREAM.SDP SDP file in the content directory of the QuickTime server could be accessed using

```
rtsp://server.company.co.uk/livestream
```

If a livestream is called, it can also be saved locally. The result is a small QuickTime movie which contains the address of the livestream.

Archiving the livestream

The Sorenson broadcaster has an option which allows the livestream to be archived. In this case a QuickTime movie is created from the encoded data, which is then saved locally.

Alternate movies and livestreaming

In accordance with the concept of alternate movies, several livestreams have to be generated in order to use different bandwidths efficiently.

It is useful here to generate a Fast Start movie from the livestream. If a stream is called using the QuickTime player, this can be saved locally, as explained on the Streaming Clips page. A reference movie can use these stored references to livestreams to cater for different user Internet settings.

Availability

Costs The Sorenson broadcaster costs around £120, and a 30-day evaluation version can be downloaded from the Sorenson Web site.

Availabilty The Sorenson broadcaster is available for MacOS and Windows 98, ME, 200 and XP.

Apple QuickTime Broadcaster

Along with QuickTime 6 Apple introduced its own free live encoding software. The QuickTime Broadcaster 1.0, together with the QuickTime Streaming Server, supports MPEG-4 live broadcasts.

The main window of the QuickTime Broadcaster contains three main control tabs, one for VIDEO, AUDIO and NETWORK settings.

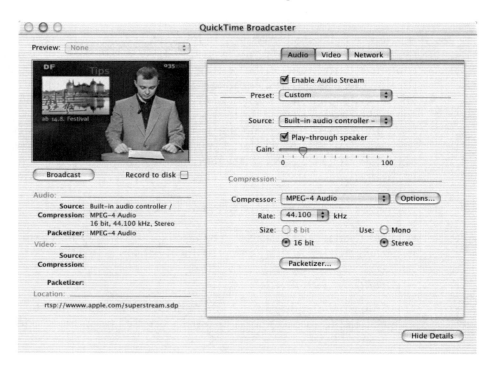

Figure 5.21 Apple QuickTime Broadcaster 1.0

The AUDIO tab

The AUDIO panel of QuickTime Broadcaster contains all controls nesessary for encoding audio streams. Just like the video panel, various presets can be selected and modified. The software supports DV audio from FireWire, USB audio and analogue audio. The input level can be regulated using the slider control.

The most important controls are, of course, the ones to select and specify the compression settings, such as codec, sampling rate, resolution and numbers of channels.

The VIDEO tab

Just like the AUDIO tab, the VIDEO tab contains controls to enable video streaming, the selection of presets, and the selection of a video source.

Using the compression settings in the VIDEO tab, the user can specify which video codec to use, the video resolution and the codec's details. The MPEG-4 codec is the most advanced video compression available in QuickTime today, but the QuickTime Broadcaster also supports the other video codecs installed.

The NETWORK tab

Clients and QuickTime Streaming Servers can request encoded streams from QuickTime Broadcaster. When just one client (QuickTime Player) is to receive the livestream, it can be requested directly from the encoder.

Unicasts to several clients require a streaming server to distribute the stream. Apple offers the QuickTime Streaming Server for this, but also other solutions, such as RealNetworks' Helix Server, can be used to distribute QuickTime livestreams. When starting a broadcast to a streaming server, the encoder first generates an .sdp-file and uploads it to a designated folder on the server. In addition, the server administrator has to set up a user account for the encoder, so that it can authenticate itself with a login and password when a livecast is started.

In multicast-enabled networks, the broadcaster can directly distribute multicast streams to a large number of clients.

Besides the VIDEO, AUDIO and NETWORK tabs, the main window of Apple QuickTime Broadcaster contains video preview, detailed information about the sources and the URL of the stream. Once the broadcast has been started, the livestream can be accessed by clients by using the URL of the .sdp-file.

5.5 Providing QuickTime content

Apple follows an interesting concept with its QuickTime Streaming Server. It is available free for MacOS X 10 and is based on open standards like RTSP and MPEG-4. While Apple develops this server as a product, it is also available as an open source server called Darwin Streaming Server. So the QuickTime Streaming Server is only one of many implementations of the same technology and additional versions based on the open source project are available for Linux, Solaris or Windows 2000/XP. QuickTime streaming is supported in RealServer 8 and Helix Server, which means that many providers will not have to install a separate QuickTime server.

Apple is shifting towards multicast transfer as a server concept more than the technical conditions of today's Internet would suggest. Though all unicast applications can be produced, focusing on multicasting should not be overlooked. MacOS servers are often used in company networks and since a multicast enabled network structure is available here, the QuickTime Streaming Server is predestined as a server solution for matters of internal corporate communication.

The improvements in the current version 4 of the QuickTime streaming server affect MPEG-4 and MP3 support, instant-on streaming for minimised buffering times, remote administration of QuickTime Broadcaster, MP3 playlists, plug-in support and improvements of the administration interface.

QuickTime streaming admin

Similar to the RealSystem Administrator or Windows Media Administrator, QuickTime streaming admin enables access and configuration of the QuickTime streaming server. To access admin, the user must have administrator rights to the server. The most important admin function is starting and stopping the Streaming Services. Remote access to the server configuration is not possible and has to be carried out locally.

Simulated livestreams

Like RealNetworks, Apple provides a tool called the 'PlaylistBroadcaster' which enables livestreams to be generated from existing clips. Similar to the RealNetworks G2SLTA (see Chapter 3), playlists are used which specify the files to be streamed and their sequence.

Playlist in PlaylistBroadcaster

PlaylistBroadcaster considers the first file in a playlist to be a reference file, and defines the livestream format (track number, track type, coding bit rates).

A playlist is a text file containing a list of files to be transferred. A playlist in the PlaylistBroadcaster always has to begin with *PLAY-LIST*, and comments can be inserted using '#'.

```
    *PLAY-LIST*
# Individual clips with path details
/media/music/clip01.mov 5
/media/music/clip03.mov 9
/media/music/clip07.mov 2
# Embedding another playlist
+ /playlists/adverts.txt
# Embedding another playlist
# with relative path
```

```
+ pop/popmusic.txt
# Blank space in paths and
# files are masked
"/media/music/rock clip01.mov"
```

The PlaylistBroadcaster enables the files listed to be played back in random order. Apple has extended this feature in that a weighting of clips between 1 and 10 can be made, which determines how often a clip is played back in the random sequence. Instead of QuickTime movies, further playlists can also be referenced, the content of which is handled like the calling list.

Version 4 of QuickTime Streaming Server includes the support for MP3 playlists and an improved web interface for an easy drag and drop editing. After setting up a playlist, the tracks selected run automatically and can be played once, in a loop or at random.

Sample Broadcaster Description File (.SDP)

In addition to the playlist of a broadcast, the PlaylistBroadcaster requires a 'Broadcast Description File' with details of playlist, play mode, streaming server or SDP file.

```
Example of a  Broadcast Description File (.sdp)

playlist_file/server/local/media/playlist1.txt
play_mode weighted_random
sdp_reference_movie/media/clip01.mov
destination_ip_address 123.135.67.9
destination_base_port 5004
recent_movies_list_size 10
sdp_file/server/QTSS/movies/playlist1.sdp
logging enabled
log_file/server/local/playlist1.log
```

If users wish to access the livestream, the Session Description Protocol (.sdp) file has to be executed. This can be carried out using a link on an Internet page, embedding the file in HTML or sending the file via e-mail. The SDP file contains information on format, timing and the stream author. It instructs the client on how to connect to the stream.

The simulated livestream is started by calling the 'PlaylistBroadcaster' file and indicating the broadcast description file.

Multicasting

The Apple QuickTime streaming server fully supports the multicast standard, and is fully prepared for the future of streaming media transfers, having focused on this technique.

Table 5.2 Keywords for SDP file configuration

Keyword	
playlist_file	Playlist to be used, addressed relatively or absolutely
play_mode	'sequential', 'sequential_looped' or 'weighted_random'
sdp_reference_movie	SDP reference movie, relative and absolute path
destination_ip_address	IP address of local server
destination_base_port	Port number, standard 5004
recent_movies_list_size	Minimum number of files which have to be streamed before one has to be repeated
sdp_file	SDP file, relative and absolute path
logging	'enabled' or 'disabled'
log_file	Log file, relative or absolute path

Splitting

Apple introduced the relay server concept in connection with Push Splitting technology. A relay server receives the livestream from an encoder or server, and makes this available to other QuickTime streaming servers in unicast or multicast environments.

Relay Server configuration file   Configuring a QuickTime streaming server as a relay server is carried out by creating or modifying the /etc/qtssrelay.conf file. Relay sources and corresponding target servers are indicated in this file.

```
relay_source in_addr=123.146.67.8 src_addr=12.165.34.2
in_ports=5002 5003 5504
relay_destination dest_addr=184.23.321.223 out_addr=242.23.12.2
out_ports=1980 1982 1984
relay_destination dest_addr=32.123.123.2 out_addr=87.213.32.1
out_ports=1010 1012 1013
```

Access protection/authentication

The QuickTime streaming server provides two modules for controlling access to streams.

As part of the QuickTime streaming server, the QTSSAccessModule enables control over supplied streams without affecting other MacOS X server access rights.

The QTSSFilePrivsModule enables access restriction when using the user and group database of the MacOS X server.

If users of QuickTime 4 or higher access a protected stream, they must enter an appropriate login and password for playback to begin. Earlier clients cannot access protected streams.

Monitoring and reporting

The Apple QuickTime streaming server creates standardised log files, which can be evaluated with any analysis software for Web server loggings. Logging can be activated and disabled in QuickTime Streaming Admin.

Streaming Ads

Advertisements can be integrated in QuickTime using SMIL. This has been supported since version 4 of QuickTime, and provides all the functions required both for integrating banners via commercial servers and inserting advertising clips in streams.

Supported formats

The QuickTime streaming server 'only' supports the QuickTime movie format. However, as a container format, this can contain the majority of major media types and compression methods.

Availability

Costs   The QuickTime Streaming Server is available as part of the MacOS X server, and can be downloaded free of charge.

Availability   The Dorwin Streaming Server has been adapted to run on MacOS 10.1 or later, Red Hat Linux 7.1, Solaris 8 and Windows NT/2000 Server.

Embedding

- When installing the QuickTime player, the user can add a QuickTime plug-in to Netscape Communicator or Microsoft Internet Explorer. In contrast to the RealPlayer or Media Player, however, there is no ActiveX control available by default, which is why users of Internet Explorer have to download it when accessing embedded QuickTime content for the first time.

The SRC, WIDTH and HEIGHT parameters are also compulsory in the QuickTime plug-in, so the simplest way of embedding a movie on the page could look as follows:

```
<OBJECT CLASSID="clsid:02BF25D5-8C17-4B23-BC80-D3488ABDDC6B"
    WIDTH="240" HEIGHT="196"
    <PARAM NAME="src" VALUE=" rtsp://qtserver.company.co.uk/clip.mov ">
    <EMBED SRC="rtsp://qtserver.company.co.uk/clip.mov"
        WIDTH="240" HEIGHT="196">
    </EMBED>
</OBJECT>
```

The <EMBED> tag Again, the <EMBED> tag is integrated into an <OBJECT> tag, so that the Internet Explorer uses the ActiveX control specified and all other browsers will use the Netscape plug-in. The embedded movie has a height of 180 pixels, and the height of the control bar comes to 16 pixels.

Figure 5.22   Sample embedding with QuickTime

Embedding a
QuickTime movie
using the
<EMBED> tag

Other parameters for embedded QuickTime movies are listed below. The parameters of the <EMBED> samples can be used the same way with an <OBJECT> tag using the <PARAM> tag:

- AUTOHREF="True" | "False"
  The link specified with the HREF parameter is executed immediately.

- AUTOPLAY="True" | "False"
  The embedded movie starts automatically when the page is opened.

- BGCOLOR="#rrggbb"
  The background colour of the plug-in can be specified by the user. As in HTML, the RGB colour model is used in hexadecimal notation.

```
<EMBED SRC="clip.mov" WIDTH="240" HEIGHT="196"
  BGCOLOR="#0000FF">
</EMBED>
```

- BORDER="width"
  Draws a border around the plug-in.

- CONTROLLER="True" | "False"
  The control bar is displayed by default. If this is not preferred, for example because the movie is to be controlled using JavaScript controls, it can be hidden using the CONTROLLER parameter.

- HIDDEN= "True" | "False"
  An audio QuickTime file can be embedded as background music for a page. The player will not be seen in this case. However, as the size of the plug-in has to be a minimum of 2×2 pixels for technical reasons, the player can be hidden. Other parameters have to be embedded for the movie to start automatically without the control bar.

  ```
  <EMBED SRC="rtsp://qtserver.company.co.uk/clip.mov"
      WIDTH="240" HEIGHT="196" HIDDEN="True" AUTOPLAY="True"
      CONTROLLER=False>
  </EMBED>
  ```

- HREF="url"
  The facility for connecting a link to an embedded movie is normally used in the production of clickable poster movies. In this case, a still frame is embedded, with a prompt saying 'Click here to play clip'. If the user follows the prompt, the movie is played back. As in HTML, the TARGET parameter can also be entered. This specifies the target frame of the link.

  ```
  <EMBED SRC="clicktostart.mov" WIDTH="240" HEIGHT="196"
      HREF="clip.mov" TARGET="myself">
  </EMBED>
  ```

'Myself' (same player window), 'quicktimeplayer' (QuickTime player) and 'browser' (standard browser) are valid targets of the TARGET parameter.

- NAME="name"
  Allows a name to be specified for the plugin, which is important for addressing using JavaScript.

  ```
  <EMBED SRC="rtsp://qtserver.company.co.uk/clip.mov"
      WIDTH="240" HEIGHT="196" NAME="QTPlugin">
  </EMBED>
  ```

- PLUGINSPAGE="url"
  Gives download information to the user if the QuickTime plug-in has not yet been installed. Example:

  ```
  <EMBED SRC="rtsp://qtserver.company.co.uk/clip.mov"
      WIDTH=240 HEIGHT=196
      PLUGINSPAGE="http://www.apple.com/quicktime/download/">
  </EMBED>
  ```

- QTNEXTx="url"
  A playlist can be played back using the parameters QTNEXT1, QTNEXT2, QTNEXT3 and so on.

  ```
  <EMBED SRC="clip1.mov" WIDTH="240" HEIGHT="196"
    QTNEXT1="<clip2.mov>"
    QTNEXT2="<song.mp3>"
    QTNEXT3="<clip3.mov>"
    QTNEXT4=<GOTO0>>
  </EMBED>
  ```

In the example, the files clip1.mov, clip2.mov, song.mp3 and clip3.mov are played in sequence, then repeated infinitely using the QTNEXT4= "‹GOTO0›" parameter. This enables playlists of up to 256 entries to be generated.

- QTSRC="filename"
  A Web browser normally decides which plug-in to use for playback by using a file extension. However, as QuickTime is also used for playing back Flash movies, the issue is raised as to whether these movies can be embedded using the QuickTime plug-in instead of the standard Flash plug-in. The solution is to embed a QuickTime movie using the SRC parameter, and address the actual Flash movie using the QTSRC parameter. Another example is embedding MP3 files:

  ```
  <EMBED SRC="clip.mov" WIDTH=120 HEIGHT=16 QTSRC="song.mp3"
  </EMBED>
  ```

The QTSRC parameter is supported by QuickTime 4 and upwards.

- QTSCRCHOKESPEED="bitrate"
  A reduction in bandwidth is a great hindrance to Internet streaming. However, the situation is quite different for provision of Fast Start movies: these are not transferred at the actual bit rate of the movie, but at the maximum possible transmission bandwidth. This enables a few surfers with broadband connections to overload a smaller server, as they only occupy the entire bandwidth for a short period, even though they may only be calling a 20 kbps movie. It makes more sense to limit the maximum transmission bandwidth, so a 34 kbps clip can only be transferred at a maximum speed of 60 kbps and the server does not become overloaded.

  ```
  <EMBED SRC="clip.mov" WIDTH="240" HEIGHT="196"
    QTSCTCHOKESPEED="60000">
  </EMBED>
  ```

- STARTTIME="starttime" ENDTIME="endtime"
  The start and end points of an embedded movie do not necessarily have to correspond to the actual beginning and end. The user can determine this using two parameters of the <EMBED> tag:

```
<EMBED SRC="clip.mov" WIDTH="240" HEIGHT="196"
  STARTTIME="00:01:30.0" ENDTIME="00:06:30.0">
</EMBED>
```

- TYPE="mimetype"
  Allows the MIME type of the embedded file to be specified. The cliently usually receives this information directly from the server or from the file extension.

```
<EMBED SRC="rtsp://qtserver.company.co.uk/clip.mov"
  WIDTH=240 HEIGHT=196 TYPE="video/quicktime">
</EMBED>
```

- VOLUME="percentage"
  The audio playback volume can be regulated using these parameters in a range from 0 to 300.

Player Controls

The QuickTime plug-in control bar controls playback functions and the plug-in itself.

The timeline is the central element, which enables navigation through the movie. In addition to the start, pause and volume functions, the opened movie can also be saved. Saving usually means that the actual media data of the movie is not stored on local drives, just its URL and user settings.

Figure 5.23 The QuickTime plug-in control bar

The accompanying web site gives an overview of the characteristics and methods of the QuickTime plug-in, as well as examples (including plug-in detection)

Plug-in control using JavaScript

Access to a plug-in in Internet Explorer requires an ActiveX control, which unfortunately does not exist for QuickTime. QuickTime plug-in control using JavaScript is therefore not possible in Internet Explorer.

However, an interface exists for the Netscape browser, and the QuickTime plug-in provides a wide range of methods and characteristics. It is important at this stage that the <EMBED> tag be named correctly using the NAME parameter.

5.6 Playing back QuickTime content

Apple provides the QuickTime player for playing back QuickTime movies. The basic version, available free of charge, plays back various media types in MacOS and Windows.

QuickTime has been an integral part of the MacOS operating system since 1990, and is now an essential system component. The player was introduced to the (then small) world of Windows with Windows 3.0, and has since staked its claim in many areas.

The QuickTime player

The QuickTime player is one of several components, all of which can be downloaded.

- QuickTime system extensions – system software for the playback and editing of QuickTime movies in word processing, graphic and other programs

- QuickTime Player – the program for playing back QuickTime movies and many other media types

- QuickTime Plug-in software for the playback and recording of QuickTime movies in Web browsers

The system extensions are the core of the system, and enable any applications to use all QuickTime functions. Extensions can also be added to complement a video codec.

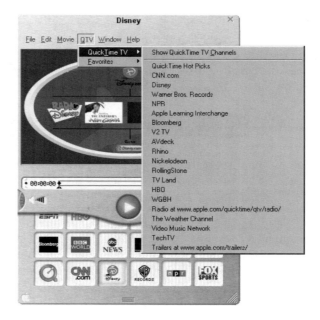

Figure 5.24 Favourites in the QuickTimePlayer

The PictureViewer was part of the QuickTime software package in previous versions, and was used to display images of different formats. As the QuickTime player itself now performs these functions, the PictureViewer is no longer included in recent versions.

Similar to the RealNetworks and Microsoft players, the QuickTime player enables access both to locally saved clips, and files and streams on the Internet. In addition to the volume, balance, treble and bass settings, the favourites are another feature of QuickTime player. They enable the graphic organisation of favourite links, and provide convenient access to users' preferred programs.

Supported formats

Digital Video:

- Apple QuickTime (.MOV, .QT, .MOOV)
- Audio/Video Interleaved (.AVI)
- DV Stream
- Movie with hint track
- MPEG-1 (.MPEG, .MPG)
- Optional: MPEG-2 (.MPEG, .MPG, .VOB)
- MPEG-4 (.MP4)

Animation:

- Animated GIF
- Macromedia Flash 5
- FLIC
- QuickDraw 3D Metafile

Digital Audio:

- Advanced Audio Coding AAC (.MP4)
- Audio Interchange File Format (.AIFF)
- Unix audio (.AU)
- Compact Disc Audio (.CDA)
- Musical Instrument Digital Interface (.MIDI, .MID)
- MPEG 1 Layer 1, 2 and 3 (.MP3)
- System 7 Sound (.SND)
- Waveform Audio (.WAV)

Still Images:

- BMP
- FlashPix

- GIF
- JFIF/JPEG
- JPEG2000
- MacPaint
- Photoshop
- PNG
- PICT
- QuickDraw GX Picture
- QuickDraw Picture (PICT)
- QuickTime Image File
- Silicon Graphics Image File
- Targa Image File
- TIFF
- Text

Availability

Costs

As mentioned previously, QuickTime playback software can be downloaded from Apple free of charge.

Availability

The QuickTime player is available for all versions of MacOS, and all Windows versions since Windows 3.0.

The QuickTime Installer is contained on the accompanying web site.

6

Further solutions

Countless streaming technologies have appeared over the past five years, yet they play a less than serious role in the market of today. They are occasionally found on earlier Web sites, or are used as niche solutions. The vast majority of commercially produced content is created and marketed by RealNetworks, Microsoft and Apple solutions, largely because these firms have the broadest base of installed players.

6.1 Further solutions for audio streaming

MP3 streaming

The transfer of files or live signals as an MP3 stream stands out by way of its simple and affordable technical implementation. The MPEG-1 Layer 3 audio format provides an optimal basis for efficient and high-quality transfer. The relatively old MP3 format can hold its own in terms of quality in contrast to the compression methods of commercial providers, and as an open standard provides an alternative for the transfer of streaming audio.

As demonstrated, RealServer, Windows Media Services and QuickTime support the provision and streaming of MP3 files. There are also other programs which enable the user to use streaming MP3 content.

The SHOUTcast plug-in   One of the most frequently used solutions for MP3 streaming is the SHOUTcast server in connection with the WinAMP MP3 player. A WinAMP player with the SHOUTcast DSP plug-in also functions as an encoder in this case. This plug-in enables WinAMP both to play back the audio data and upload it to a SHOUTcast server.

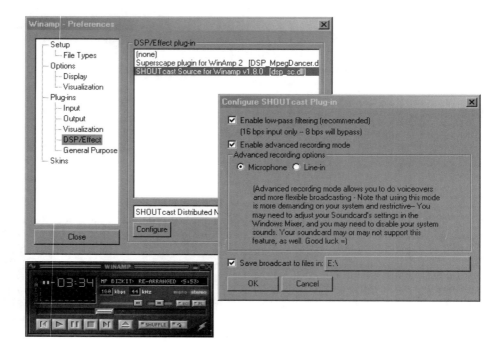

Figure 6.1 WinAMP with the SHOUTcast DSP plug-in

Configuration of the SHOUTcast plug-in is quite straightforward: the address (name or IP) of the server and format in which the MP3 stream is to be distributed have to be indicated. The port used for the upstream is important here, as this has to be configured at the server for receiving the MP3 stream.

A title can also be entered for the stream. By default, this is identical to the title of the file just sent, but can also be entered manually. Once configuration is complete, the connection to the server can be established.

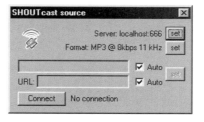

Figure 6.2 Configuration of the SHOUTcast plug-in

One interesting feature of the WinAMP player is the facility to generate audio streams using other plug-ins. As the player plays back other media formats in addition to MP3, such as WAV, AIFF or audio CDs, these can also be provided as MP3 streams.

The SHOUTcast server

The SHOUTcast server is a simple software package which has a graphic interface, but is usually configured using the SC_SERV_GUI.INI text file in the installation directory. All relevant settings on ports, user numbers, passwords, logging or splitting can be configured here. Once the server starts, it receives the incoming streams and makes them available via the compatible client port. Every instance of the SHOUTcast server can only distribute one stream. If several streams are to be made available using one server, several instances of the SHOUTcast server have to be opened.

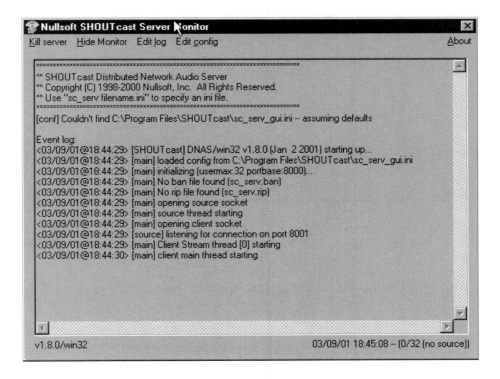

Figure 6.3 The SHOUTcast server monitor

Teles Audioactive

Another well-known MP3 streaming solution is Teles Audioactive, which enabled high-quality audio transfer long before SHOUTcast. In contrast to SHOUTcast, both on-demand and live streaming are possible. The Pro Version of the system is required for live streaming, but the availability of SHOUTcast free of charge tends to be a more preferable solution.

The main advantage of MPEG-1 Layer 3 compression paradoxically gives rise to its key weakness: its status as an open standard allows any developer to program a separate client which can also be used to record streamed material. This method is therefore more suitable for smaller project development and radio stations, but is unlikely to gain acceptance in commercial spheres. Furthermore, the MP3 format today is nearly ten years old. Although it can compete quite well with the younger compression standards, competitors like Windows Media Audio, RealAudio or AAC use much more developed coding algorithms.

Liquid Audio

Liquid Audio was developed from the outset to correspond to the interests of the music industry in the provision and sale of music on the Internet. Watermarks and RSA encryption are used to prevent illegal copying. This not only controls the downloading of clips, but also restricts the distribution of music files after the download.

Like most streaming media packages, Liquid Audio comprises an encoder (Liquifier), server (Liquid Music Server) and player (Liquid Music Player).

Liquifier The Liquifier enables track meta data to be entered, including artist, title, composer, text, cover, images and so on. When defining the various bit rates of a stream, it can also be defined whether it should be available for download. When defining the downloadable section of a track, the recordable sections of a song can also be specified. In addition to the effective encryption and specification of the validity period, songs can also be assigned a watermark, which identifies it as marketed content, even after burning onto CD.

Liquid Audio Tracks include the following features:

- Modern compression methods (Dolby AC-3, Fraunhofer AAC) enable flexible data reduction from under 10 kbps up to 1.4 Mbps (uncompressed).

- RSA encryption of audio data.

- Use of inaudible watermarks which enable identification of protected audio data, even after compression.

- Validity periods for audio tracks also enable the restricted sale of audio tracks.

- Identification of tracks with the 'Genuine Music Mark' to guarantee optimal audio quality uncorrupted by illegal copies.

- Tracks can be given cover images, texts, information, URLs, credits and so on.

- Player skins can be adjusted to the respective track.

Liquid Music Server The Liquid Music Server was developed for the controlled provision and secure sale of coded music content. Tracks coded with the Liquifier can only be transferred using this software, as the mechanisms outlined below are required for the implementation of Liquid Audio access protection:

- Intensive logging of all server access

- Download of released or marketed content

- Different access restriction methods

- The Liquid Music Server is currently available for SUN Solaris, SGI Irix and Windows NT.

Liquid Player The Liquid Player was developed for the playback and recording of audio data in Liquid Audio Format, and is available free of charge for Windows and MacOS. The most important feature is of course the playback of audio streams and displaying track information such as covers, promotional images, texts, notes and discography. If released or marketed tracks are to be recorded, the player downloads them and can burn the audio data direct to CD. The transfer of data to mobile devices such as the Diamond Rio Player is also possible.

Figure 6.4 Liquid Player

Another key feature is the facility for obtaining audio files under controlled conditions. If the user decides to acquire one or several tracks, there are two ways of registering:

- Only the name, e-mail and country is entered, and any files downloaded can be played for a period of one year on the same computer (FastTrack Security).

- A passport file is created on the Liquid Audio Web site, and file playback is connected to the availability of the passport file created (Full Passport).

This enables the Liquid Audio Player to provide a flexible platform for the secure and convenient sale of music over the Internet.

Liquid Audio has for a long time provided mechanisms for the sale of music over the Internet, which large providers have only begun to produce in more recent versions of the streaming media solutions, and so was a forerunner of this market of the future. MP3 compression in particular presents the music industry with enormous challenges, and one wonders how the Internet could reasonably be used to bring together the interests of the industry and consumers. It remains to be seen whether the problem of illegal copying can be solved through the provision of a secure sales platform for digital music for Liquid Audio.

6.2   Further solutions for video streaming

MPEG-4

The MPEG group   The Moving Picture Expert Group (MPEG) first met in 1988, and nobody would have guessed at that time what a big impact its work would have in the future. The members of the MPEG are specialists representing the TV- and home-entertainment -industry, telecomunications and relevant research institutes. At the end of the 80s algorithms for coding audio and video reached the necessary complexity to compress a TV signal for transfer using CDs. It was therefore the perfect time for the MPEG to establish open, flexible standards that gave developers enough clearance for optimisation and differentiation. So one of the key factors for the success of MPEG standards is that they only standardise the decoder of content. Developers can define their own encoder to contrast with the ones of competitors, and nevertheless all encoded content can be used with every decoder. In addition, all three released MPEG standards (MPEG-1, MPEG-2 and MPEG-4) are specified independent of the underlying transport medium (e.g. computer networks or storage medias) to be most flexible.

MPEG-1   MPEG-1 was released in November 1992 and defined a standard for compressing audio and video for storage on a CD with bit rates of about 1.5 Mbps. It uses temporal and spatial redundancy of video images for reducing the bit rate (see chapter 1). Sequent images are predicted using motion compensation and the difference between the predicted image and the sources is stored using lossy image compression. Using these methods, MPEG-1 provides VHS-like image quality at bit rates of about 1.15 Mbps. The audio compression of MPEG-1 was supplemented several times so that three MPEG-1 audio layers are available today to encode audio with bit rates of 196, 128 or 96 Kbps (Layer I, II or III).

One well known application of MPEG-1 is VideoCDs (VCD), that were formerly used in home entertainment and even today can be played with every DVD player. But the most famous application of MPEG-1 is definitely MP3 (MPEG-1 audio Layer III), which is the de-facto standard for audio compression these days.

MPEG-2   The next MPEG standard was released in November 1994 after four years of development. Design goals of MPEG-2 were the digital transmission of interlaced tv signals via terrestrial, satellite and cable networks. Based on the video compression algorithms of MPEG-1, MPEG-2 provides a much more flexible coding ranging from low-resolution content with 2 Mbps up to 4:2:2 HDTV material for professional use. The audio coding specified in MPEG-1 is fully back and forward compatible with MPEG-1. Advanced Audio coding was later added to MPEG-2, which provides the same quality as Layer II at half the bandwidth. So only 64 Kbps are needed to encode one 48 kHz signal, whereas MPEG-2 supports up to 48 channels surround sound.

Both the European standard, DVB, and the American standard for digital tv, ATSC, used MPEG-2 compression technology. However, proprietary audio coding was chosen in the US. In Japan AAC is used for audio coding of the digital tv. In addition to the implementation in millions of set-top boxes, MPEG-2 is the basic technology underlying the Digital Versatile Disc (DVD) and Sony's professional tape format, IMX.

MPEG-4   MPEG-4 especially meets the demand for robustness in error-prone environments, higher interactivity, the encoding of natural and synthetic data, and an improved compression factor compared to MPEG-2, in which estimated bandwidths are very low at up to 10 kbps. As well as optimised playback, MPEG-4 also has enhanced copyright protection, a requirement often discussed by the industry. The following points are central issues in the development of MPEG-4:

- Figure 14   Universal usability and robustness in error-prone environments
  Audiovisual data must be able to be transferred and played back in different networks, whilst tolerating various errors in transit (Catchword: Mobile Computing).

- Figure 15   Higher interactive functionality
  Future multimedia applications offer the user a high degree of interactivity, in which flexible and interactive access, and the manipulation of audiovisual data takes a central significance. The user should not only be able to play back audio and video data, but also edit and save content at will.

- Figure 16   Compression of natural and synthetic data
  The flexible encoding of traditional pixel-based audio and video data, and synthetically generated audio/speech signals and video images in combination makes certain demands of the compression procedure which produces MPEG-4.

- Figure 17   Compression efficiency
  Saving and transferring audiovisual data requires the procedure to be highly efficient in order to produce optimum playback quality. This is given particular consideration in MPEG-4 with low bit rates of under 64 kbps.

Video objects in MPEG-4   In contrast to previous multimedia standards, MPEG-4 allows the segmentation of a scene in several audio-visual objects. The separate description of objects in the bit stream using a special description language makes it possible to manipulate the content at the decoder via user interaction. MPEG-4 was released in October 1998 and has been supplemented many times since then.

One key feature of MPEG-4 is the possibility to code video obejcts that are coded in separate Video Object Layers (VOL). Features such as form, transparency, positioning, rotation and translation are encoded in this bit stream, and enable the user to reconstruct the entire scene comprising all elements, or to manipulate the individual parameters of certain objects. This approach allows the scene to be manipulated by editing object parameters, without having to transcode the entire bit stream. As the entire data stream is described as object-oriented, objects are added or deleted by the corresponding VOLs being added or deleted – again without having to transcode the entire data stream. A scene encoded in MPEG-4 can also consist of several objects, described in outline, movement and texture. In contrast to MPEG-1 and MPEG-2, coded image content does not necessarily have to be rectangular.

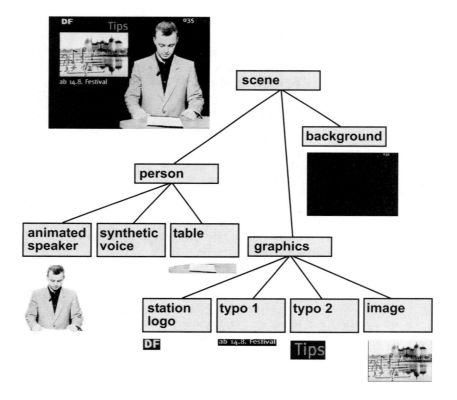

Figure 6.5 Video objects in MPEG-4 (example)

The information required to reconstruct the entire scene – identification and composition of various video objects – is encoded alongside the actual image data in the bit stream. Isolating individual VOLs is therefore as easy as the manipulation itself. However, optimum identification of individual objects and encoding them in VOLs is not part of the MPEG-4 standard, and should be carried out separately.

It is thought that, in the future, objects will be encoded in MPEG-4 format in different qualities, sizes or frame rates, in order to guarantee the most flexible data playback possible, similar to SureStream technology.

MPEG-4 AAC   When it gets to audio coding, MPEG-4 first of all relies on AAC to encode high quality audio at low bit rates. In addition to AAC, MPEG-4 provides special functionality for compressing speech data at bit rates between 4 to 24 Kbps at 8 or 16 kHz. For music-optimised coding, the HILN-algorithms (Harmonic and Individual Line plus Noise) work even with 4 Kbps, because they (the HILN - algorithms) differentiate between harmonic and dominating frequencies and save the noise-properties seperately. All these methods can be combined to an efficient, scalable audiocoder.

Structured Audio Orchestra Language (SAOL) also aims for object orientation and reusability. It is used in combination with Structured Audio Score Language (SASL) to describe synthetically created speech, sounds and effects. Synthetic speech output is generated independently of language, age and gender. This approach makes the audio data of an MPEG-4 stream writable and reusable in any new group.

Like all MPEG standards, the MPEG-4 specification is structured in several parts (part 1: system, 2: video coding, 3: audio coding, 4: compatibility checks, 5: reference software, etc.). The system part, for example, describes the .MP4 file container. This binary format makes it possible to describe scenes with several objects in it, and is based on the Virtual Reality Modeling Language (VRML).

To adapt the complexity and numerous features of MPEG-4 to different kinds of applications (and hardware types), the standard can be configured. Just like MPEG-2, MPEG-4 uses various profiles that summarise several tools.

MPEG-4 implementations

MPEG-4 today has become an attractive alternative to proprietary solutions, such as RealMedia or Windows Media. It combines the flexibility of open standards with the latest improvements of audio/video coding. Different manufacturers today are starting to use MPEG-4 coding, even though there are only very few implementations available that use advanced features like video objects.

Since QuickTime 6 Apple supports standard-conform MPEG-4 video coding and AAC compression, MPEG-4 livestreams can be encoded with the Apple Broadcaster and content can be distributed using the QuickTime Streaming Server. On www.apple.com a linklist to MPEG-4 content is provided.

Envivio MPEG-4   One of the leading MPEG-4 implementations comes from Envivio. It offers a complete streaming solution based on MPEG-4 technology, which even supports video objects. The Envivio Broadcast Studio can be used to generate MPEG-4 content, that consists not only of audio and video data, but also contains various objects. So it is more a multimedia authoring solution that enables users to generate multimedia presentations, which are stored using the MPEG-4 format. In addition to this, Envivio offers a player and a server software. An Envivio plug-in for RealOne Player is also available.

Emblaze MPEG-4   Emblaze Systems was formerly known for a streaming solution that uses a java applet for decoding video streams. Since a Java Virtual Machine is available on every web browser, downloads of complex player software was not necessary to access Emblaze content. As the products for conventional streaming could not compete with RealMedia or QuickTime, Emlaze Systems decided to change the business model. Today, Emblaze concentrates on solutions for mobile devices and interactive TV, based on open standards like MPEG-4.

Microsoft and MPEG-4   Microsoft was the first company to offer MPEG-4 technology to a wide range of users. Older Windows Media video codecs, such as Windows Media MPEG-4 Video V3 used a proprietary MPEG-4 implementation. Windows Media 9 Series contains an ISO-compliant MPEG-4 video codec to be used with .ASF files.

DivX   The DivX codec was formerly based on the proprietary MPEG-4 implementation of Microsoft. Version 5 of the DivX codecs is claimed to be fully compatible with MPEG-4 technology.

VivoActive

Together with RealNetworks (Progressive Networks at the time), VivoActive was one of the pioneers in the transfer of moving images on the Internet. The facility for producing small video transfers suitable for slow modem connections guaranteed Vivo a rapidly expanding user base from 1995 onwards. The status of video compression and reduced bandwidth at the time made image quality comparably poor, but VivoActive were among the first to recognise the potential of video streaming.

A separate server is not required for transferring Vivo movies, as HTTP streaming is exclusively used. Vivo clips are created using the VivoActive Producer, which can be purchased for around £350. In contrast to other developers, only Vivo provided playback using browser plug-ins, and did not provide a standalone player.

The takeover of Vivo by RealNetworks in 1998 brought the success story of the format to an abrupt end. However, RealNetworks provides support for VivoActive users, but sales and further development have since been discontinued in favour of the RealSystems.

6.3   Further streaming technologies?

Streaming 3D?

Conventional Internet content is two-dimensional: images, video or animations may be able to simulate three-dimensional representation, but the third dimension remains out of reach. However, technologies have existed for several years which bring the third dimension to the Internet. As three-dimensional depictions of objects are transferred here, the user can move freely through the virtual environment.

VRML   The third dimension made its official Internet entrance in 1994: VRML (Virtual Reality Modeling Language) enables the cross-platform representation of virtual environments as an open standard for depicting three-dimensional objects. VRML files consist of text-based characterisations of objects, enabling the creation of separate WRL files with a text editor. However, the development of more complex three-dimensional worlds is only realistic using genuine 3D programs such as Discreet 3D Max, Caligari Truespace or Avid Softimage.

Figure 6.6 VRML in the Web browser

VRML has yet to experience its big break, but the potential of the technology cannot be denied: the user can move through virtual worlds in which images, audio, video or links are integrated.

One of the reasons for the lack of success of VRML is the size of the files: a complex environment often requires over 500 KB, which has to be transferred in its entirety. The latest versions of VRML enable the file to be displayed while being downloaded.

However, three-dimensional environments contradict nature, in that they are transferred using streaming methods. The streaming of data requires the user to follow a specific strand. The point is, users would no doubt want to be able to move freely in three-dimensional space. As much information as possible therefore has to be available for the user to enjoy total freedom of movement. This contradicts the character of a streaming application, where the only information transferred and output is that perceived by the spectator.

The fact that not all data in a VRML environment has to be loaded for information to be displayed is closer to the concept of Fast Start Movies in QuickTime.

True streaming 3D applications are therefore only developed for the user to move around the 3D world on a predefined route. In this case, the data required can be transferred in the correct sequence and displayed. However, this contradicts the principle of a 3D environment: free navigation.

Streaming Animation?

Of the many technologies which transfer animations over the Internet such as Sizzler, WebMotion, mBED, Scream or WebAnimator, only a few have become established. Macromedia Flash and Shockwave are the most important technologies which have been successful in this area.

Figure 6.7 Macromedia Flash

Vector animation: Macromedia Flash — Macromedia Flash produces vector-based animations on the Internet. Two-dimensional objects are not depicted by individual pixels here, but by contours, surfaces, lines and points. For example, a monochrome rectangular surface can be represented by a fixed number of image dots (e.g. 300x150 pixels), but can also be represented by the position of its corners, lines and colours, and shown in full colour. The facility for defining complex curves enables animations to be created without having to transfer memory-intensive individual pixels.

One advantage of vector-based animations is the scalability of the animations. The 'step effect' common in bitmap images does not occur when scaling vector graphics. The disadvantage of vector animations is that photos or video images cannot be transferred. Only generated vector graphics are suitable for use in Macromedia Flash.

However, streaming does not actually occur here. Flash animations have to be competely loaded before playback can begin. The fact that Flash movies can be loaded in several sections and played back does not constitute genuine streaming.

6.4 Further tools for generating content

The tools provided by RealNetworks, Microsoft and Apple for producing clips and streams may offer the functions required for creating respective formats, but also allow third party providers space to develop their own tools. The boom in streaming media has produced a flood of new products in this area, and below we will discuss both traditional ones and newcomers.

Discreet Cleaner 5

The professional production of on-demand content is only one of many possible applications of Cleaner. All types of movies, sounds and images can be created for distribution on CD-ROM, DVD or on the Internet. In streaming QuickTime production, MediaCleaner is the only tool for using the extended features of the Sorenson video codec.

In the production of on-demand clips, Cleaner provides extensive facilities for preprocessing the output material before compression, and an option to save these settings for later use. The user therefore comes across some of the effects used in RealNetworks, Apple or Microsoft encoders, such as cropping, resizing or de-interlacing; but also some which are not, such as blurring, noise reduction, masking and watermarks.

The following video and audio filters can be added to the facilities for optimising output material:

Video:
Figure 6	Gamma correction
Figure 7	Brightness
Figure 8	Contrast
Figure 9	Black and white comparison
Figure 10	Hue and saturation
Figure 11	Up to three QuickTime effects
Figure 12	Video fades

Audio:

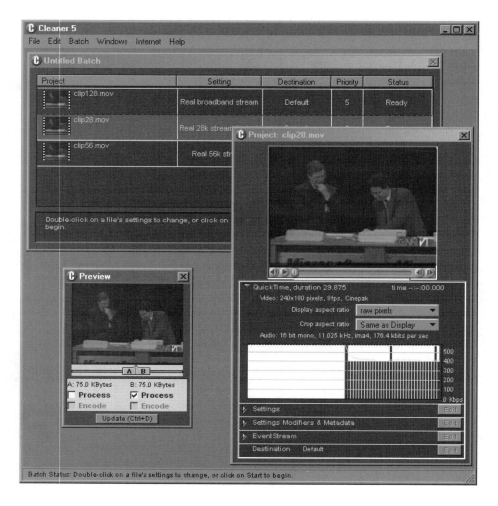

Figure 6.8   Discreet Cleaner 5

Specific use of these filters enables optimum production of streaming media clips while taking into account the deficiencies of respective compression methods. More so than the standard encoder, MediaCleaner enables optimal encoding, but, on a negative note, restricts the correction of errors in the output material.

The convenient production of batch processing allows several clips to be encoded in sequence automatically. Even when producing many clips at high quality, an encoder can run constantly, and only requires attention when new batch lists are configured and when results are checked.

As mentioned previously, Sorenson contributed to the development of Cleaner, which was the only program that used the extended features of the Sorenson video codec. Temporal scalability, automatic key frames, media keys or 2-pass encoding are required for competitive use of the Sorenson codec, which makes Cleaner essential for QuickTime encoding with this compression method.

In addition to the three streaming formats of RealMedia, WindowsMedia and QuickTime, the MediaCleaner can also be used to create AVIs, MPEGs, MP3s, FLCs, WAVs, AIFFs, JPGs, GIFs, PICTs and DV streams. A particular feature of the current version 5 is the facility for coding MPEG-1 and MPEG-2 files, so even DVD-compatible streams can be generated.

Another improvement in Cleaner 5 is the facility for capturing video and audio via a Firewire connection, and creating a batch process directly from the clips generated. After encoding, the generated file can be saved or uploaded to a server via FTP.

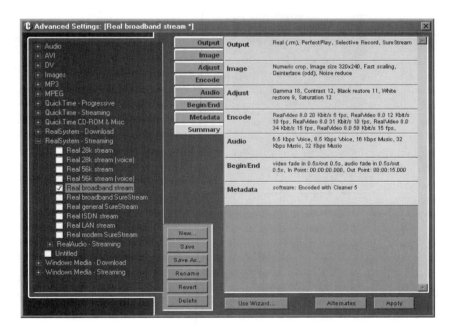

Figure 6.9 Advanced settings in Cleaner 5

The full version of the Cleaner costs around £550, and the full version of the Sorenson video codec and the QDesign audio codec are available for around £450.

Canopus ProCoder

Just like Discreet Cleaner, Canopus' ProCoder presents itself as a universal converter between all kinds of digital video formats.

The key feature of ProCoder is the possibility to transcode between all installed .AVI- and QuickTime-codecs. MPEG-1/2 and DV-formats are also fully supported. Just RealMedia and Windows Media are available as target format, since RealNetworks and Microsoft do not want their content to be easily transcoded into other formats. The program also supports batch endcoding and can convert videos to several target formats simultaneously.

Figure 6.10 Canopus ProCoder

Wizards make it easy for users to begin working with the program. To provide automatisation of encoding jobs, ProCoder provides 'Droplets'. These are small executable files that start the main program with predefined settings as soon as files are dragged-and-dropped on them. A plug-in for Adobe Premiere is also included, although ProCoder itself provides some basic editing functions.

For MPEG coding, Canopus has integrated its own codec into ProCoder, which supports VBR- and 2-pass-encoding. An MPEG-2 mastering modus is also included to produce MPEG-2 content that can be used for DVD authoring.

Compared to Discreet Cleaner, the Canopus ProCoder offers better performance, although version 1 is quite unstable and often crashes.

In version 1.03, ProCoder does not support RealVideo 9, Windows Media 9 Series or QuickTime 6 MPEG-4 codecs. A demo version is free for download at www.canopus.com and the full version costs around £580.

6.5 Hardware

Encoding several streams for various bandwidths or in different formats, especially in real time (live encoding), requires a high computing capacity. To increase reliability and efficiency, many developers have developed hardware which can considerably simplify compression, either as system extensions or integrated solutions.

Pinnacle StreamGenie

The increasing number of live broadcast, and the more professional approach to it, has generated a growing demand for integrated solutions which support the production process on the basis of optimised hardware and software. The Pinnacle StreamGenie goes one step further, as its efficient portable hardware is complemented by a pure streaming media encoder, and includes transmission handling facilities.

StreamGenie is based on (dual) Pentium III-550 processors, mounted with an audio mixer and video capture cards in a stable portable aluminium case. In total size, video and four audio inputs can be mixed, provided with real time effects and encoded as RealVideo or Windows Media streams. These features enable up to six sources to mix a signal and encode them in two different formats (SureStream/ Multibit) simultaneously – extremely useful with live events. In addition, 3D real time effects are also available, using which transition or picture-in-picture effects can be produced. Professional title, graphic injections and chroma keys can also be mixed into the picture signal. The output signal is therefore not only encoded, but also output in uncompressed format, for archiving using the Composite and Y/ C output. A 15.1 " TFT display is used.

The key feature of the StreamGenie is that signal processing is carried out entirely in 4:2:2 PAL or NTSC resolution, and encoded at the last step. This enables the streamed signal to be archived in full resolution, and high quality broadband streams to be created. Its price may seem high at £20,000, but is qualified by the background of powerful hardware components.

Chyron DualStreamer

In livestream production, the reliability of hardware and software is an essential criterion in the purchase decision. The usual solution for encoding RealVideo and Windows Media is a powerful PC running Windows, and using the encoding software of both manufacturers.

If you have doubts about the reliability of Windows, with its overload of drivers and libraries, you can rely on the Chyron DualStreamer. This is a PC in a 19 inch truss which runs a special encoder based on a Windows kernel. Its exclusive optimisation for encoding, complete lack of unnecessary interfaces and system extensions, and its special encoders guarantee maximum program efficiency.

An HTML-based interface can be used to control ongoing processes. In addition, an LCD display on the front of the case provides access to all functions of the device. Clari-Net accepts Composite Video, balanced and unbalanced analogue audio as input signals. These signals are encoded in real time and output via the Ethernet interface on an ISDN hub, or directly on the Internet. The user only has to configure the stream, specify the target server and start the livestream. As the name suggests, the DualStreamer can encode the input signal into two different RealMedia or Windows Media streams. Encoded streams can be either broadcast directly to streaming servers, be broadcast live and archived at the same time, or the encoded material is stored to local or network storage for later use as on-demand material.

The advantage of this and similar devices is a real Plug&Play architecture, which guarantees uncomplicated and reliable livestreaming in mobile or static use. There is no need to constantly configure a standard PC or software, and the DualStreamer can be integrated into professional broadcast studios using its GPI interface.

ViewCast Osprey

ViewCast is the leading developer of capturing cards for streaming video applications. Like its competitor, Winnov, it offers a wide range of solutions, from a simple capture card to real time encoding of broadband MPEG.

Osprey-100

The Osprey card is specialised for capturing video signals, for which three Composite inputs and one Y/C input are available. These inputs can be used for connecting various video sources, which can be digitised at a resolution of 320×240 at up to 30 fps (maximum 15 fps at 640×480). The Osprey-100 is one of the most common solutions for simple video streaming, video conferences and small capturing, and is available for around £100.

Osprey-200

The Osprey-200 (around £140) includes an audio input at the expense of one of the Composite video inputs. This means that a separate system sound card is not required to capture video and audio. In addition, the Osprey-220 provides professional XLR audio connectors for balanced stereo input.

Osprey-500

The Osprey-500 cards are designed for professional streaming purposes and are provided in three different versions with various features for optimised encoding of analogue or digital sources.

Besides Composite and S-Video video and balanced and unbalanced audio inputs, an IEEE-1394 Firewire signal can be used as signal input with the Osprey-500 DV (around £570).

The Osprey-500 DV Pro costs around £1,300, but for this also provides digital AES/EBU audio and SDI video inputs.

The most advanced capture card of Viewcast today is the Osprey-540 for around £1,450. It provides the same inputs like the 500 DV Pro, but supports de-interlacing, scaling, cropping and colour conversion. Since these effects are directly implemented in the card's hardware, the encoder's cpu is not required here.

Concluding remarks

7.1 Comparing systems

Given the current market situation, deciding on a streaming video solution is usually a choice between RealSystem, Windows Media and QuickTime. Only these products provide the quality, security, development and support of a comprehensive solution capable of satisfying the current requirements of streaming media.

Discussion of the various products can often become very heated, just as discussing the 'best operating system'. In the case of Microsoft and Apple, the debate between the two is very close. The fact is that all developers try to keep up with their competitors. This competition is currently fairly balanced, which makes future versions of programs all the more interesting.

Video and Audio quality

The first and most important point, in which RealMedia, Windows Media and QuickTime need to compete with each other, is the quality of compressed audio and video signals. The further development of the codec plays a central role in the competition for best results, and the demands on streaming video codecs have increased with the growing distribution of fast Internet access in the direction of broadband.

In practice, any objective assessment of encoding results is usually misleading, as these results are highly dependent on optimised preprocessing. As this is not possible in the case of live broadcasts, it is inappropriate to compare on-demand or simulated live broadcasts with live broadcasts or their archive files.

A balanced picture emerges when comparing the image and audio quality of RealMedia 9, Microsoft Media 9 Series and QuickTime 6. Nevertheless, Microsoft has integrated many additional features to optimise the user's experience.

Table 7.1 Important features of RealMedia, Windows Media and QuickTime

RealMedia 9	Windows Media 9 Series	QuickTime 6
Video Coding		
+ support for interlaced video, HDTV resolutions	+ support for interlaced video, HDTV resolutions	+ use of the open standard MPEG-4 (simple profile and advanced simple profile)
+ high interoperability: best support of different platforms	+ high-quality frame interpolation with low bit rate content	+ Open source server available
- proprietary standard	- low interoperability: encoder and server for Windows only, no player for Linux available	- max. resolution of 352x288 and 2048 Kbps
	- proprietary standard	- live-encoder only for MacOS, player only for MacOS and Windows
Audio Coding		
+ support for surround sound (non-discrete audio channels)	+ support for up to 7.1 multichannel audio and multiple languages	+ support of the open standard AAC
- proprietary standard	+ support of mathematically lossless and high quality (24 bit, 96 kHz) audio encoding	+ VBR audio encoding
	+ VBR audio encoding	
	- proprietary standard	
Format		
+ support for Audio- and Video-Surestreaming since RealSystem G2	+ support of Multiple Bit Rate video with several video resolutions (Scalable Video)	+ open-standard file container
Format		

RealMedia 9	Windows Media 9 Series	QuickTime 6
- proprietary standard	+ availability of secure digital rights management (also for live content)	
	+ wide industry support	
	- proprietary standard	
Costs, Compatibility		
+ industry-leading interoperability	+ free encoder and player	+ free encoder, player and server
- high costs for server licenses, no free encoder	- server only available in Windows Server version	+ open source server
- ad-contaminated, insistent player software	- no support for Linux and Unix systems	- no support for Linux and Unix systems

Windows Media vs. RealMedia The large number of new features of Windows Media Audio and Video 9 makes it very attractive in comparison to RealMedia. Since both systems use proprietary codecs, neither is best choice in terms of future-proofness. The enormous efforts of Microsoft during the development of Windows Media 9 make it a very attractive alternative to the former market leader, RealMedia.

QuickTime and MPEG-4 The new QuickTime MPEG-4 codec fails with regard to quality compared with its competitors. At the same bit rate, the simple profile MPEG-4 can often not keep up with RealMedia or Windows Media. However, the use of MPEG-4 as a future-proof, open standard is a weighty argument for the use of QuickTime 6.

Moreover, the preceived quality of QuickTime video on the Internet is often very high. This is due to the widespread use of Fast Start Movies in QuickTime, which, when played back, do not drop in quality during interruptions in transmission bandwidth, but stop altogether or buffer underrun. The concept of transfers cannot be compared with genuine streaming, which is also possible in QuickTime. However, the fact remains that the image quality of QuickTime MPEG-4 films is positively lacking in some respects.

RealMedia When comparing RealAudio, Windows Media Audio and Advanced Audio Coding (AAC) at bit rates of 64 Kbps and more, the difference between competitors is negligible. This is because all codecs represent a similar state of the art of audio/video coding, and none can present a genuinely unique patent solution. The real decisive arguments here are others than pure quality, such as coding efficiency, device support, future proofness or user basis.

Operation/Implementation

Users rarely expect surprises when creating and implementing RealMedia content. Due to the long history of RealNetworks in streaming media, there is extensive documentation and many informative articles available. These help with very specific queries and problems. However, only brief instructions are usually required for producing simple streaming media pages. Problems rarely occur when using content on different systems, thanks to the many reliable supported platforms. Players, encoders and servers are well thought-out and very clear.

Windows Media   Although there were certain areas where Windows Media could not hide its young development history, Windows Media 9 Series changed this. Encoding quality, a rich set of features in encoder, server and player, improved DRM components, and an unrivalled user basis are important arguments to consider.

Existing documentation is good, and can be used to create complex streaming media content as well. Creating cross-platform content is made particularly difficult with Windows Media. Microsoft is naturally interested in promoting its own operation systems, and so there is no player available for Linux, Unix, FreeBSD or Windows 95 and NT that supports playback of Windows Media 9. However, Windows Media has undergone a notable development in this area, and the Windows Media Player is now available on many platforms.

QuickTime   With QuickTime 6, Apple has evolved to the proponent of open standards in the trio. The use of RTSP, MPEG-4 and AAC is a secure investment into the future of streaming media technology. The QuickTime file format is also an open file format, that was even chosen as the basis for the development of the MPEG-4 file container. After Microsoft and RealNetworks took the lead in the competition for the best streaming media system, Apple brought itself back into the race by choosing to support open standards and open source initiatives.

If one has to identify a weakness in QuickTime's operation or implementation, it is the lack of support of operating systems other than MacOS. But unlike with Microsoft, this deficit is compensated, since every developer can program compatible encoders, clients or servers by using the open standard specifications. However, QuickTime's lack of platform variety is a stumbling block: the player is only available for MacOS and Windows.

Distribution

RealNetworks and Microsoft have an extremely wide basis of players installed among users. Microsoft's lead is explained by the availability of the player in every current Windows installation. The disadvantage is the lack of portability to other (especially Unix and Linux) platforms. This distribution on all relevant systems is the clear advantage of the RealPlayer. Widespread distribution brings interoperability and the full-coverage availability of RealMedia content.

QuickTime cannot keep up with its two competitors in relation to the high number of installations, even though QuickTime is an integral part of every Mac operating system and is claimed to have been downloaded over a 100 million times since the release of QuickTime 5. Providers who place special emphasis on uncomplicated user-access to content without large downloads cannot rely on QuickTime in this sense.

Costs

Player software costs are minimal in all systems. All three competitors offer free downloads of at least a basic version.

QuickTime 5 content

However, creating content is a different matter. Microsoft provides its encoder free of charge, and the cost of the RealEncoder is fairly modest at around £100. The costs for QuickTime livestreams are not excessive – the Apple Broadcaster is free and the Sorenson broadcaster costs around £140. However, anyone wishing to create professional QuickTime 5 on-demand content requires Cleaner 5 (around £550), the full version of the Sorenson video codec (around £200) and the full version of the QDesign audio codec (£250). Even though the user gets far more than a simple encoder with Cleaner 5, a more affordable tool should be available for encoding optimised QuickTime 5 clips.

Expensive RealServer

RealNetworks heads the price list in streaming server costs. Depending on the number of simultaneous streams, it can cost up to £5,000 and over. For this amount of money, providers get a highly flexible server platform that delivers every streaming media format relevant on the market today.

Outsourcing

Microsoft has integrated its Windows Media Services into the Windows 2000 and .NET servers. These operating systems are definitely not free of charge, and large content providers in particular have to face big expenses due to the setup of Windows servers.

However, the licence costs for streaming media servers should not be overvalued. There are currently many companies in Europe which offer hosting facilities for streaming media content. These services usually provide load balancing and guaranteed availability of hosted content. When using these services, the user also has the right to use server licences. In addition to simplified technical implementation of server services, guaranteed quality of service and reduced administrative effort, there are no licence costs to be calculated initially for the server.

Conclusion

However great the temptation to give some rating to the striking technical parallels between RealSystem and Windows Media, it would appear that the two main competitors will have to resign themselves to a neck-and-neck race. RealNetworks used to have the lead in this race, but with Windows Media 9 Series, Microsoft took first place, leaving RealNetworks only the advantage of better interoperability and a more flexible server.

Unfortunately the pressure of innovation seems so high in this market segment, that in the case of all developers, new features are often implemented before existing versions can be debugged. As a result, the clients and browser plug-ins of RealSystem, Windows Media or QuickTime sometimes do not run reliably. The most notable developments of recent months seem to have to be paid for with stability.

RealMedia

The classic software package in the provision of streaming media is RealSystem, which is available on many different platforms. No other developer offers player, encoder and server on so many different platforms. Despite a few weaknesses in live broadcasting and in the provision of on-demand content, the long history of the system and know-how of the company arguably made it the most interesting streaming media system for a long time.

Windows Media

Compared to RealSystem and QuickTime, Microsoft Windows Media is the newcomer among streaming media systems. It coped with the adoption of feature programs from rival systems, but the latest version (Windows Media 9 Series) took the technical market lead from RealNetworks. With version 9 of Windows Media, RealNetworks is definitely condemned to reacting on new innovations instead of setting the industry standards as it did in the past.

The financial aspect should not be overlooked: Microsoft and Apple provide all necessary software components free of charge. This can be a weighty argument in its favour when making a decision on a provider, especially given the expensive RealServer licence costs.

Even though market competition is currently in full flow, we may well ask the question as to whether RealNetworks can successfully defend its position against the conglomerate. Microsoft seem firmly decided to support the worldwide advent of streaming media through further technical development and intensive marketing. It seems logical that this breakthrough should be made using Microsoft technologies. Given the current situation, Windows Media can be earmarked as a safe bet for the future.

QuickTime

In contrast, innovation is the concept underpinning Apple QuickTime, and only because of the development of its long-established multimedia standard and the implementation of open standards. Due to the production of its own technical concepts, QuickTime is particularly suitable for the optimal provision of on-demand content. This is not necessarily restricted to the bandwidth of current Internet connections. The major weakness of QuickTime is its lack of availability on systems other than MacOS and Windows. The Apple Broadcaster is only available for MacOS, which is a clear disadvantage for QuickTime, largely because of the costly PowerMac G4 that is needed for every live encoding job. Windows or Linux computers provide a far better price-performance ratio in these applications. If Apple's market share were to increase, clients and encoders would have to be ported urgently to other platforms.

7.2   The future...

Whichever format is used, streaming media has already changed the face of the Internet. And the use of time-based media on the Internet will increase in importance in the next few years, especially in Europe, and clearly influence the continued growth of the Web.

Key factors: broadband and flatrate

The two key factors for the future growth of streaming technologies are broadband Internet connections and flatrates in private households. The opportunity to enjoy streaming media at a higher quality without having to worry about call charges is decisive for future development. According to a report by the Forrester Institute, the quota of European households with broadband access is set to increase to over 20% by the year 2005, up from just 0.2% in 1999. The course of development will be very exciting to watch against this backdrop, both from a technical point of view and as regards content.

If the audio transfer currently available with modem and ISDN connections is quite acceptable, streaming video reels from such restricted transmission bandwidths. This technology will only become established if TV quality can be transferred, which it currently can at around 250 to 350 Kbps. Technologies such as DSL, cable modems or satellite connections are available to fill this gap. However, we will have to wait a while for their use to become more widespread. Content providers should examine their target group accurately and select the streaming media supply accordingly. RealSystem, Windows Media or QuickTime, narrowband, broadband or both, video or audio only: the reason for using streaming media on a Web page should not be the technology in itself, but rather its implications in terms of delivery. The user must have the chance to be able to use this information meaningfully, irrespective of context. Technical requirements such as bit rates or compulsory plug-ins should not present a handicap, and the content should be an integral part of the overall concept of supply.

The future development of RealMedia and Windows Media will depend on the strategy of RealNetworks and if they can stand up to the competition of Microsoft. This is questionable, due to the dimensions of the multinational Microsoft corporation in contrast with the small software developer, RealNetworks.

Newcomer with future: MPEG-4

Much more than any proprietary technology, MPEG-4 is the long awaited new player in the game. As it is developed by the MPEG committee, many of the most important companies, institutions and experts contribute to its ongoing development. Much more than RealMedia, the MPEG is serious competition to the future of Windows Media as the dominating streaming media technology.

Apple recognised the potential of MPEG-4 and changed its product strategy as a result.

But in any case, streaming media technology will play a key role in the future of the Internet: opening the entire dimension of time-based media to the Internet in times of content syndication and media convergence. Multimedia content extends the hitherto static Internet into becoming an interactive platform, through which any form of media communication can take place.

Index